THE PROMISE OF SALVATION

THE PROMISE OF SALVATION

A Theory of Religion

MARTIN RIESEBRODT

Translated by Steven Rendall

THE UNIVERSITY OF CHICAGO PRESS

CHICAGO AND LONDON

MARTIN RIESEBRODT is professor in the Department of Sociology and the Divinity School at the University of Chicago. He is the author of *Pious Passion: The Emergence of Modern Fundamentalism in the United States and Iran* and *Rückkehr der Religionen: Fundamentalismus und der "Kampf der Kulturen."*

STEVEN RENDALL has translated more than fifty books from French and German, and has won two major translation prizes. Among his recent translations are Harald Weinrich's *On Borrowed Time*, Wolfgang Sofsky's *Privacy: A Manifesto*, and Jon Elster's *Reason and Rationality*.

The University of Chicago Press, Chicago 60637
The University of Chicago Press, Ltd., London
© 2010 by The University of Chicago
All rights reserved. Published 2010
Printed in the United States of America

18 17 16 15 14 13 12 11 10   1 2 3 4 5

ISBN-13: 978-0-226-71391-5 (cloth)
ISBN-10: 0-226-71391-1 (cloth)

Originally published as *Cultus und Heilsversprechen: Eine Theorie der Religionen*, © Verlag C. H. Beck oHG, München, 2007.

Library of Congress Cataloging-in-Publication Data

Riesebrodt, Martin.
     [Cultus und Heilsversprechen. English]
     The promise of salvation: a theory of religion / Martin Riesebrodt; translated by Steven Rendall.
         p. cm.
     Includes bibliographical references and index.
     ISBN-13: 978-0-226-71391-5 (cloth: alk. paper)
     ISBN-10: 0-226-71391-1 (cloth: alk. paper)   1. Religion—Philosophy.   2. Salvation.
I. Title.
     BL48.R45313   2009
     210—dc22

                                                                    2009020836

♾ The paper used in this publication meets the minimum requirements of the American National Standard for Information Sciences—Permanence of Paper for Printed Library Materials, ANSI Z39.48-1992.

FOR BRIGITTE

Let us consider the unmistakable character of the present situation. We have heard the admission that religion no longer has the same influence on men that it used to have (we are concerned here with European Christian culture). And this, not because its promises have become smaller, but because they appear less credible to people.
—Sigmund Freud, *The Future of an Illusion*

CONTENTS

In addition to a certain naïveté, without which one can hardly approach so great a subject, it was chiefly the unsatisfactory state of research on religion that led me to propose a theory of religion. Conventional theories of religion have proved incapable of explaining the persistence of religion in the modern world and its increasing strength all over the globe during the past thirty years. The anticipated secularization has not taken place; or at least it has not taken place as had been widely expected. Moreover, the concept of religion is in crisis. Some people dilute it to the point of futility, considering barbecues with guitar music, soccer games, shopping in supermarkets, or art exhibitions to be religious phenomena. Everything becomes "somehow" or "implicitly" religious. Others criticize the concept of religion as an invention of Western modernity that should not be applied to premodern or non-Western societies. In their opinion, Hinduism, Buddhism, and Confucianism are Western inventions that cannot be termed religions without perpetuating colonialist thinking. When soccer games are seen as religious phenomena and the recitation of Buddhist sutras is not, something has obviously gone wrong.

Given this situation, it is time to reconceptualize religion in a critical perspective and, in view of its dramatic revival, to reconsider it from a theoretical perspective. Ultimately, scholars are not expected to reproduce or even increase confusion but rather to lend intellectual structure to the chaos of phenomena, to understand and explain, even if only provisionally and imperfectly.

How does my theory of religion differ from its predecessors? It builds upon them, of course, and is in many respects indebted to them. So much has already been written about religion that there's probably nothing fundamentally new that can be said about it. Neither my definition and explanation

of religion nor my thesis that religion is based on communication with superhuman powers and is concerned with warding off misfortune, coping
with crises, and laying the foundation for salvation is new. Nonetheless, I
believe that my theory goes beyond conventional approaches in the structure of its argumentation, its inclusion of East Asian religious traditions, its
orientation toward practice, and its empirical grounding.

The book begins with a discussion of the concept of religion. I reject the
postmodern critique of a universal concept of religion and offer a historico-
sociological justification for the latter. In all ages people have distinguished
interaction with superhuman powers from other forms of action. In different times and cultures, religious actors and institutions have seen each
other as similar, no matter whether this perception was expressed in competition and polemics or in cooperation, assimilation, and identification. In
addition, all rulers of religiously pluralistic empires—the Achaemenids, the
Sassanians, the Romans, the T'ang, Ming, or Qing dynasties, the Japanese
emperors, the Fatimids, or the Mughal dynasty—have pursued a politics of
religion.

My theory is based on a coherent, practice-oriented concept of religion
that distinguishes religion from religious tradition, on the one hand, and
from religiousness, on the other. I deal with religions not as worldviews systematized by intellectuals, but rather as systems of practices that are related
to superhuman powers. Religions represent concrete systems of practices
and must be distinguished from the concept of religious traditions that refers to the historical continuity of systems of symbols. My approach renders
superfluous the debates whether "Judaism," "Christianity," "Buddhism,"
or "Hinduism" are religions. I discuss them as religious traditions in the
sense of cultural ways of life that no doubt contain systems of religious
practices, but also transcend them. My approach is concerned not with the
"purity" of doctrine and practice in the sense of theological adherence to
a tradition, but rather with the concrete reality of religion, including all
its overlaps, syncretisms, and local peculiarities. On the other hand, I also
distinguish religion from religiousness, which I understand as an individual
appropriation of religion. As important as the study of religiousness may
be for understanding religious actors and communities, it is of little use
for developing a theory of religion. Religiousness does not produce religion;
instead, religions produce various forms of religiousness.

Theories of religion often make metaphysics or ethics the center of their
analyses. In contrast, my theory is centered on worship, that is, on the relations between humans and superhuman powers. For that reason I infer the
meaning of religious practices not from worldviews ("theologies") or sub-

jective interpretations but rather from "liturgies," that is, institutionalized rules and guidelines for humans' interactions with superhuman powers. The meaning of religions is developed less in theological discourses than in performance.

My theory pursues a consistent interpretive approach and thus bridges the gap between religious, internal perspectives and scholarly, external perspectives. My external perspective consists in the selection and systematization of internal perspectives. Whatever I say about religions is taken from their own self-representations. I give East Asian religions the same attention as the Abrahamic religions that arose in the Mediterranean region. My examples and illustrations are taken, on the one hand, from the Jewish, Christian, and Islamic traditions, and, on the other, from the Buddhist, Daoist, and Shinto traditions. Although I am not a specialist and my discussion of these materials is surely inadequate, I hope that bringing them into the discussion will broaden the understanding of religion as a whole.

In contrast to functionalist approaches, I am concerned not with the function of religion but rather with its promise. Religion's functions are as various as its different social and political conditions. Religion's promise, by contrast, remains astonishingly constant in different historical periods and cultures. Religions promise to ward off misfortune, to help cope with crises, and to provide salvation. Religions are less about "the holy" than about blessings, salvation, and protection from misfortune, as well as about the providers and mediators of salvation. However, my theory does not represent an "essential definition" of religion. It does not seek to prove that all religions are "ultimately" the same, but rather to make it possible to compare them in relation to a structure of meaning that underlies them.

My approach does not derive its knowledge of contemporary religions from assumptions regarding "modernity" borrowed from philosophies of history. Actual or alleged characteristics of "modernity" are not used to predict the secularization and marginalization or the privatization and de-privatization of religion. I am laying out no theory of religious development, and certainly not one that explains how religion rises out of the depths of magic to the heights of ethics, from polytheism to monotheism, or from religious to scientific thinking. Instead of overloading the study of religions with premises drawn from anthropology or the philosophy of history, we should use it to discover something new about humans, society, history, and "actual, existing modernity."

I hope that my theory of religion will not only clarify—and enlighten—but also lead readers to raise new questions. Anyone who rejects my definition and theory of religion should at least be able to say what he or she disagrees with and on what grounds. I hope anyone who does empirical work on religion will find here a useful conceptual, methodological, and theoretical framework.

The writing of this book can best be compared with a long hike in the mountains, during which one sometimes gets lost in the mist and takes shortcuts that turn out to be long detours. On this lengthy hike, various institutions and persons have supported and accompanied me. Looking back far down the trail, I must first of all thank Walter Bühl, M. Rainer Lepsius, Lorenz G. Löffler, and Wolfgang Marschall. The Institut für die Wissenschaften vom Menschen in Vienna and the Franke Institute for the Humanities at the University of Chicago supported my work with research fellowships.

I wrote this book at the University of Chicago, where I have been teaching since 1990. What I owe to this institution in general, and in particular to its Divinity School, my colleagues and students, can scarcely be expressed in words. Richard Rosengarten, the dean of the Divinity School, has constantly encouraged my work. I laid out my theory in my classes and I am indebted to my students for challenges, corrections, and clarifications. Aaron Bradley, Kelly Chong, Amanda Huffer, Rory Johnson, Mary Ellen Konieczny, Loren Lybarger, Sunit Singh, Michaela Soyer, Nelson Tebbe, and Geneviève Zubrzycki served as my research assistants. I thank them all for their support.

Intellectual exchanges with colleagues in Chicago over the years were of inestimable value to me. In order not to reproduce here a complete address book, let me mention above all Prasenjit Duara, Bruce Lincoln, Moishe Postone, Marshall Sahlins, Anthony Yu, Malika Zeghal, and especially Andreas Gläser, who read one chapter in great depth and discussed it with me. In Germany I benefited particularly from exchanges of ideas with Friedrich Wilhelm Graf, Hans Kippenberg, and Detlef Pollack, and in Japan from conversations with Koizumi Junji, Kurimoto Eisei, and Shimazono Susumu.

I have set forth parts of the theory in lectures at the universities of Basel, Copenhagen, Frankfurt-an-der-Oder, Graz, Illinois (at Urbana), Osaka, Stockholm, Tokyo, California (at Los Angeles and at Santa Barbara), Uppsala, Vienna, and Yale. I thank Hubert Seiwert for his help with the transcription of Chinese characters and names. I wish also to thank Steven Rendall for the excellent collaboration during the translation process. The greatest debt of gratitude I owe to my wife, to whom this book is dedicated.

CHAPTER ONE

Religion as Discourse:
On the Critique of the Concept of Religion

The concept of religion is so much taken for granted in our everyday language that we can hardly imagine that only about two hundred years ago it was far from widespread. "Religion" is an abstract concept through which concrete "religions" can be compared with one another. Many processes contributed to the elaboration of this concept, such as the schism of Western Christendom during the Reformation and the religious wars that followed it, the spread of trade and the colonial expansion connected with that spread, and the revolution in the sciences with its ensuing process of disenchantment or demystification. All this contributed to the development of discourses in which people sought to situate religion between revelation and reason and to understand the newly discovered plurality of religions. With the increasing theoretical and practical rationalization and critique of religion, the concept of religion evolved into a medium in which cultural and social debates on fundamental problems were conducted. It is probably no exaggeration to say that nearly all the Enlightenment's central questions, from metaphysics to epistemology, from ethics and aesthetics to anthropology, were raised in relation to the concept of religion. For these reasons, in the discourses of Western modernity the concept of religion was far more clearly defined and systematized than in the premodern West or than comparable concepts in non-Western societies.

Even if we recognize the specific character of the concept of religion in Western modernity, this in no way means that the concept of religion expresses a cognitive distinction that is specifically Western. The distinction between religious and nonreligious is lacking neither in the premodern West nor in non-Western cultures, and the religious in the sense of institutions that are associated with superhuman powers has existed in all ages and cultures. Religious activity has always been distinguished from nonreligious activity, religious specialists from other specialists, sacred places from profane places, and holy times from profane times. Premodern emperors in the West and in Asia always conducted religious politics and often created specific offices for this purpose. It is true that in other cultures and ages there was less cause to define and systematize religion as an abstract concept, but as early as the twelfth century a complex system for classifying religions was created by the Muslim scholar Shahrastani (1086–1153).[1] In addition, in some non-Western languages there are concepts that are at least similar to the concept of religion.[2] In comparison with the modern West, however, the sharp differentiation between religious and nonreligious institutions and the contrast between the religious and the secular are for the most part lacking.[3]

Nonetheless, the strong symbolic content of the concept of religion in the modern West has not led to the elaboration of a single, dominant concept of religion but, instead, in accordance with the diversity of worldviews, institutional contexts, and interests, to a diversity of definitions that are still difficult to sort out.[4] Depending on preconceptions, religion is a revealed truth, an indispensable component of society, a human capacity that is given a priori and serves as the foundation for any morality, or, on the contrary, a symptom of alienation, a remnant of a prescientific age, an ideology in the service of worldly interests, an infantile illusion, or a kind of romantic escapism. Some people have defined religion so generally that everyone has to be "somehow" religious, and others have defined it so narrowly that hardly anyone can be "really" religious.

In other words, the definition of religion already decides whether religion is a universal phenomenon that simply varies in form or a historically determined phenomenon that emerges and passes away.[5] The evolutionary approaches of the nineteenth and twentieth centuries assumed that religion was based on a process of transformation that concerned not only its form but also its content. For instance, evolutionary and historical models from Hegel to Robert Bellah postulated that religion developed from emotionality to rationality, from magical beginnings to religio-ethical heights, from natural religion to revealed religion, from particularism to universalism, or from immanent to transcendental salvation.[6]

Which phenomena are subsumed under the concept of religion also implies overt or covert value judgments. Are religions always morally "good," or can they also be considered, from another standpoint, as "evil" if they justify, for instance, cannibalism, oppression, or violence by referring to the will of superhuman powers? Are only conventional and orthodox forms of "religion" really religion, while all deviations from them are either "magic," "superstition," or "witchcraft"? Are only ecclesiastically organized communities "genuine" religions in contrast to "sects" or even "cults" that ecclesiastical monopolists of "true religion" seek to control through special functionaries? And what should we say about "quasi-religious" phenomena? Did nationalism temporarily replace religion, and is religion now returning with the decline of the nation-state in the age of globalization? Are soccer games and rock concerts "somehow" also religious, since they produce enthusiastic communities? What is "spirituality," and what should we think about it? Should any experience of "self-transcendence" be regarded as religious?[7] All such questions and problems are involved in any definition of religion, whether or not we want them to be.

Modern Religious Discourses

In the history of Western modernity, one can somewhat simplistically distinguish four epochs of religious discourse: an Enlightenment discourse, a Romantic discourse, a secularization discourse, and a postmodern discourse. The Enlightenment discourse was concerned primarily with the question of whether and how reason and religion could be reconciled. The radical Enlightenment, especially in France, used reason to criticize religion, in which it saw a prescientific mode of thought that belonged to the past.[8] In contrast, more moderate representatives of the Enlightenment sought to reconcile reason and religion by rationalizing religion itself. They dreamed of a reasonable religion in the form of a natural religion, or a reasonable Christianity in which the emphasis was on ethics.[9]

As a reaction to the Enlightenment discourse, the Romantics put religion beyond the reach of rational criticism by assigning it a special place in the heart or soul [Gemüt]. The Romantic approach thus created an enclave for religion within human nature that was analogous to that for aesthetics. On this view, religion was naturally inherent in humans as a potential that could be developed or allowed to wither away. At the same time, this view made religion sui generis, that is, irreducible to other phenomena and impossible to explain by means of social or psychological factors. Religion was characterized as a form of intuition that could be the bearer of both individual "genius" and the "genius" of a "people." The now widespread notion of "spirituality" continues the individualistic orientation of Romantic discourse.[10]

The secularization discourse, which dominated the past century, continued the Enlightenment discourse in a modified way. Now it was primarily a question of the alleged retreat of religion from state and society to the social periphery and the human private sphere. Historically, this view was always only partly correct, and given the massive increase in religious movements and the return of religions into the political public sphere, it rightly entered a crisis that favored the emergence of postmodern discourse.

In the Enlightenment, Romantic, and secularization discourses, the goal was to determine the "essence" of religion and its role in modernity. Is religion primarily a worldview, a morality, or a feeling? Is it an irrational reaction to threatening phenomena, or does religion sanctify society's key cognitive and normative ideas? Is religion an instrument used to strengthen domination or emancipation, or is it neutral with regard to social coordination and integration? Is religion a phenomenon of human alienation or the full realization of the human person? Although in all three discourses the object and function of religion are defined quite differently, hardly any doubts arise about the concept of religion itself.

The postmodern perspective leaves this common foundation behind. Shaped by the "linguistic turn" in the humanities and by the Foucauldian interpretation of Nietzsche, this discourse deconstructs ingrained notions by locating them in the context of power structures and strategies of legitimating domination. To a certain degree these approaches develop further central insights of Karl Marx, Émile Durkheim, and Max Weber. The Marxist dictum that the ruling ideology is the ideology of the rulers is deepened empirically and theoretically by investigating the ways in which linguistic rules and classification systems not only express positions of super- and subordination but help create them by facilitating their internalization, reproduction, and naturalization.[11] This can be connected with Durkheim's insight that society is possible only on the basis of shared categories of thought, and also with Weber's postulate that domination is stable over time only if it succeeds in eliciting and maintaining belief in its legitimacy.

Shaped by the theory of discourse and by the criticism of concepts, this perspective has now been extended to the concept of religion as well. But instead of merely investigating the function of religion in the construction of ideologies of domination or resistance, postmodern debate has taken as the object of analysis the changing discursive construction of the concept of religion.[12] Stimulated by the reading of Nietzsche, many writers now see the category of religion itself as a historically specific attempt to establish structures of power. As a result, the former conviction that religion was a universally applicable analytical concept, or even a concept for which there are linguistic equivalents in all cultures, has in recent decades given way to a widespread skepticism or even rejection. Religion is now considered a category that was first developed in the secularization discourse of Western modernity and thus cannot be universalized. Anyone who persists in universalizing it naïvely misunderstands its role in the production of power/ knowledge.

Postcolonial theories develop this perspective still further by investigating the ways in which the concept of religion is used in colonialism. They assert that it is inappropriate to apply the concept of religion to other cultures and complain about the manipulation of this concept in the interest of the colonial powers. Thus classifications—for example, the classification of Hinduism, Buddhism, or Confucianism as "religions"—are often said to be Western "inventions" that arose from the specific interests of Western colonial powers or missionaries.[13]

Authors who consider themselves in no way indebted to Foucauldian thought, postcolonial theory, or "subaltern studies" have also criticized the specifically Christian heritage of the concept of religion. Because Christianity came to see itself as a religion and took as its starting point the unquestioned assumption that religion was universal, "religions" that could be constructed on the analogy of Christianity had to be discovered everywhere. However, this obviously involved a specifically Western cognitive ordering of social and cultural reality that is supposed to be inapplicable to non-Western cultures.[14]

From my point of view, no sharp distinctions—whether in terms of content or of chronology—can be drawn between the four debates that I have associated with the Enlightenment, Romanticism, secularization, and postmodernity. Neither have they replaced each other; rather, they have overlapped in the course of time. None of these approaches has really come to an end, and all four raise questions that have to be considered if one wants to formulate a theory of religion.

The Indispensability of the Concept of Religion

At this point it may be asked why I cling to the concept of religion and why I am interested in a theory of religion at all. I could, after all, simply be satisfied with the postmodern demystification of the concept of religion and accept that it has now historically reached its end. Other concepts, such as fetishism and totemism, have undergone this fate, and no one misses them. Why should it be any different for the concept of religion? Nonetheless, I believe there is a whole series of good reasons not to adopt this conclusion and to retain the concept of religion, though not just any concept of religion, as I will explain later in greater detail.

It seems to me unnecessary to abandon the concept of religion, for the criticism of it is insufficiently persuasive. Its critics overemphasize the

Western origin of the concept and fail to consider all its definitions and modes of usage. Critics always argue as if there were only one modern Western concept of religion, marked by an indelible stain that cannot be corrected by redefinition. As a rule, no alternative concepts are offered that either lack such connotations or constitute the object in a different way. On the contrary, critics deconstruct the concept of religion and then cheerfully continue to make use of it.

My adherence to the concept of religion is based on neither theological nor religious but solely pragmatic grounds. Its critics are right in saying that the concept cannot be universalized on the basis of either a theory of discourse or a theory of institutions, but they overlook approaches founded on a theory of action. From my point of view, the concept of religion as action makes sense and is indispensable. Subsuming religious action under other concepts would result in an analytical loss with regard to our ability to understand and explain the specificity of religious phenomena. Given the great significance of religiously motivated action in our time, not to mention in other centuries, an abandonment of the concept of religion would represent a loss for knowledge. I do not assume that religion was implanted in humans through a divine act of creation or provided a priori by nature. In humans' interaction with their environment, religion developed as a relationship to superhuman powers. I will therefore propose a definition and a theory of religion that will make possible a better understanding of religion as a specific type of meaningful social action and, at the same time, account for its universality.

Not least, I oppose my theory of religion to deconstructionism, which, fashionable as it is, hinders serious research and has confused a whole generation of students. I consider the constant repetition of these debates quite banal, once one has understood what is at issue. Such a position cannot be maintained in the long run, for in deconstructing a given concept one has to make use of other concepts, which either have already been deconstructed by others or at least are similarly deconstructible. This obviously holds for all concepts that might be substituted for the concept of religion.

From now on we could, of course, study ideologies, discourses, cultures, or "cosmographic formations."[15] But we already know that these concepts have also been "constructed" through historically specific discourses and are thus nothing but instruments in the linguistic battle between classes or cultures. Ultimately we could do away with the concept of discourse itself, having finally seen through that too. Then we would simply go on writing while avoiding analytical concepts or relativizing them. In some disciplines this goal has already been achieved, based loosely on the motto "Yesterday we were still standing at the edge of the abyss, today we've gone a step further." Since no theory of religion can be formulated without a concept of religion, I must first discuss in greater detail the postmodern critique of the concept of religion.

On Discourse-Theory Criticism

In its serious versions, postmodern criticism has provided a positive stimulus and has thereby helped to elevate thinking about the concept of religion. Despite my rejection of most of the points made by these critics, the debate has certainly sharpened everyone's awareness of the problem. Unfortunately, however, the fate of postmodern and postcolonial discourse-analysis criticism is in some respects similar to that of Marxist ideological criticism: in being popularized, it has often degenerated into simplistic theories of power struggle and conspiracy.

Nonetheless, arguments regarding the sociology of knowledge that are worth considering are found not only in Marx and Nietzsche but also in Foucault and a few postcolonial theoreticians. How concepts and linguistic rules originate, how they shape our thought, how they produce or reproduce social, political, and psychological structures, are certainly not trivial questions. But although serious theorists understand that the trajectory from the context in which such linguistic rules emerge to their actual or alleged effects is a complex and contradictory process, epigones often draw hasty teleological conclusions. Linguistic rules and classification schemata are seen as the result of deliberate manipulation on the part of the "ruling class," as if members of this echelon could themselves simply escape the power exercised by categories of thought. From this point of view, the task of knowledge is to "unmask" concepts as "constructed." This "constructedness" of concepts will, however, be news only to those who thus far have naïvely assumed a direct correspondence between reality and concepts. How anyone might make this assumption, given the tradition of nominalism or the neo-Kantian debates around the turn of the twentieth century, I cannot imagine.[16]

The most interesting criticism of the concept of religion was elaborated for the most part by poststructuralist and postcolonial authors operating largely under the influence of Foucauldian discourse theory. The first writer who subjected the concept of religion to rigorous criticism from this point of view was the anthropologist Talal Asad. His critique of the definition of religion dates from 1983, but first gained a wide audience when it was published ten years later in his book *Genealogies of Religion.*[17] Asad draws on

Foucault in arguing that the concept or religion itself is a product of social discourse. According to him, religion has no immutable essence; rather, the essence of religion is discursively constituted in each case and is thus just as mutable as are social structures, power relations, and processes from which it stems. To that extent there can be no universal concept of religion but, at most, an archaeology of changing concepts of religion. Western modernity, for instance, has produced a concept of religion entirely different from those of the Christian Middle Ages or of Islam.

The predominant modern, liberal concept regards religion as a separate sphere, distinct from politics and economics. This allows secular liberalism to limit religion's scope, and it allows liberal Christians to defend religion. However, applying this liberal concept of religion to Islam or even to medieval Christianity leads to distortions. Instead of understanding these religions as they were constructed in their historical context, it measures them against the modern liberal concept of religion and thus misunderstands them. For this reason, Asad argues not for a better universal concept of religion but, rather, for insight into the impossibility of any such concept. Using Clifford Geertz's definition of religion, he then seeks to prove how culturally specific, ethnocentric, and constructed in relation to Christian belief this allegedly universal concept of religion ultimately is.

Asad's historico-relativistic perspective represents an understandable reaction to crude overgeneralizations. It attempts to do justice to the cultural dimensions of societies, the political embeddedness of cultural phenomena, and the specific shaping of subjects. There is much in Asad's critique that is noteworthy and justified. I absolutely share his opinion that religion is not a transhistorical phenomenon that is sui generis and inherent in the human species or that slumbers in human inwardness.[18] I also agree with Asad's view that in each case the institutionalization of religion must be analyzed in connection with a society's political structures of power. We can even observe without reservation that Max Weber already did this in his analyses of religion. We have only to consider his studies on the religions of China, India, and ancient Judaism, on the concept of charisma, and on political and hierocratic domination. Still, Weber's model of religious and political domination and his identification of oppositional mentalities and interests is more complex than Asad's discourse theory.

Asad seems to start out from the assumption that in every religious tradition and historical period there is a dominant understanding of religion that is distinct from that of other traditions and periods. Thus, the modern, liberal understanding of religion is discursively constructed in a way different from those of Islam or the Christian Middle Ages. I consider this view to be erroneous for a number of reasons. Asad reduces interpretations of religion to discourses and pays no attention to religious practices; he also ignores the diversity of parallel discourses and overlooks transcultural structural parallels.

In the West, the concept of religion has a long history that does not begin with the Enlightenment, and can in no period be limited to a single definition.[19] In modernity, as a rule, there is a diversity of parallel discourses and perspectives that exhibit opposing ideas regarding religion and the appropriate way of institutionalizing it. Even within religious studies there is no consensus as to whether the concept of religion ought to be used at all. Decades ago, W. C. Smith questioned the concept from a Romantic point of view.[20] Asad's claim that the liberal concept of religion is dominant in Western modernity is also problematic historically. If we say that the liberal understanding of religion dates from about 1800, then we must note that during the intervening two centuries there have been long and vigorous conflicts regarding the public role of religion, and these conflicts are still going on. The question of the separation of church and state, of religion and politics, has given rise to quite different solutions depending on the social system and the religious tradition in various Western countries, and is still in flux.[21]

The Catholic Church has, at least until the twentieth century, opposed the liberal concept of religion and sought wherever possible to defend its own dominance and legal privileges. In countries in which it represented the interests of the state, Lutheranism has also advocated a view of religion that is in no way liberal. We more commonly find a nationalization of religion than a secularization. The Prussian king Frederick William III forced the Lutheran and Reformed churches to merge and even wrote liturgies for the newly unified denomination. In Scandinavian countries, Lutheranism is still largely an established church even in the twenty-first century. Only in Sweden has it recently been disestablished. The role of the Catholic Church in Spain, Ireland, or Poland offers further examples that do not simply follow the liberal understanding of religion.[22] Clearly, discourse analyses are insufficient for the investigation of the actual institutionalization of religion in Western modernity (or elsewhere).

Even within Western modernity we find no monolithic discourse on religion but, rather, a diversity of discourses that must be attributed to specific contexts and institutions—for example, to a political-legal context, a normative-moral one, an intrareligious one, and an analytical-scholarly one.

In each context the concept of religion is expected to produce different distinctions, and in each case different interests and perspectives are involved in its formulation.

In the normative-moral discourse, it is a matter of distinguishing between good and bad, legitimate and illegitimate forms of religion. This distinction may be manifested, for instance, in the classification of certain practices and communities as superstition, cult, magic, or witchcraft. It is principally members and representatives of religious institutions who make use of this discourse, though an interested public and the media may also participate in it.

In the political-legal discourse, it is a matter of distinguishing between legal and illegal forms of religion, between those that are legally permissible and those that are not, between those that politically desired and those that are not. In this discourse it is decided which forms of religion are in the interests of the political order or should be allowed or forbidden in accordance with the established principles inherent in that order. Here jurists and politicians are dominant, for it is they who write, amend, and interpret the constitution. Lobbyists for religious groups and academics are listened to, but as a rule they do not make decisions.

In intrareligious discourses, it is a question of appropriate religious practice, right belief, or legitimate authority. Which kinds of practice correspond to the assumed will of superhuman powers? How should one, and how can one, communicate with these powers? What are the consequences for our everyday activities? In addition, references to other religious communities are also found here. Issues involving delimitation and polemics are involved, but commonalities are also sought through assimilation or identification. From a practical point of view, it is a matter of clarifying interactions with members of other religious communities. In which kinds of worship may one participate, and with whom may one share a meal, enter into marriage, or engage in social intercourse?

The social sciences and the humanities define religion as an analytical concept in accordance with empirically verifiable characteristics. Here it is a question of interpreting and explaining social action and tracing it back to its supposedly universal anthropological, psychological, or social foundations. This discourse is dominated by academics. Yet even in these secular disciplines the liberal-secular concept of religion has been in no way established; rather, various academic disciplines favor quite different interpretations of religion, which depend partly on specific disciplines and partly on philosophical and political premises. The sociology of religion, religious studies, anthropology, cognitive psychology, neurology, and theology do not work with a single, unified concept of religion. And critics of Western modernity tend to conceive religion differently than its supporters do. Although these discourses obviously have porous boundaries and thus influence one another, they manifest differences in the interests of those concerned and in the way they see the problem.[23]

Asad's argument reveals a general weakness in discourse analyses: they tend to focus on the discourses of political and intellectual elites, while ignoring the deviating practices of large population groups. In fact, however, these practices represent a commentary that must not be overlooked. Here I agree with Edmund Leach, who once pertinently remarked that not only language but also social behavior represents a means of communication, and that the anthropologist should keep both forms of communication simultaneously in view.[24]

Max Weber's outline of the affinity between various classes and their experiences of rationality as well as their typical forms of religiousness also implies that the social division of labor alone can lead to the development of different understandings of religion within the same society. In his view, peasants and craftsmen, bureaucrats and soldiers, have in all periods and regardless of cultural boundaries understood religion differently and practiced it differently than the cultural elites have. At the same time, these different understandings of religion exhibit structural similarities beyond the boundaries of religious tradition. To that extent, there is no "medieval Christianity" as a homogenous phenomenon. At the same time, the religions of farmers or soldiers resemble each other beyond the boundaries of religious tradition.

Finally, Asad's claim that there could be no universal concept of religion is neither sufficiently grounded nor logically valid. On the contrary: even if one adheres to the view that religion has a different structure, function, and meaning in different social formations, this view requires a concept of religion on which such a claim can be grounded. If religion always means something different in different contexts, how do the critics of the concept of religion know that what is different in each case still represents "religion," especially in societies that have no concept of religion? Either the phenomena present such great differences that a common concept for them cannot be justified and the concept of religion should be abandoned, or they represent only different forms of something that remains definable in terms of shared characteristics. If one accepts the premises of discourse theory, then all concepts are gradually dissolved into ultimately incomparable particularisms. In my view, we cannot adequately describe the uniqueness of social phenomena without general concepts and comparisons. Moreover, in contrast to this historically relativist view, it turns out that types of discourse are quite similar over and beyond periods and cultures.

On Postcolonial Criticism

Postcolonial theories pick up where discourse-theory criticism of the concept of religion leaves off and develop it further. According to them, the application of the category of religion to the cultures of India, China, or South Africa, for instance, amounts to a kind of ideological colonization. From a postcolonial point of view, this involves imposing on non-Western societies a concept that prevents an adequate understanding of them and falsely reconstructs them in accordance with Western categories.

Within postcolonial criticism there are some writers who fundamentally reject the use of the concept of religion, since "religion" is an inappropriate category for understanding, for instance, Hinduism. Others reject the specifically Christian connotations of the concept of religion, yet cling to the concept itself.[25] Both groups, however, agree that during the colonial period the concept of religion was misused to interpret or even to organize non-Western religions in accordance with the model of Christian religion instead of understanding them in accordance with the way they are interpreted and embedded in their own cultures. Out of this critical view have developed studies that emphasize the manipulation of the concept of religion for the purposes of colonial projects or Christian missionary work. In them, Hinduism, Buddhism, or Confucianism are considered inventions of colonial officials, missionaries, and orientalists.[26]

This criticism of the concept of religion is not, of course, entirely off base. Colonial projects themselves were often religiously conceived as "missions to the pagans," in which other cultures were seen as either lacking religion or adhering to inferior forms of religion. Such characterizations could, moreover, be made to serve the interests of the colonial powers, as David Chidester has shown in his studies on the use of the concept of religion in South Africa. Furthermore, missionaries often found themselves in a complicated situation with regard to the similarity of religious practices. For example, José de Acosta (1540–1600), a Spanish Jesuit missionary, was astonished by the parallels between the Incas' religious practices and those of the Catholic Church and saw in them an intentionally confusing tactic on the part of the devil to discredit Christianity: "What is most astonishing about Satan's envy and desire to compete with God is that not only in idolatries and sacrifices but also in certain kinds of ceremonies he has mimicked our sacraments, which our Lord instituted and his Holy Church employs, especially the sacrament of communion, the loftiest and most divine of them all."[27]

A question arises, however: from the fact that the concept of religion was involved in colonial projects and interests, must one necessarily conclude that any scholarly use of that concept is impossible, or that it merely helps mask political intentions? Like discourse theories, the postcolonial approach suffers from a lack of specificity. The claim that outside the West there was no "religion," or that, before they were invented by the West, there was no "Hinduism" or "Confucianism," requires more precise analysis. The rejection of the concept of religion as a matter of principle invites us to ask: in what sense did religion not exist before the encounter with the West? In what sense are Hinduism, Buddhism, or Confucianism not religions or religions "invented" by the West?

In his comparative studies on Chinese religion, for example, Jordan Paper argues that the use of the Western concept of religion is problematic for three reasons. He claims first of all that there is no linguistic equivalent, second that religion cannot be generally distinguished from culture, and third that in China religious and state institutions are not differentiated.[28] I consider all three objections invalid. Linguistic equivalence will always be debated, and has also varied widely. The claim that religion cannot be distinguished from culture is simply the result of an inadequate differentiation between religious practices and religious traditions. Paper mentions, however, that one of the questions in China that is comparable to the concept of religion is "To whom are you sacrificing?"[29] This certainly provides a starting point for an analytic concept of religion insofar as it is related to practices of establishing contact with superhuman powers. And this corresponds exactly to the action-theory approach that I am pursuing here.

An interesting illustration of postcolonial criticism is found in an analysis of the Indian debate between Hindus and Christians regarding religious conversion. Sarah Claerhout and Jakob de Roover argue that this debate cannot lead to any conclusion because each side has a completely different understanding of religion. Hindus and Christians are not talking about the same thing when they discuss "religion" and "conversion." For Hindus, religion represents something entirely different from what it does for Christians.[30] Christians, according to these authors, maintain that some religions are untrue, that religions compete with one another, and that one religion leads to heaven and all others lead to hell. In contrast, Hindus consider no religion to be false, do not see religions as rivals, and believe that they lead to the same goal.[31] What Claerhout and De Roover don't say, however, is that for Hindus, religion is the tradition of a community. Its justification

lies in the fact that it is venerable and has helped countless earlier generations regulate their lives and orient themselves in the world. They thus experience Christian religious propaganda as a form of aggression.

When the authors claim that from the Hindu point of view no religion
could be false, their argument again requires clarification. If all religions are
true, no objection could legitimately be made to missionary work. However,
the Hindu position maintains that each religion is appropriate for a specific
social group. In other words, it involves not a universal but a particularist
concept of truth. According to this ethnic understanding of religion, Christianity is false for Hindus, and Hinduism is false for Christians. This Hindu
position is, however, not essentially different from Christian traditionalist
positions.

Here it may help to consider the history of the European Enlightenment.
Joseph II's reforms included an edict of tolerance (1781), whose chief effect
was to legalize Protestantism in the Habsburg Empire and to allow it to
carry out missionary work among Catholics. The edict was met with bitter
resistance, however, especially from the Catholic Church and the rural population. A letter of protest addressed to Joseph II by Tyroleans complains
that by tolerating other religions "the bonds of Christian unity" would be
torn asunder. The Catholic Church's monopoly is founded on the argument
that "the Roman Catholic religion, the religion of our fathers [. . .] should
remain the only one in the country." Only in this way, the letter says, will
it be possible to avoid "besmirching our morals and our way of thought."[32]
Because of such protests, the freedom to convert was once again restricted,
six years after the edict of tolerance was issued. Here, too, reference to the
community and tradition was the ground for rejecting conversion. And here,
too, religion and culture merged. Claerhout and De Roover's description of
the Indian debate may be accurate, but they err when they assume that they
are also describing general differences between Christianity and Hinduism.

In any case, I consider unfortunate the question whether Hinduism,
Buddhism, or Confucianism are religions. As I will later show, a religion
is an empirically given system of practices related to superhuman powers.
Concepts such as Christianity, Buddhism, or Hinduism refer not to a single
system of practices but rather to religious traditions and continuities of
symbolic systems. To that extent, religious traditions are more comprehensive than religions in the sense of systems of practices, and often include
ethnicity or culture in the broader sense.

Thus, instead of trying to decide whether Hinduism or Confucianism
are religions, one should ask whether these traditions contain, or contribute
to, systems of practices that could be called "religious" insofar as contact

with superhuman powers is established in such practices. This question can certainly be answered in the affirmative. To that extent, these traditions also do not constitute something "invented" or "imagined" by Western colonial officials, scholars of religion, or missionaries, but rather contain changing systems of meaningful practices with a long history.

From my point of view, postcolonial critics also go wrong when they ascribe to the cultures of colonized peoples a role that is ultimately passive, and assume that the construction of "religions" must be attributed to Western intervention alone. Rather, what are involved are interactions in which both sides, both the colonizers and the colonized, took part, though with differing chances of achieving their goals. Historically, however, this was nothing new. For example, in the course of its spread to China, Indian Buddhism was transformed by its encounter with Confucianism and Daoism.[33] And Confucianism, Hinduism, and Buddhism each reacted differently to Christian missionary activity and to Western colonialism.[34] So the development of reform movements within these traditions in response to Western challenges does not mean that the West thereby "invented" these religions; instead, such movements represent reactions of indigenous cultures and institutions against the penetration of Western colonial powers, traders, and missionaries.[35] Even if this encounter might have provided the initial impetus for systematizing and rationalizing Hinduism, Buddhism, and Confucianism and determining them on the Christian model, the result is still an Indian Hinduism, a Chinese Confucianism, and a Singhalese Buddhism.

Certain critics seem unaware that by insisting on the absolute otherness of non-Western cultures they are demoting them to the status of passive receivers of what the West is supposed to have made out of them. These critics are clearly following naïve Romantic notions by interpreting the encounter with the West as a kind of contamination through which cultures have lost their authenticity. In so doing, however, they make Western modernity not only a watershed in world history but also its only real actor.

On the Necessity of Analytical Concepts

Postmodern criticism's most important contribution consists in examining general concepts to see how far they universalize historically particularist ideas and thereby misunderstand other cultures and especially non-Western cultures. Dipesh Chakrabarty, for example, has shown that it not enough to gauge the solidarity of Indian workers by the standard of the Marxist model of a class-conscious working class that emerged in the context of the liberal capitalist development of the West.[36] And Talal Asad has pointed out that the idea of religion as a privatized, depoliticized social sphere cannot be applied universally. I fully agree with these arguments, which ultimately continue and further develop the Marxist critique of ideology. Western development must not be normatively applied to other societies, as are both liberal theories of modernization and Marxist schemata of development. All concepts need to be reflected upon critically before they can be generalized.

The postmodern debate, however, includes arguments that far overshoot the target. For example, it is often argued that the concept of religion is not universalizable and cannot be applied to other cultures because it is a Western concept. If this is supposed to imply that scholars, in analyzing society and culture, should use only universal concepts that are also linguistically universal, it is a position that would spell the end of all scholarly work. Every concept has proceeded at some point from culturally specific discourses in a specific language. In addition, such a position would make comparison impossible and would end in the senseless and inaccurate view that all cultures are incomparably "different" but that their "difference" cannot be expressed in language.

General concepts are indispensable for any cognitive ordering of the world. Scholarship seeks not only to communicate an immanent interpretation of a culture, but also to understand, compare, and explain cultures in their social and historical contexts. Yet we can understand the peculiarities of cultures only if we can establish their relations to other cultures. We need a conceptual framework that allows us to make comparisons and thus to precisely describe and qualify similarities and differences.

Moreover, it is not at all clear what a purely "culturally immanent" observation would actually be and who would be capable of making it. "Culture" is, after all, an achievement of systematization. Viewed realistically, each individual usually understands only a certain part of his own culture, the part that is accessible to him in the world as he experiences it. "Cultures" first become comprehensible as "wholes" when viewed from a distance that no longer takes them as given or natural and makes it possible to discern difference. But difference implies comparison, and comparison requires general concepts.

The necessity and inevitability of applying Western scholarly concepts to other cultures certainly does not mean that this should be done carelessly or thoughtlessly. The question whether and, especially, which concepts are applicable to other cultures and societies is not a trivial one. Naturally, when culturally specific concepts are naïvely applied, there is a danger of fundamental misunderstandings and erroneous interpretations. Marx rightly reproached the bourgeois economy for having falsely conceived earlier eras by using bourgeois categories, as if man had always been *homo oeconomicus*. The same holds for the concept of religion. But the concept of religion, like the concepts of "economy" and "mode of production," can be formulated so that it does not bear specifically modern characteristics.

While it is a universal fact that humans physically reproduce themselves in society through the social organization of labor, the specific forms of this organization are not universal but vary immensely. Modern capitalist economic structures differ, for example, from ancient capitalism, from feudalism, or from a subsistence economy. Furthermore, each of these forms is extremely diverse internally. The concept of "economy" can be applied to all these phenomena so long as the definition does not imply any assertion regarding the specific form of production and its position in the social fabric. A general concept of economy must, of course, also take into account the fact that in other historical epochs and cultures the economy was embedded in society in a way entirely different from the way it is embedded in Western modernity.[37] Thus in precapitalist periods the economy rarely represented an institutionally differentiated social subsystem. The interests of the actors were differently constructed socially and culturally, and solidarities were founded differently than they are in modern, liberal economic systems. In other words, the legitimacy of the application of Western concepts of the economy is essentially dependent upon how precisely it is extracted from its specific historical, social, and cultural context.

The same holds true for the concept of religion. It too must be defined so that its modern, Western shaping is not simply universalized. The definition must contain neither culturally specific religious ideas and practices nor the specific institutional embedding of religion in the social system. Neither God, nor church, nor the relative autonomy of religious institutions or subjects constitutes an appropriate foundation for a general concept of religion. For this reason, Daniel Dubuisson's criticism of the concept is misplaced. He claims that the existence of religion is connected with its institutionalization as a social subsystem. In his opinion, one can speak of religion only when it exists as an autonomous social realm with a definite structure. Since this is not universally the case, religion, in Dubuisson's view, is a modern phenomenon.[38]

I consider this objection ungrounded because the criterion of institutional differentiation obviously relativizes all social phenomena historically. For example, if music is defined the way Dubuisson defines religion, we arrive at the absurd conclusion that only the modern West has produced music, because only in the modern West was a relatively autonomous music culture differentiated. The institutional point of view is clearly inappropriate for general definitions because it necessarily describes differences. From my point of view, it makes more sense to ask whether other cultures distinguish between religious and nonreligious actions or between musical and non-musical performances. This kind of orientation toward practice or performance crucially alters the way the question is raised, and the change in perspective from the social system to social action also resolves central problems in the concept of religion.

Not only is an institutional definition of religion inappropriate, but so is a discourse-theory determination of the concept. Here, the concept of religion has a problematic no different from that of other concepts in social and cultural studies. The lack of an explicit concept of social structure, of social inequality, or of gender relationships ultimately does not prevent us from investigating these subjects in other cultures and societies. The concept of gender, for instance, refers to the fact that all cultures have different ideas of what counts as "male" or "female" without this being always explainable in terms of biological differences between the sexes. This distinction is encountered everywhere, but in entirely different forms and with differing effects on meaning and social behavior. I believe that few scholars would be prepared to forgo the concept of gender and the investigation of this subject in various cultures and historical periods just because the concept has no equivalent in other cultures or because it can be shown that it was only recently constructed discursively in the West and forged as a weapon in the "war between the sexes."

This is why a universal concept of religion represents a legitimate form of science fiction so long as it takes up fundamental facts of human action or social relations without making their specific shaping part of the definition. For example, if religion is defined as practices that are based on a belief in superhuman powers that can provide blessings or ward off misfortune, this still leaves plenty of room for a variety of forms and interpretations of such practices. Such a definition does not bind religion to specific forms or objects of belief, practices, or organization. It also respects cultural room for maneuver in interpreting blessing and misfortune. Nor does the definition imply that all societies necessarily have such ideas and practices or even a concept of religion.

The continuing relevance of Max Weber's sociology consists not least in the fact that he was fully aware of this problem and took it into account in his own conceptual construction. His elaboration of types constantly distinguishes between general types of action and culturally specific forms. Furthermore, Weber's ideal types are deliberately constructed to serve not as classification schemes but as instruments for the precise description of historically specific formations. Thus, in applying modern Western concepts to the premodern West or to non-Western societies, one must take care to critically examine those concepts, using the tools of an interpretive historical sociology. What is often overlooked is that, conversely, the same is true for the application of premodern Western or non-Western concepts to the modern West. Many concepts in our modern scientific and scholarly language go back to premodern philosophical and religious traditions. Regarding the formation of scholarly concepts, neither an ahistorical universalism nor a culturally relative particularism can be taken for granted.

If one nonetheless wanted to abstain completely from general scholarly concepts because of their cultural and social "constructedness," one would have to give up not only scholarship but also any kind of communication over cultural boundaries. The ability to use language is naturally given to human beings, but language is still a cultural product that changes in the course of history. To that extent, scholarly concepts are obviously part of the cultural repertory of a cognitive ordering of phenomena. At the same time, all humans belong to the same species. This means that cultural repertoires develop in relation to universal characteristics of the species and thus are not arbitrarily or infinitely variable or unbridgeably different. Human beings can understand each other despite cultural differences. We are not simply foreign to each other; we have the ability to overcome foreignness through communication.

With respect to the concept of religion, then, its universal application as an analytical concept is neither unproblematic nor doomed from the outset. Postmodern criticism of the concept of religion is partially correct. As earlier writers pointed out, "religion" is not a name for an unproblematic, given object, which one could simply point to. "Religion" involves a dual process of abstraction, in that abstractions such as Judaism, Christianity, Islam, Buddhism, or Hinduism are transposed into another, higher-level abstraction.

"Religion as such" is not an empirically accessible object. It can be studied only in its concrete forms and practices. Accessible only are concrete actions, religious ideas, institutions, and communities—that is, historically and culturally concrete religions. "Religion as such" also founds no communities that share symbols, practices, and religious ideas. In other words, "religion" is an analytical concept that requires justification.

From Language to Social Reference

My rejection of the postmodern critique of the concept of religion does not yet solve the problem of definition. How can we arrive at a general concept of religion, and how can it be justified? The easiest solution would seem to consist in a positivistic turn according to which we can define as we wish, with success or failure determining the outcome. But this way out of the problem is unsatisfactory from the point of view of an interpretive sociology, because in that sociology definitions are guided not by functions but by structures of meaning. Are there structures of meaning that can be used, over and beyond cultural boundaries, as the foundations for such a definition of religion? I think there are.

In order to recognize them, we have to replace a model based on linguistic criteria by one based on action. Then it becomes clear that distinctions between religious and nonreligious phenomena tend to be universal. This is true in two respects. First, actors draw at least a rudimentary distinction within their own culture between religious and nonreligious actions: namely, religious actions involve personal or impersonal superhuman powers and thus commonly require charismatically qualified specialists, while nonreligious actions do not. In his studies on the Trobriand islanders, Malinowski showed that they certainly distinguished between everyday techniques of gardening, on the one hand, and the accompanying magico-religious interventions, on the other.[39] Second, we know that even societies living in relative isolation from one another distinguish between their own religious beliefs and practices and those of others.[40]

If this is true, then distinctions comparable to the concept of religion should appear outside the modern West as well. Instead of looking for concepts in other languages into which the concept of religion could be translated or even those that are identical with it, we should be looking for cognitive classifications and distinctions that find expression in human action. There are plenty of indications that members of different religions mutually compare their practices and religious ideas and thereby become aware of certain differences as well as similarities. Thus relations between different practices and religious ideas are produced that are in no way incompatible with the concept of religion. Moreover, those who perform functions in different religions perceive themselves as models for cooperation or competition. In other words, a scholarly concept of religion can be justified not least by the fact it specifies activities of coordination and differentiation that appear in the everyday life of many cultures and societies—not exclusively Western or modern Western ones. In the following chapter I will further develop this argument, illustrating it and making it more precise.

CHAPTER TWO

Religion as Social Reference:
On Justifying the Concept of Religion

The universality or general applicability of a concept of religion depends not on the universality of discursively produced concepts but rather on the existence of certain types of meaningful action. I now turn, therefore, not to the analysis of concepts or classification systems but to the investigation of social practices and references. For interpretive sociology, what is really at stake in the conceptualization of religion is the perception of a difference between religious and nonreligious actions, actors, and institutions. This perception may be manifested in a diversity of situations and configurations.

All societies and cultures distinguish between charismatically gifted persons and "normal" ones, or between religious specialists and laypersons, and the corresponding social distance can take various forms. Moreover, religious groups and institutions perceive each other as points of reference. This mutual connection is manifested in phenomena of demarcation and rapprochement, in the claiming of sacred times and places by religions that have replaced earlier ones, in religious politics, and in comparative descriptions made by outside observers. Similarities and differences can either be expressed descriptively or evaluated polemically. They can be organized in structures of competition or parallelism, in egalitarian or hierarchical orders. Every religion that reforms itself or is newly constituted necessarily distinguishes itself from preceding and alternative religions, or else it claims their legacies for itself. Religions adopt and superimpose themselves on the holy places and holy times of other religions.

A plurality of religions forced premodern empires to develop a politics of religion. Thus Chinese, Indian, Persian, and Roman rulers regulated public rituals and through their edicts influenced the balance of power between various religious groups and institutions. In all ages, travelers have described religious practices and institutions and compared them with each other. If religions have mutually related to and shaped one another in very different cultural contexts and historical periods, if rulers have pursued politics of religion and travelers have compared religions, then one can legitimately introduce a concept of religion that is based on structures of meaning that are compatible with universal patterns of social relations.

In order to justify the concept of religion, in this chapter I will investigate mutual connections between religious actors and institutions as they are manifested in religious polemics, syncretisms, identifications, and superpositions, and in edicts and in travelers' reports.[1] I have generally limited myself to materials from premodern Western or non-Western societies, since the question whether the concept of religion can be legitimately applied to them is especially controversial.

The goal of my discussion is certainly not to find a universal concept of religion. There can be no such concept, because this degree of conceptual systematization is obviously not universal. What I try to show is the widespread existence of social relations and mutual references that are compatible with the concept of religion. Which aspects of religion are emphasized in the sources depends on the writers' interests. Thus in one case, worldview may be central; in another, morality, orthodox belief, or orthodox practice. For rulers and bureaucrats, the issue is often the effects of religion on the legitimation of their authority, the stability of the social order, or tax revenues. In the examples to be examined, which aspects of religious complexes are emphasized depends less on the historical period than on the respective social position and interests of the actors. Max Weber's sociology of religion contains many references to such perspectives as they are shaped by social class or by their role in the field of religion.[2]

This diversity of perspectives with regard to religion did not emerge only with Western modernity but is a structural feature of all complex societies. At the same time, the differing emphases placed on various aspects of religion in no way imply that certain other perspectives are not also understood as religious. Here we must distinguish among description, interests, and evaluation. Even a peasant whose religious interests may consist primarily in carrying out rituals having to do with harvests, weather, and health will recognize the religious practices of other strata and groups as such. The chanting of Christian monks in a church, the recitation of sutras in a Buddhist monastic community, or the ritual of sacrifice in the temple represent religious phenomena that even peasants can distinguish from nonreligious phenomena in that they are directed toward superhuman powers. A Calvinist will recognize a Giotto fresco as a religious painting, even while rejecting such pictorial representations. And Catholic missionaries in Latin America perceived the natives' "idols" as competitors, even if they condemned them as works of the devil.[3] The classification of such phenomena as religious must be distinguished from their evaluation.

In the following sections I will show how religions constitute themselves in relation to each other. On the one hand, religions often become conscious of themselves by demarcating themselves from and arguing against other religions. On the other hand, interacting religions also borrow elements from one another and assimilate to one another. The identification of one religion with another sometimes occurs when both are seen as expressing the same message. Phases of demarcation and polemics, on the one hand, and phases of assimilation, unification, or identification, on the other, often flow seamlessly into one another or overlap.

Demarcation

Perception of differences between groups constitutes the presupposition of any "identity." We become aware of our own peculiarity and culture by distinguishing them from those of others. For example, the Trobriand islanders had a very particular view of their neighbors on the island of Dobu. As Bronislaw Malinowski reported, the Trobrianders saw the inhabitants of Dobu as superior because they had more deadly magical powers, while at the same time despising them as barbarians because they ate human beings and dogs.[4]

Perceptions of difference, however, always express subliminal commonalities. The Trobrianders did not eat human beings, but they did eat animals and practiced "sorcery." They did not eat dogs, though, and their sorcery was less powerful. As Georg Simmel acutely noted, conflict too is a form of socialization that points to a common basis without which the conflict would have no meaning.[5] Clearly, this also holds for religions. Richard Fletcher, describing the Christianization of northern Europe, rightly notes that missionary work is a kind of competition. In rural areas there were old rituals for controlling the forces of nature. Christian saints had to prove that they had access to powers more effective than those of the native populations. This competition produced a certain degree of comparability and made compromises necessary.[6] Similar configurations can be found in the expansion of Buddhism to China, Tibet, and Japan.[7]

Every religion needs a perception of difference of this kind in order to see itself and represent itself as a religion. All newly constituted or expanding religions therefore resort to polemics or are the object of polemics. But polemics does not aim solely at demarcation from the outside; it often serves

primarily to increase internal pressures to conform. In many of the following examples it will be clear that setting boundaries with other religions is
considered necessary because these boundaries are in practice ignored by
many "believers." Bureaucrats and intellectuals are usually the people concerned with the purity of practice and doctrine, whereas ordinary believers
are clearly less interested in such boundaries. At the same time, this initial
boundary-setting and the systematization that follows from it begins to create a self-conscious tradition out of a vague collection of practices and beliefs. These mutual references will be documented by some examples taken
from the history of Abrahamic and East Asian religions.

Abrahamic Religions

From its beginning, ancient Judaism constituted itself in contrast to other
religions.[8] The invisible and pictorially unrepresentable God of the Hebrew
Bible is compared with the gods and idols of other tribes, his power with that
of other gods, his way of being worshipped with other religious practices.
The First Commandment already distinguishes the god of Judaism from
other gods, whom it is strictly forbidden to worship: "I the Lord am your God
who brought you out of the land of Egypt, the house of bondage. You shall
have no other gods besides Me. [. . .] You shall not bow down to them or serve
them. For I the Lord your God am an impassioned God."[9] The Promised Land
is also based on the rejection and even destruction of alien religions. "When
my angel goes before you and brings you to the Amorites, the Hittites, the
Perizzites, the Canaanites, the Hivites, and the Jebusites, and I annihilate
them, you shall not bow down to their gods in worship or follow their practices, but shall tear them down and smash their pillars to bits."[10]

Christianity also constitutes itself in contradistinction to other religious groups and positions. As a Jewish sect, it initially engaged in polemics
primarily against the dominant Judaism of its time.[11] Thus, for example,
several verses in Matthew begin with the cry, "Woe to you, scribes and
Pharisees, hypocrites!"[12] There are polemics against "false prophets," apparently referring to competing messianic groups.[13]

With the spread of Christianity in the Hellenistic world, the "pagans"
also became relevant as a reference group.[14] This becomes particularly clear
in the Pauline epistles. Thus, for example, Paul calls upon pagans newly
converted to Christianity to avoid "worshipping idols" and sacrificing animals to them.[15] With reference to the people dancing around the "golden
calf" in Exodus 32:19, he warns the Corinthians to "shun the worship of
idols."[16] And he goes on: "What pagans sacrifice they offer to demons and

not to God. I do not want you to be partners with demons. You cannot drink the cup of the Lord and the cup of the demons. You cannot partake of the table of the Lord and the table of the demons."[17]

The whole early history of Christianity is characterized by similar internal and external processes of demarcation. Thus, for example, the synod of Elvira (ca. 306) approved a prohibition on Christians' marrying Jews and pagans or eating with them.[18] These tendencies persisted in later synods and councils, and are present in the writings of classic Christian theologians from Augustine to Thomas Aquinas, Luther, and Calvin.

Like Judaism and Christianity, early Islam also was constituted in reference to other religious communities, and especially to Jewish, Christian, and "idolatrous" groups and practices.[19] It distinguishes between (other) "religions of the Book," that is, Judaism and Christianity, on the one hand, and polytheism and idolatry, on the other.[20] In the light of this distinction, religions are to be accorded differing levels and authenticity. For one thing, religions of the Book function as higher-order religions, as victors over the lower, idolatrous form of religion. Within religions of the Book, Islam sees itself as comparable to Judaism and Christianity and, at the same time, as superior to them because it defines itself as the restoration of their original message.

With regard to polytheism, Islam essentially continues the polemic begun in Judaism and Christianity. In Islam as well, the primary goal is to prevent Muslims from relapsing into polytheism. In sura 109, which is about "disbelievers," we still find a relatively tolerant juxtaposition of Islam and polytheism: "Say [Prophet], 'Disbelievers: I do not worship what you worship, you do not worship what I worship, I will never worship what you worship, you will never worship what I worship: you have your religion and I have mine.'"[21]

Nonetheless, Islam and polytheism are incompatible: "God does not forgive the joining of partners with Him."[22] Islam considers itself the true monotheism in contrast to both Judaism and Christianity. Thus, for example, we find this criticism of the Christian doctrine of the Trinity: "So believe in God and His messengers and do not speak of a 'Trinity'—stop (this), that is better for you—God is only one God, He is above having a son."[23] Finally, in sura 98 a more radical view of the opposition between Islam and other religions is expressed: "Those who disbelieve among the People of the Book and the idolaters will have the Fire of Hell, there to remain. They are the worst of creation."[24]

This reference to other religions is also found in the whole history of Islamic religion. Thus, for instance, in his book *Religion and Empire*, the Muslim scholar Ali Ibn Rabban al-Tabari (833–870) asks hypothetically how one would enable a foreign traveler from India or China who wants to become acquainted with the empire's various religions to find the right path. One would explain to him, he writes, that in the empire there are Zoroastrians, Manichaeans, Christians, and Jews; and there are also Muslims, who adhere to Islam, the purest and most sublime religion.[25] Tabari describes these religious communities, rating them on a scale ranging from "erroneous, impure, and stupid" in the case of the first group, to "good and pure" in the case of Islam.[26] It is obvious that if he were in his right mind, the fictitious Indian or Chinese would inevitably make the right choice. For our purposes, however, all that matters is that a Muslim scholar compares these different communities and does so using categories that are fully compatible with the concept of religion.

Beyond these somewhat polemical or apologetic discussions, in which the superiority of Islam with regard to other religions is central, there is also a rich literature that deals with these subjects in a more descriptive way. Franz Rosenthal even says that the comparative study of religions is one of the greatest achievements of Muslim civilization.[27] Among the most important contributions to this is the work by al-Shahrastani (1086–1153), *Kitab al-milal wa al-nihal*.[28]

Al-Shahrastani's ranking of religions is largely based on a well-known model, their proximity to Islam; but he further differentiates them by categorizing them in four groups: "(1) those who possess a revealed book [. . .], i.e., Jews and Christians; (2) those who possess something like a revealed book, i.e., Magians and Manichaeans; (3) those who subscribe to laws and binding judgements without benefit of a revealed book, i.e., the ancient Sabians; and (4) those who have neither a revealed book nor fixed laws, i.e., the ancient as well as the materialist philosophers, the star- and idol-worshippers, and the Brahmans."[29]

These examples drawn from Judaism, Christianity, and Islam provide sufficient evidence that all three of the Abrahamic religions defined and constituted themselves in contrast to other religions. Essentially, this mutual, often polemical reference continues in later Judaism, Christianity, and Islam.[30]

Asian Religions

Mutual perception and competition are also found in the cradle of the Asian religions known to us, whether we are speaking of Buddhism, Jainism, Sikhism, Daoism, or Shinto. Indian Buddhism emerged as a movement that distinguished itself both from Brahmanism and from other ascetic movements. The Buddha, like other wandering *samanas*, had turned to extreme asceticism, but he found enlightenment only after he had moderated his self-mortification.[31] To five monks who had questioned him, he announced the doctrine of the Middle Way. According to this teaching, there are two dead ends to be avoided in searching for the path to salvation. Ordinary lay-persons, villagers who seek sensual pleasure, end up in one of these, whereas extreme ascetics who have become addicted to self-inflicted pain end up in the other. The Middle Way leads to truth, inner peace, the highest knowledge, and Nirvana.[32]

In this text the Buddha thus excludes from his doctrine the laity, on the one hand, and extreme ascetics, on the other. He goes on to describe in greater detail how he demonstrates his superior power to ascetics with matted hair, and ultimately makes them monks who follow him. The length of this story already suggests that it is of special importance. Here we see the competition defeated.[33]

Another polemic, the *Brahmajala Sutta*, is directed against the false theories and practices of hermits and Brahmins. The Buddha complains that at least a few of them do not live solely on alms given by believers but engage in all sorts of secondary activities that bring in additional revenue, such as reading palms, prophesying, and interpreting dreams; and that they participate in games, sleep in luxurious beds, or attend entertainments.[34] In addition, he criticizes their alleged errors and contradictions. Thus, for instance, he mentions Brahmins who indulge in senseless philosophical speculations and claim to remember details of their previous lives. He criticizes hermits who wriggle out of things like eels, believe everything and its opposite at the same time.[35] The arguments begin with the constantly repeated words, "There are a few ascetics and Brahmins who . . ." or "Although a few ascetics and Brahmins . . ." In the *Kutadanta Sutta* the Buddha rejects animal sacrifice as it is carried out by kings and wealthy Brahmins.[36] All this clearly shows that early Buddhism constituted itself in a specific religious system of references. In accordance with its character as a virtuoso movement, other virtuosos represent the primary negative reference groups.[37]

In the course of Buddhism's expansion toward China, it was transformed by its encounter with Confucianism and Daoism. One can hardly imagine a greater contrast than that between the principles of Indian Buddhism and those of Confucian China, between the ideals of Buddhist monasticism and those of the Chinese bureaucracy. Whereas one of Buddhism's ideals is homelessness, that is, the abandonment of one's family and the graves of one's forefathers, among the highest values for Chinese culture is the pious relationship to one's ancestors.[38] Whereas Chinese culture is essentially life-affirming and believes in the possibility of reforming people and the world as well, Buddhist monasticism rejects the world, and holds that salvation is possible only through flight from the world, through inner indifference to the world and to life. Whereas in Chinese culture the ruler is the supreme father, who alone is allowed to sacrifice to the Lord of Heaven and to whom everyone else is literally subordinate, Buddhist monks frequently openly display their scorn for kings and refuse to bow down to them.[39]

For all these reasons, when Buddhism was introduced into China, it met with continual polemics, which were based on a series of deeply rooted conflicts of value. At the same time, these polemics, like the Buddhists' attempts to refute them, contributed to the transformation and sinization of Buddhism, on the one hand, and to a merging of Confucianism, Buddhism, and Daoism, on the other.

In the *T'ai-p'ing Ching*, a work from the late Han period, Buddhism is criticized for its lack of piety toward ancestors, which is shown above all in its not having a homeland and children.[40] The Buddhists' reaction consisted not only in rejecting such polemics, but often also in formulating a counterpolemic. Thus they falsified texts and presented sutras in which filial piety was stressed. They carried out this strategy in so masterly a fashion that many of these stories achieved great popularity. In addition, the Buddhists argued that there could be no more perfect expression of filial piety than helping one's parents to achieve salvation by converting to Buddhism.[41] On top of that, they argued that the Buddhist concept of piety was superior to the Confucian because Buddhism aimed at universal salvation and thus honored all ancestors, not just an individual's own.[42]

Buddhism bore a different relation to Daoism. At first, the similarity between the two was striking, and Daoism even invented an explanation for it. Buddha was said to be an incarnation of Lao-tzu, who converted the western barbarians. At other times, however, that same doctrine allowed the Daoists to describe Buddhism as an inferior and corrupt imitation of Daoism, and to oppose it.[43] Unlike Daoism, Buddhism was said to be not of Chinese origin and, moreover, to have distorted Daoism's teaching.[44] For their part, the Buddhists sharply attacked Daoism, which some authors found ludicrous, not least because of the claim that the Buddha was an incarnation of Lao-tzu.[45]

The *Konjaku Monogatari*, a Japanese historical collection from the eleventh century, explains the introduction of Buddhism into China by way of a legend, according to which two Indian monks brought relics of the Buddha, along with a few scrolls, to the court of the Chinese emperor Ming in the late Han period. Although the ruler was delighted with them, determined resistance arose among the Daoist masters and government officials. This led to a contest in the palace garden. The two sides faced each other and, as a first test, set the other side's scriptures on fire. While the Daoists' scriptures simply burned up, the Buddhist texts hung in the air along with the luminous relics of the Buddha. In their confusion, the Daoist masters either died or embraced Buddhism.[46]

A collection of Chinese legends about the Daoist grand master Wang and his pupils, written down during the Ming dynasty, refers to the competition between Daoist "immortals" and Buddhist monks.[47] This competition was frequently expressed in contests in which the two sides demonstrated their prophetic or miracle-working abilities; here, naturally, the Daoists always won.[48]

The way religions that were initially opposed end up influencing each other is also shown in Buddhism's spread to Japan.[49] According to tradition, sinified Buddhism first reached Japan in the form of a gift from the Korean king of Pèkché to the Japanese emperor Kimmei. This gift contained a copper and gold image of the Buddha as well as a few "enigmatic" sutras. The emperor confirmed that although Buddhist doctrine was superior to all others, it was difficult to explain and understand.[50]

The emperor and some of his courtiers were very taken with Buddhism and were inclined to introduce it, not least because it offered an opportunity for political centralization. The parallel with Tibet is obvious here.[51] But there were some who warned that this would arouse the wrath of the kami, the traditional superhuman powers, the ancestors, heroes, and gods.[52] Emperor Kimmei therefore suggested an experiment. A statue of the Buddha was given to Iname no Sokune of the Soga clan, Buddhism's strongest supporter, so that it could be venerated.[53] But when a plague broke out, it was interpreted as a punishment inflicted by the kami. The statue of the Buddha was thrown into a ditch and the Soga family's Buddhist temple destroyed.[54] The experiment of establishing Buddhism in Japan was ended. The kami had won the first round.

The second attempt was far more massive. Korean Buddhist monks came into Japan and founded monasteries. They brought with them ritual objects, vestments, and literature. They were accompanied by carpenters and craftsmen to erect and equip the temple. In the course of this development, Buddhism underwent a remarkable adaptation to Japanese conditions, which I will examine later. The result was the coexistence and, ultimately, partial fusion of Buddhism with traditional religious practices that were later known under the name of Shinto. As George Sansom observed, the introduction of Buddhism and Confucianism stimulated the earlier religion and led its believers to regard their previously nameless corpus of religious practices as a system comparable to the two organized faiths. Not until the

Japanese became acquainted with "Butsudo," the Buddha's Way, did they begin to speak of Shinto as the Way of the *kami*.[55]

Thus it was only in the course of its clash with Buddhism that Shinto first became established as a collective concept for traditional practices of venerating the *kami*.[56] The experience of religious difference and competition led to the formulation of mutual references. At first, the perception of differences was dominant, such as the emphasis on doctrine (*kyo*) in Buddhism and on practice (*to*) in Shinto.[57] Also, an awareness developed that different superhuman powers were competing with one another. Over the centuries, representatives of the two religions engaged in polemics against each other. The priests and adherents of each tradition sought to gain the ascendancy. For hundreds of years, Buddhists and supporters of Shinto argued about which objects of veneration were the more important.[58]

Reports of arguments between Buddhism and Confucianism have come down to us from the Edo period. In this debate, both parties seem to assume that they were still stigmatized as foreign and that they would gain legitimacy only by establishing their compatibility with Shinto.[59] Anticipating the persecution of Buddhists in the nineteenth century, the Buddhist priest Ryuon described the groups united in anti-Buddhist polemics. Buddhism was attacked by bigoted Confucian scholars, so-called Shinto scholars, astronomers, and Christian missionaries. They were all enemies of Buddhism.[60]

The reciprocal constitution of religions, their reciprocal recognition as competitors, is also found in the thirteenth-century conflict between Indian Buddhism and an expanding Islam. Whereas the Muslims saw Buddhism as idolatry, the Buddhists regarded Islam as a barbaric religion that still sacrificed animals and made salvation dependent on circumcision.[61]

Superposition

Reciprocity is also evident in religious superpositions, by which I mean the appropriation of sacred places and times by subsequent religions. If pre-Christian shrines and holidays can be transformed into Christian ones, Buddhist holy sites transformed into Hindu sites, or pre-Islamic holy sites transformed into Islamic sites, then a religion's claim to replace its predecessor implies a fundamental recognition of similarities. This often seems to be connected with a belief in the charismatic quality of certain places whose potency a later religion wants to appropriate for itself. The Spanish *reconquista* was not content to demolish mosques, but always built its own churches on the same spot. Even if the act of superposition is held to demonstrate superiority, it still expresses the relatedness of the two religions.

If the successor religion considers its predecessor to belong to another category altogether, superimposition makes little sense.

Syncretic innovations are often involved in the process of superposition. A few examples will suffice to illustrate this process. In the course of Buddhism's decline in India, many Buddhist shrines were Hinduized, and the Buddha of Amaravati was venerated as an incarnation of Vishnu.[62] In 354 CE, Pope Gregory set the Christian Christmas holiday on December 25. Thus the birth of Christ coincides almost exactly with the celebration of the sun god and its irresistible force after the winter solstice (*Sol Invictus*). The Christian Sunday is also derived from the Roman day of the week devoted to this god. Later on, the coincidence of the birth of Christ with the winter solstice also proved successful in missionary work in northern Europe.[63]

A well-known example of the superposition of religions is the conflict over the Ayodhya mosque destroyed by Hindu nationalists in the 1990s. The nationalists' goal was to build a Hindu temple devoted to Rama on the site where, they claimed, another had stood before it was razed by the Muslim conquerors. What interests me here is the reciprocal recognition of Islam and Hinduism. The destruction of Hindu temples once served to humiliate what was, from an Islamic point of view, a conquered and inferior religion. However, the use of the same space for a mosque shows in particular that a holy place of one tradition can be made into a holy place of another tradition. In that case, Islam thus treated Hinduism as a competing religion. The same pattern reappears in the attempt to reverse this process by razing the mosque and (re)building a Hindu temple in its place. Had it been a factory instead of a mosque that stood there, the nature of the conflict would have been entirely different, because it would have lacked symmetry. In this case, members of two religions were competing for the same holy place and thus for symbolic representation and dominance.

An alternative to superposition and competition is peaceful coexistence, sharing spaces and times. Although many religious conflicts arise out of rivalry for control of public spaces, relatively peaceful juxtaposition and shared spaces have also existed in which superpositions have led not to erasure but rather to parallelism. An interesting example is the Kataragama temple complex in Sri Lanka, where Hindus, Buddhists, and Muslims have long coexisted in relative peace.[64]

Assimilation

Polemics, conflicts, and superpositions represent only one side of the coin. Even if religions are often constituted in opposition to each other, they frequently borrow from each other, assimilate to each other, and incorporate elements of the religious ideas, practices, aesthetic representations, and vocabulary of their rivals. Assimilation itself is often connected with competition, which may involve strategies through which one religion incorporates others into its own frameworks while integrating and subordinating them. Or a religion may be compelled to offer the popular benefits and attractions of the others as well as those of its own. Whatever the grounds may be, even syncretisms show that religions mutually perceive and present themselves as comparable.

Asian Religions

The relationship among Confucianism, Daoism, and Buddhism in China could be discussed under all our rubrics, because we find, as already noted, not only demarcations and persecutions but also fusions, syntheses, and identifications. What dominated was frequently determined by political interests.[65] The introduction of Buddhism into China did not merely represent an experience of difference; rather, as early as during the Han period there were syntheses and identifications, especially between Buddhism and Daoism. The similarities between these two religions—such as the lack of sacrificial acts, the central role of meditation, and the belief in the possibility of overcoming death[66]—appeared obvious to contemporaries. Daoists even developed the story of Lao-tzu's conversion of the barbarians, mentioned above, which presupposes that Daoism and Buddhism have a common origin (hua hu). Since both religions had the same ancestry, there was no difference between them, so that it was entirely appropriate to venerate the divinities Buddha and Huang-Lao at the same altar.[67]

Contrary to this myth of origins, however, the Daoists often seem to have been inspired by the Buddhists. They adopted, among other things, figurative representation, the systematization of doctrine, and the canonization of the scriptures. In addition, they used the Buddhist texts flowing into the country to enrich their own canon.[68]

Tendencies toward assimilation and synthesis are also manifest in the writings of the Ming emperor Taizu, who emphasizes the compatibility of Confucianism, Buddhism, and Daoism. He writes that it "is well known that under the Heaven there is (ultimately) no duality in the Way and that the sages are essentially of one mind. They differ only on the question of personal praxis or participation in public life. In that they deliver real benefits, they are in principle all one. Let it be known to ignorant people that all three teachings are indispensable!"[69] The collection of legends known as

The Seven Taoist Masters, too, occasionally refers to parallels between Buddhist, Confucian, and Daoist teachings and practices, and stresses the true knowledge that underlies them all.[70]

A particularly striking illustration of the harmony among Confucianism, Buddhism, and Daoism dates from the eighteenth century and can be found in the Parma Museum. It is a silk painting that represents the emperor Kien Lung (1736–1795) and "three friends." The emperor is depicted surrounded by three plants—a pine tree, a plum tree, and a clump of bamboo—which symbolize Confucianism, Daoism, and Buddhism.[71] Even in present-day China the integration of Buddhist and Daoist elements can be seen in local cults, as Kenneth Dean shows in his interesting study.[72]

The relations between Buddhism and Shinto, likewise, were in no way characterized only by enmity or rivalry but rather, for centuries, by peaceful coexistence and fusion. This harmony was favored in part by political interests. Buddhism's universalism provided the foundation for a unified government, whereas Shinto provided the legitimating charismatic heritage but was clan-bound and therefore locally rooted. Without Buddhism, authority could not be centralized; without traditional Shinto practices, local authority would have weakened.

Buddhist monasteries also had an interest in integrating Shinto practices into the temple complexes, because their taxpaying peasants were attached to these traditional practices and in this way could be spatially bound to the Buddhist temple.[73] To that extent, powerful interests ultimately supported the peaceful coexistence or even a partial synthesis of the two traditions. Buddhism and Shinto were brought into line with one another and institutionally connected.

In 743, the emperor Shomu issued an edict according to which his subjects were to erect a large statue of the Buddha in order to protect the country. The Todaiji temple was completed in 745, and the enormous statue of the Buddha in 751. In this phase of Buddhism's triumph, the question arose, from the Shinto point of view, whether this venture was legitimate. A high-ranking delegation was sent to the Ise shrine to ask the Shinto powers for advice. The oracle announced that the Sun Buddha and the sun goddess venerated in Ise were identical.[74] It added that the *kami* Hachiman wanted to have his shrine erected near the temple so that he could protect the Buddha.[75]

This synthesis, widely supported by the aristocracy, was complemented by a Buddhism comparable to shamanism (*ubasoku-zenji*), which was widespread, especially in rural areas. The *ubasoku* moved from village to village, consoled the sick and the oppressed, and offered prophecy and prayers in the name of the Buddha, the great miracle worker.[76] This movement grew so large that the ruler came to regard it as dangerous, but since his edicts failed to keep it under control, he finally co-opted it. The leading representative of "shamanistic" Buddhism, Gyogi Bosatsu, was appointed to the highest religious office at the court.[77]

Although there were at first repeated attempts, especially on the part of Buddhism, to claim superiority, Buddhism and Shinto increasingly merged. Shinto *kami* were interpreted as local manifestations of a Buddha or Bodhisattva. A system of pairing emerged that was broken up only in the nineteenth century, when Japanese nationalism was developing.[78] Indigenous gods were increasingly given Buddhist titles and venerated by having Buddhist priests recite sutras in their shrines.[79] So the association of Buddhism and Shinto did not remain merely a way for the court to achieve centralization and legitimation but was anchored in the ideas and practices of a larger population groups, as indicated by the temple complexes and shrines with their artistic representations.[80] The monk Saicho, for example, who founded the Buddhist Tendai school, chose as the site of the Enryakuji temple Mt. Hiei, which was protected by the *kami* Sanno.[81] Because of their intersection and merging down into the modern age, it is often difficult to distinguish between Buddhism and Shinto in Japan. In the minds of those practicing these religions, at least, there was no conflict or even contrast between them.

Was There a Christian-Confucian Synthesis in China?

Another interesting example of the mutual recognition of religions is furnished by the Jesuits' adaptation—primarily tactical—first to Buddhism and then to Confucianism in China. As they had already done in Japan, the first Jesuit missionaries, among them Michele Ruggieri, Matteo Ricci, and Antonio Almeida, appeared in China looking like Buddhist monks, with close-cropped hair and Buddhist-like robes. As a result, they were warmly welcomed by their Buddhist "coreligionists," since the latter regarded the Jesuits as a Buddhist sect.

Almeida wrote: "We are surrounded on all sides by monks who treat us in a friendly manner and every evening come to hear about the things of God [. . .]; we show our altar to the most important of them and they do reverence to the image of the Saviour."[82] But it was not only the Buddhists who were astonished by the similarity of the two religions; the Jesuits too discovered surprising parallels. As Jacques Gernet has noted,

Ricci notes many resemblances in dogmas and rituals: the Buddhist monks recognize a kind of Trinity and existence of paradise and hell. They practice penitence, observe celibacy and follow the practice of alms-giving. Their ceremonies are reminiscent of Christian masses: "When they recite, their chants seem just like our plainsong." Ricci also notes the religious images and lamps lit in the temples, and handgear similar to that of the Christian priest. The five Buddhist prohibitions to be respected by lay believers are reminiscent of the Ten Commandments of Christianity.[83]

The deterioration of the relationship on both sides was accompanied by mutual recriminations. The Buddhists said that the Christians had stolen most of their ideas from them, whereas Christian converts tried to show that Buddhism was a degenerate form of Christianity, an opinion Ricci shared. Thus the pattern of polemics that appeared earlier in Japan was repeated in China. Chinese not involved with either side noted the two religions' similarity, and some found them equally absurd and dangerous.

When the Jesuits learned that Buddhism was held in no great esteem by the Chinese elite, they began to play a different role. They let their hair grow and donned the robes of Confucian scholars. Above all, they allied themselves with the Confucian Donglin Academy, which was anti-Buddhist. Matteo Ricci suddenly discovered similarities between classical Chinese philosophy and Christianity. "During the last few years, whilst interpreting their works with good masters, I have found many passages which are favourable to the things of our Faith, such as the unity of God, the immortality of the soul, the glory of the elect, etc."[84]

In his treatise *The True Meaning of the Lord of Heaven*, Ricci adopted a systematic approach to the appropriation and reinterpretation of Confucianism.[85] But this work of synthesis met with a mixed reception. Some readers saw it as a blatant misinterpretation and were either furious, if they regarded the distortion as intentional, or amused, if they saw it as reflecting Ricci's ignorance and lack of education. One critic wrote: "Nevertheless, their comments on the Master of Heaven are altogether inadequate as far as a true idea of Heaven is concerned [. . .]. Furthermore, what they say about paradise and hell appears to differ barely at all from what Buddhists maintain and they go even further than the latter when it comes to extravagance and nonsense"[86]

Other readers, however, defended Ricci's interpretation as a contribution to the synthesis of Confucianism and Christianity. In this vein, David

Mungello argues that such syntheses were in tune with the spirit of the late Ming dynasty. But here we are not talking about a synthesis of the Confucian Wang Yangming school with Buddhism and Daoism, but about an attempt to meld Confucianism with Christianity.[87] This attempt ultimately failed because of its claim to have an absolute monopoly on truth. All Christian missionaries believed that their religion alone represented "the Way, the truth, and the life." They saw all other religions as either fundamentally false or hopelessly corrupt. Furthermore, they saw themselves as representatives not only of a superior religion but also of a superior culture.[88] The Christian missionaries' intransigence went too far even for Chinese converts to Christianity. "Most Chinese would have liked to combine the Christian religion with the Chinese cults and regretted the fact that the missionaries forbade them to do so. A Buddhist-Christian syncretism would have found favour with many Chinese."[89]

What Ricci really wanted was not a genuine synthesis but a Chinese Christianity that would be Chinese in form but strictly Christian in content. In view of the organizational structure of the Catholic Church and the internal conflicts within Christianity involving the pope, monastic orders, and monarchs, it was just a matter of time before this synthesis dissolved. The conflict that broke out between Jesuits and Dominicans over Christians' participation in ancestor worship and the veneration of Confucius was ultimately resolved by Clement XI in favor of the Dominicans.[90] Nonetheless, this episode shows that the Christian missionaries were not the only people who regarded the two religions as similar.

Akbar's Religious Synthesis

A particularly interesting example of an implicit concept of religion in premodern Asia is provided by the debates at the court of the Mughal emperor Akbar the Great (1542–1605) and the religious synthesis that resulted from them. In 1575–76, Akbar caused a "house of worship" to be built in which religious matters were discussed after the Friday prayer and often late into the night.[91] He began by inviting representatives of various Islamic groups, such as legal scholars, Sufi mystics, and heterodox sects. Later on he broadened the discussions to include representatives of non-Islamic religions, such as Brahmins and Christian missionaries. The latter were even allowed to teach Akbar's own son.[92] The list of participants that Akbar consulted over the years reads like something taken from a religious studies curriculum. The subjects include Islam, Hinduism, Jainism, Buddhism, Zoroastrianism, and Christianity. The emperor was also interested in magical practices,[93] and conducted personal discussions with representatives of all religions, probably because since childhood he himself had felt drawn to a variety of religious traditions.[94]

Akbar became increasingly doubtful about Islam's monopoly on truth. Why, he asked, should truth be limited to one religion and, moreover, to a relatively new religion like Islam, which was less than a thousand years old?[95] As a result of his many conversations and broad studies, he finally arrived at the conviction that in all religions and peoples there are individuals who are endowed with reason or charisma. In some ways, Akbar's religious synthesis anticipated a position that would much later be propagated by Lessing, during the Western Enlightenment.

The Roman Empire and the Silk Road

Periods of crisis often lead to religious persecutions. But there are also contrary tendencies, such as the importation of foreign forms of worship with the goal of calming people agitated by chaotic times. Thus, for instance, in the late Roman Empire the Greek practice of placing images of the gods on couches and then having a banquet in front of them was borrowed. During the plague of 293 BCE, the worship of Aesclepius was introduced; in 217 BCE, during the second Punic War, the worship of Venus Erycina was imported from Sicily; and in 205 BCE, when Hannibal was on Italian soil, threatening Rome, the cult of the Earth Mother Cybele was brought to Rome from Pessinus.[96]

The Silk Road, of course, offers an exceptionally instructive venue for syncretisms of every kind, for many religions came into contact with each other. In particular, Manichaeism presented itself as a synthesis by appropriating symbols and concepts of other religions like Nestorian Christianity and Buddhism. In a hymn to Mani, for instance, we find the formula "My precious, venerable father, my Mani Buddha."[97] The Nestorian monument in Xian is also a wonderful example of syncretistic skill. It is crowned with a Maltese cross resting on a Daoist cloud, and underneath it is a Buddhist lotus flower. The inscription reflects a synthesis of Christianity, Buddhism, Daoism, and Confucianism.[98]

The Politics of Religion

The viability of the concept of religion is evidenced not only by the mutual references of religious actors and groups but also by the fact that all great

empires, with their cultural and religious diversity, have conducted a politics of religion. As a rule, even in great empires the relationship between
religious practices and institutions and political institutions tends to be a
rather tense one, the separation of the two spheres being quite rudimentary.
Domination constantly requires legitimation, and religion plays a central
role in providing it. Even if the ruler himself has a religious function, to
carry out certain public and private rituals he needs religious specialists,
whether these are shamans or priests. Large empires are usually heterogeneous religiously, since their populations include a diversity of conquered
peoples. Insofar as the balance of power among different social groups
is closely connected with the political regulation of religious institutions,
it is clear that political institutions have a basic interest in controlling
them.

In situations of religious plurality and competition, two solutions are
conceivable. Either one religion is given precedence and the others are marginalized or even persecuted, or the ruler tries to integrate a plurality of
religions into the political system. The grounds for this kind of integration may be multiple, but two of them seem of particular importance. First,
legitimation by several religions may be deemed necessary, especially in
large empires.[99] Second, it may be in a ruler's interest to create a balance
of power that he or she can manipulate, one in which the various religious
groups compete for the ruler's favor. Many examples of this kind of politics
of religion are found in premodern periods as well. Here I will mention only
a few.

The politics of religion pursued by the Achaemenids is widely known
because of its effects on post-exilic Judaism and the reconstruction of the
temple in Jerusalem. Generally speaking, the Achmaenids very skillfully
used a flexible politics of religion to integrate subjected peoples into their
empire, but they brutally put down any challenge to their power.[100]

Both models—precedence and balance of power—are also found in the
religious politics adopted by the Sassanian Empire. After the Sassanian victory over the Parthians in 224 CE, they initially continued their tolerant
policy with regard to non-Iranian religions. Shapur I issued an edict declar-
ing that members of all religions were to be allowed to pursue their own
beliefs.[101] Later on, the Sassanians became more closely associated with
Zoroastrianism, a rapprochement reflected in, for example, the polemics
conducted by the high priest Kartir against all competing religious groups,
especially Christians and Jews.[102]

It is obvious that the Roman Empire pursued a politics of religion. One
example was the emperor Decius's edict regarding sacrifice or the so-called

Edict of Milan.[103] Lactantius reports on a meeting held in Milan in 313, at which the emperors Constantine and Licinius decided to put an end to the persecution of Christians. The formulation of this circular is extremely instructive for our purposes here, because it put Christianity on the same legal footing as other religions. Not only does this document expressly use the concept of religion (*religio*), but it also subsumes Christianity and other religions under the rubric. In the Edict of Milan we read:

> When I, Constantine Augustus, and I, Licinius Augustus, happily met at Milan and had under consideration all matters which concerned the public advantage and safety, we thought that, among all the other things that we saw would benefit the majority of men, the arrangements which above all needed to be made were those which ensured reverence for the Divinity, so that we might grant both to Christians and all men freedom to follow whatever religion each one wished, in order that whatever divinity there is in the seat of heaven may be appeased and made propitious towards us and towards all who have been set under our power. We thought therefore that in accordance with salutary and most correct reasoning we ought to follow the policy of regarding this opportunity as one not to be denied to anyone at all, whether he wished to give his mind to the observance of the Christians or to that religion which he felt was most fitting to himself, so that the supreme Divinity, whose religion we obey with free minds, may be able to show in all matters His accustomed favour and benevolence towards us.[104]

In India, the politics of religion was part of political reality for millennia. Take, for example, the edicts of the Indian king Asoka, the twelfth of which calls for religious tolerance among different religious groups. In it we read:

> Beloved-of-the-Gods, King Piyadasi, honors both ascetics and the householders of all religions, and he honors them with gifts and honors of various kinds. But Beloved-of-the-Gods, King Piyadasi, does not value gifts and honors as much as he values this—that there should be growth in the essentials of all religions. Growth in essentials can be done in different ways, but all of them have as their root restraint in speech, that is, not praising one's own religion, or condemning the religion of others without good cause. And if there is cause for criticism, it should be done in a mild way. But it is better to honor other religions for this reason. By so doing, one's own religion benefits, and so do other religions, while doing otherwise harms one's own religion and the religions of others.

Whoever praises his own religion, due to excessive devotion, and con-
demns others with the thought "Let me glorify my own religion," only
harms his own religion. Therefore contact (between religions) is good.
One should listen to and respect the doctrines professed by others.
Beloved-of-the-Gods, King Piyadasi, desires that all should be well-
learned in the good doctrines of other religions.[105]

The Ganga dynasty (350–550) pursued a religious policy that was manifested, for instance, in the regulation of forms of worship and the construction of temples.[106] A similar policy was continued much later after the
Muslim conquest of India, though the criteria changed. Expanding Islam
still distinguished different social groups on the basis of their religious af-
filiation,[107] and for the most part the distinction between religions of the
Book and other religions was applied. In general, non-Muslims were required
to pay a special tax.[108] Under the Delhi Sultanate (1206–1526) also there was
a religious policy that, according to Sharma, was of prime importance. The
sultans and governors tried to keep the peace and bring in tax revenues.
Otherwise they left their subjects alone, except when the religious policy
was concerned.[109]

   Although "Hinduism" is said to be a Western invention, the religion of
the Hindus was subject to government regulation as early as the reign of the
founder of the Mughal dynasty, Babur (1483–1530), when Hindus were forbidden to build temples and to worship their gods in public. Babur enacted
a law against blasphemy that was intended to protect and favor Islam and
to regulate conversions and re-conversions.[110] In the course of the Muslim
conquest, a number of Hindu temples were destroyed, such as a temple in
Ayodhya that had been erected in honor of Rama on the site of his birth and
served as a center for pilgrims. Mosques were often built on the ruins of
these Hindu temples.[111] As we have already seen, religious policy under Akbar became far more tolerant and inclusive.[112] But there can be little doubt
that in both pre-Islamic India and the Mughal Empire the politics of religion
was known and actively pursued.[113]

   For almost two thousand years, China has experienced a religious pluralism that has usually been organized by the ruler in the form of coexistence or rivalry. There too, competition among religions was manifested
in a multiplicity of edicts that essentially concerned the balance of power
between, on the one hand, Confucianism as the state religion and ethical
ideal, and, on the other hand, Daoism, Buddhism, and other religions.

   In 568, during the northern Chou dynasty, Daoists and Buddhists discussed in the presence of Emperor Wu and Confucian scholars the Sutra

on the Conversion of Barbarians, that is, the previously mentioned Daoist claim that Buddha was simply a later incarnation of Lao-tzu. This debate had short-term and long-term implications for the politics of religion. Initially, it led to an official ranking of religions in which Confucianism came first, Daoism second, and Buddhism third. But in 574, both Buddhism and Daoism were prohibited because of their deceptions. The Buddhists had so clearly shown the Daoists to have engaged in forgery that the emperor now decided that Daoism was just as bad as Buddhism. The Daoists had stolen and forged sutras, taken away people's money and property, and practiced magic in order to trick people.[114]

During part of the Tang dynasty there was also intense competition between Daoism and Buddhism that was significantly influenced by their respective interests and by the emperors' personal preferences.[115] Emperor Wu-tsung, for example, granted priority to the Daoists. On the occasion of his birthday he organized a debate between Daoist and Buddhist priests regarding their respective scriptures, declared the Daoists the winners, and publicly honored them.[116]

Persecution of the Buddhists began a few years later, based on an edict issued in 845 that declared Buddhism to be a foreign, barbarian religion that had undermined Chinese customs and traditions and was responsible for current problems.[117] The edict called for radical secularization: monasteries were confiscated and destroyed; monks and nuns were forced to resume secular lives. Although the edict concerned primarily Buddhism, other foreign religious groups—namely, Nestorians and Zoroastrians—were also persecuted. More than three thousand were forcibly secularized so that they would not "corrupt China's customs and traditions."[118] The Manichaeans had suffered the same fate a few years earlier.[119]

These events manifest how an interpretation of religion is brought to bear according to which Buddhists, Nestorians, and Zoroastrians are lumped together as members of foreign religions and—in this specific case—distinguished from the native Daoist religion. A particularly interesting aspect of the Chinese politics of religion is the multilayered legitimation of the ruler of an ethnically pluralistic empire, as under the Qing dynasty. On political grounds, the ruler cultivated the ethnic and cultural diversity and the particularist identities of the different peoples within his empire. At the same time, he was able to use each group's own religious frame of reference to present himself as a legitimate ruler.[120]

These diverse examples show that the politics of religion is not an invention of Western modernity. On the contrary, all non-Western and premodern empires have known and made use of a politics of religion, insofar as they classify social groups on the basis of their membership in a religion and regulated their practices and institutions. Without an implicit understanding of religion, this cannot be explained.

Travelers' Reports

In conclusion, I turn briefly to texts of another kind, namely, travelers' reports. I begin with Herodotus, who is more interested in observing and describing other religions and their practices than in judging them. Although he does not make specific use of the concept of religion, he does describe gods, priests, sacrifices, festivals, temples, and statues—that is, phenomena that can easily be subsumed under that concept.[121] On the whole, Herodotus notes many similarities and a few differences among religions. Many of the religions seem familiar to him, others strange, especially in Egypt. He notes small differences in the genealogy of the gods. Regarding the age of the gods, for example, he observes that "in Greece, the youngest of the gods are thought to be Heracles, Dionysus, and Pan; but in Egypt Pan is very ancient."[122]

In the festival of Dionysus, Herodotus also finds many parallels between Egypt and Greece:

> Everyone, on the eve of the festival of Dionysus, sacrifices a hog before the door of his house. When the animal is slaughtered, it is given back to the swineherd from whom it was procured. The swineherd then removes the carcass. In other ways the Egyptian method of celebrating the festival of Dionysus is much the same as the Greek, except that the Egyptians have no choric dance. Instead of the phallus they have puppets, about eighteen inches high; the genitals of these figures are made almost as big as the rest of their bodies, and they are pulled up and down by strings as the women carry them around the villages. Flutes lead the procession, and the women as they follow sing a hymn to Dionysus. There is a religious legend to account for the size of the genitals and the fact that they are the only part of the puppet's body which is made to move.[123]

Herodotus describes not only the names and genealogies of the gods and religious rituals, but also the architecture of shrines and their equipment, as well as the habits, duties, and privileges of priests.[124] He seeks, moreover, to understand practices that are more alien to Greeks, like those of the Persians, and compares them with Greek religious practices and ideas. "The following are certain Persian customs which I can describe from personal knowledge. The erection of statues, temples, and altars is not an accepted practice among them, and anyone who does such a thing is considered a fool, because, presumably, the Persian religion is not anthropomorphic like the Greek."[125]

As these descriptions show, Herodotus classifies and distinguishes certain phenomena that are fully compatible with a concept of religion. In addition, he repeatedly compares Greek and non-Greek religious ideas, institutions, and practices, emphasizing similarities far more than differences, and he frequently seems to assume that foreign religious ideas and practices are generally translatable into Greek ones.[126]

A second example of premodern religious comparison is offered by the important Muslim religious scholar Muhammad Ibn Ahmad al-Biruni (973–1048) in his book on India.[127] In the preface, he mentions the founder of a religion who had examined many different religions before developing his own. He had studied and compared Judaism, Christianity, Manichaeism, Hinduism, and Buddhism. Since his knowledge of Hinduism was inadequate, al-Biruni decided to go to India so as to inform himself at firsthand about the religion of the Hindus. His book is thus explicitly nonpolemical and has no apologetic intentions. He reports on the religion of the Hindus, whom he describes as "our religious antagonists" (Biruni, 7), not in order to refute their ideas but rather to describe them with as much factual accuracy as possible. He is interested in facts. For that reason he cites the Hindus' doctrines verbatim. "If the content of these quotations happen to be utterly heathenish, and the followers of the truth, i.e. the Muslims, find them objectionable, we can only say that such is the belief of the Hindus, and that they themselves are best qualified to defend them" (7).

In the course of his account, al-Biruni compares subjects such as the concept of God in Islam, Judaism, Christianity, and Hinduism (36–34). He describes the Hindus' religious beliefs and practices in a highly detailed and differentiated manner, with special attention to the practical aspects of the way the Brahmins and other castes conduct their lives (130–38). He also describes sacrifices and pilgrimages and compares them with the pilgrimage to Mecca (146). In a chapter on ways of dealing with the bodies of the dead, both those who have died of natural causes and suicides, he compares the ideas and practices of ancient Greece with those of the Hindus, Manichaeans, and Buddhists (167–71). From the kind of descriptions he gives, it is clear that al-Biruni distinguishes religious ideas and practices from one another as well as comparing different religious groups.

Conclusions

After offering so many examples, I should now recall their significance. The goal of this chapter is obviously not to present a world history of religious polemics, borrowings, syncretisms, edicts, and travelers' reports. Neither is it to prove that "religion" is a category of the human mind that is given a priori. I have been concerned here solely to justify the universal use of a concept of religion. Since I agree with the critics of this concept who argue that analytical concepts should be compatible with the cultural meaning of social action, these examples aim to justify the use of the concept of religion outside the modern West. As I hope to have shown in this chapter, a perception of differences between the religious and the nonreligious is expressed in the thought and actions of people of diverse historical periods and cultures. Religious actors behave as competitors or potential partners with one another. Religious practices are mutually demarcated or fused with one another. Governments issue edicts that usually concern more than one religious group. And travelers draw parallels between foreign and familiar religions, their religious ideas and practices.

The examples refute the postmodern assumption that "religions" were first constituted in contact with the West and its concept of religion. That assumption is simply false historically. What is true is that the encounter with the West led to a systematization and canonization of religious practices and ideas. But it is false to conclude from this that previously existing practices did not represent a religion and that the West thus became a universal creator of religions. British imperialism and Anglicanism did not invent Hinduism, and Buddhism did not invent Shinto. Instead, these processes manifest the structural characteristics of religious competition. In such situations the more weakly organized participants are sometimes forced to increase their efficiency in order to be competitive. A typical strategy consists in showing that one's own religion already has everything offered by the rival, for example, holy scriptures, pictorial representations, or a pantheon. Alternatively, one's own religion can place a taboo on certain aspects of the competing one, such as priests, statues of the gods, or hair on one's head. No matter what strategy is selected, competition powerfully shapes every religion in both its positive and its negative self-definition.

To be sure, no unified concept of religion emerges from the examples given above. That is not to be expected, since such conceptual unification is a result of intellectual systematization. But the various perspectives illuminate aspects of religious phenomena that are absolutely compatible with the concept of religion. In these complex institutions, different social groups emphasize what is primarily relevant for them: religious intellectuals emphasize worldviews and doctrines; religious officials emphasize correct practice; bureaucrats emphasize religion's contribution to state welfare, security, and public morals. For religious laypersons, however, the influence of superhuman powers on their everyday lives is central.

Up to this point, I've shown that the concept of religion can legitimately be used outside the modern West as well, if it is sought not in language but in social behavior. But not every concept of religion can claim to be universally applicable. In chapter 3, therefore, I summarize typologically the most widespread scholarly interpretations of religion and investigate their universalizability. I then introduce and ground my own practice-oriented concept of religion.

CHAPTER THREE

Scholarly Imaginations of Religion

An initial survey of other attempts to define and explain religion will show by contrast what is different about my own approach. I have no desire to discredit other views; since all social phenomena are complex, they can always be analyzed from various points of view. To that extent, all perspectives have their own advantages and disadvantages, strengths and weaknesses. But that does not mean that all concepts of religion are equally generalizable or that all theories of religion have the same explanatory powers. On the contrary, I am setting forth my theory in the belief that it is superior to other theories.

My goal is to present, on the basis of the experience we have gained over time with other approaches, a perspective in which a certain systematic unity emerges from the diversity of religious phenomena. For me, it is of central importance to propose a definition and a theory that are not simply disguised versions of Christianity or of current trends among members of the middle classes in Western industrial countries. My chief interest is to present a general theory worthy of the name. Someone pursuing other cognitive interests and seeking, for example, to provide a theory of religious transformation or of religious particularities will proceed differently. At this point, therefore, I offer a brief account of approaches to which my own is indebted and those I have not adopted.

Since this book argues for a particular theoretical perspective on religion, I have not conceived this chapter as a history of the theory of religion. First, a short chapter would not suffice, and second, there are already outstanding treatments of this subject from various points of view.[1] I will limit myself here to approaches that have been especially influential in the areas of religious studies, anthropology, and sociology. Although I occasionally refer to specific texts, I will focus not on particular authors and their works but on various types of approaches, their premises and points of view.

The differences among approaches to the theory of religion can often be discerned in the central metaphors and analogies they use. Beginning with the deistic interpretation of religion as a divine gift of reason, I go on to identify interpretations of religion as an experience of revelation, as a proto-science, as affect and a means of controlling affects, as a brain function, as a sanctification of society, as an interest in salvation, and as a commodity.

It is often asked whether religious studies go back to the Enlightenment or to the Romantic period. This question presupposes an opposition between the Enlightenment and Romanticism that may skew the problem from the outset. An interest in religion that goes beyond theological discourse is found not only in the writings of those associated with the Enlightenment and with Romanticism, but also in the writings of their respective predecessors. Whereas Enlightenment writers offered either a "reasonable religion" or a rational critique of religion, the Romantics emphasized the aesthetic and emotional quality of religion in shaping personality. However, one should not understand early Romanticism as an anti-Enlightenment movement, even if later it sometimes took that direction. I agree with Hans Kippenberg, who finds the origins of religious studies as an academic discipline in the Romantic period, but traces the sociology of religion back to the Enlightenment, although here as well we must be wary of undifferentiated oppositions.[2]

Religion as a Divine Gift of Reason

The starting point for theories of religion in the social sciences was probably deism and the critical debates surrounding it. Deism—which Ernst Troeltsch called the Enlightenment's philosophy of religion—represented a concept of religion that gave expression to a rational morality and worldview.[3] In its logically consistent form, it rejected as irrational all "positive" religions that claimed to be based on special revelations, or at least rejected them insofar as they were irrational. Deism constituted a "reasonable" belief in God and a "reasonable" morality. From the time of Herbert of Cherbury down to the literature of the Enlightenment in the late eighteenth century, this approach became increasingly widespread among intellectuals. Most positions in the theory of religion, such as Hume's skepticism and the Romantics' aesthetic conception of religion, were shaped in the debates over deism.

Herbert of Cherbury maintained that God had given the gift of reason to all humans. Reason, according to him, contained a few essential fundamental truths, such as the existence of a creator-God, the duty to venerate him primarily through moral conduct, the obligation to repent and avoid sins, and the belief that a just punishment for sins would be meted out in this life and in the next.[4] On this view, all revealed religions represented later overlays or even falsifications of this original natural religion.

Thus deism interprets religion as essentially a naturally given, universal metaphysics and morality. The world is an ordered cosmos whose laws mirror divine reason. Humans can recognize God in the laws of nature and morality. Kant's famous formula "the starry heavens above me and the moral law within me" encapsulates the deistic view. Almost all later concepts of religion can be interpreted as reactions that affirm, modify, or reject this understanding of religion.

Religion as an Experience of Revelation

Among these reactions to rationalism is the pietistic-Romantic concept of religion. It opposes the rationalistic view of religion as ethics and metaphysics, and makes aesthetics central instead. For the pietistic-Romantic concept, religion is primarily an individualized experience of revelation. A significant portion of religious studies first developed on the basis of this concept, which was further developed in the twentieth century into a phenomenological concept of religion. In any case, it is impossible to overlook the high degree of continuity between Romanticism and phenomenology in religious studies; sometimes the boundary between them is difficult to determine.[5] For example, Rudolf Otto's 1917 book *The Idea of the Holy* (*Das Heilige*) was very positively received by Edmund Husserl, and later such authors as Gerardus van der Leeuw and Mircea Eliade explicitly drew on phenomenology. I therefore feel justified in attributing this understanding of religion to writers ranging from Friedrich Schleiermacher, Jakob Friedrich Fries, and Wilhelm Martin Leberecht de Wette to Rudolf Otto, Van der Leeuw, and Eliade despite historical and systematic differences among them.

What do these approaches have in common in terms of content and methodology that would allow us legitimately to subsume them under a single type? From my point of view, they share a way of understanding religion primarily as an "experience of revelation." Religion is an "experience" of "the holy." Not all these writers use the concept of "the holy," but they use other terms that are compatible with it. The kind of experience may vary, taking the form of mystical contemplation, ecstatic possession, or simply a more highly cultivated religious sensibility with regard to the cosmos or the infinite.

This approach sees in religiousness a human capability that is given a priori and that differs from any other kind of experience. It sees the human being as having a disposition toward religion, as *homo religiosus*. Nonreligiousness is regarded, like being tone-deaf or not being sensitive to art, as a lack of cultivation of the general human potential, as Schleiermacher long ago emphasized. Eliade also criticizes modern culture for its deficiency in this regard, and contrasts it with a fictive "archaic humanity," which is supposed to have lived in constant relationship to "hierophanies," i.e., revelations of the sacred.

Representatives of religion understood in this sense are seldom religious officeholders or laypersons; usually they are individuals who have particular religious gifts. Hence Romantic and phenomenological studies have paid far more attention to religious virtuosos than have other approaches. The emphasis on virtuosity suggests, at least implicitly, a cultural criticism of a modernity whose materialism and utilitarianism have suppressed and marginalized this kind of experience.[6]

This view of religion is often manifested in authors who see themselves as virtuosos or initiates and present their studies with prophetic or mystical affect. Rudolf Otto's statement that anyone who has never had a religious experience himself need read no further is a famous example of such a view.[7] Here I will illustrate the foundations of this approach in greater detail by referring to Schleiermacher's early writings as well as to those of Van der Leeuw and Eliade.

As I have already mentioned, the modern origin of this concept of religion lies in Romanticism. The young Friedrich Schleiermacher gave it enduring expression with prophetic pathos in his *On Religion: Speeches to Its Cultured Despisers*. Since in the course of time the Romantic concept of religion took on increasingly conservative characteristics, it is often not realized that Schleiermacher's understanding of religion was originally radical, if not revolutionary. His early Romantic concept of religion undermined the religious basis of existing authorities. With his rejection of religion as metaphysics, ethics, dogma, and the fetishization of holy scripture, he also rejected as inauthentic all claims made by the state, orthodoxy, and organized religion. Schleiermacher thus introduced a concept of religion that had radical implications. Religion was not supposed to explain the world or provide a foundation for morality; it served neither church nor state; it was not in competition with science and did not function to produce social

discipline. Neither did religion mean following the injunctions of a holy
scripture, especially not literally. For Schleiermacher, holy scriptures were
"mausoleums" of religion. A religious man was one who needed no holy
scripture but could write his own.[8] Even the concept of God is not necessarily connected with religion. It represents merely an anthropomorphic
metaphor for the universe. Religion is based on human creative potential,
which escapes any instrumentalization and serves to promote the individual's full development. In religion, humans transcend themselves and their
species with regard to the experience of a higher order. By insisting in this
way on the autonomy of the subject, Schleiermacher is in no way opposing
the emancipatory potential of the Enlightenment but, rather, seeking to
broaden the significance of individual autonomy.

This view rejects deism's "natural religion," with its emphasis on morality and its critique of positive religions. Religion cannot exist as a bare
abstraction; it needs a concrete, living form. All such forms, however, are
overloaded with components that have been superimposed on the essence
of religion—metaphysics, morality, institutional interests, dogmas, "dead
letters,"[9] and the resulting intolerance. Nonetheless, one can discern true
religion in the forms of positive religion, since every religious experience is
ultimately expressed in concrete practice. The difference between the various forms of religion thus lies primarily in the particular religious experience that is made central.[10] As a whole, then, religion consists in the sum of
possible religious experiences, which tend to be infinite in number.

Schleiermacher distinguishes his concept of religious experience from
that of "natural religions." Religious experience has nothing in common
with the fear of thunder and lightning felt by "unrefined sons of the earth"[11]
or with being moved by the beauty of nature. Such experiences may serve
to prepare the human race for true religion, but do not yet express it. In contradistinction to Eliade, Schleiermacher is far from idealizing the "archaic,"
and instead endorses the growth of civilization and mastery over nature.
Carrying out mechanical labor hinders people from religious contemplation
and enslaves them. The solution to this problem is to be found in the future,
not in a return to the past.

The early Romantic concept of religion does not move beyond the privileging of Christianity, but it relativizes the differences between various religious traditions by interpreting them as differing ways of giving form to the
essence of religion. It thereby contributes significantly to the dismantling
of crude value judgments and to the preparation for religious tolerance and
pluralism.[12] Since, for this view, true religion represents an inner experience that ultimately resides in all religions and that may be more or less

adequately expressed by any particular religion, in principle the Romantic concept rejects the notion that any one religion embodies the "truth." Religion is an individualized, even subjectivized revelation. It can, indeed must, take diverse forms. Each individual living within a religious community expresses his or her experience in a unique way. Individual experience can and must be shared, thereby enriching others. The same holds true for experiences within other religions. Thus the Romantic concept of religion is not only deliberately relativizing and individualizing but also pluralizing, social, and communicative.

At the same time, Schleiermacher deplores his age's lack of religiousness. He blames this lack not on those who are deficient in faith or in morals, the atheists or the "immoral" (Sittenlosen), but on the Enlightenment bourgeoisie, with its moralism and utilitarianism, its unimaginativeness, sobriety, and tediousness. With almost prophetic foresight, he identifies Western modernity's tendency to the blind worship of action: "Design and purpose must be in everything; prudent and practical people must always accomplish something, and when the spirit can no longer serve, they are fond of exercising the body; work and play, only no quiet, submissive contemplation."[13]

Variations on the Romantic model were now produced by authors such as Fries and his pupil De Wette or, later on, Max Müller. It was above all the revival of interest in Kant, Schleiermacher, and Fries that led to further revisions toward the end of the nineteenth century, such as the position taken by Rudolf Otto, who, at first a follower of Schleiermacher, became a neo-Friesian.[14] Then came Husserl's phenomenology, which was adopted at least in name by religious studies, thus making Gerardus van der Leeuw a pioneer in the field. Van der Leeuw introduced the concept of religious phenomenology in a brief work published in 1924, and explicated the approach nine years later in his magnum opus.[15] At the center of his work are concepts such as "experience," "revelation," and homo religiosus, all of which are later found in a similar form in Eliade.[16] I will therefore discuss these two authors together, as representatives of the phenomenological approach in religious studies.

For Van der Leeuw and Eliade, the religious "shows itself." The "sacred" is revealed in religious objects. Humans experience the appearance of the sacred through interpretation. "For in its 'reconstruction,' experience is a phenomenon. Revelation is not; but man's reply to revelation his assertion about what has been revealed is also a phenomenon from which, indirectly, conclusions concerning the revelation itself can be derived (per viam negationis)."[17] Van der Leeuw and Eliade both see in the sacred primarily a phenomenon of power or strength, and they see the original ground of being or of life as a search for power and salvation through union with the sacred. Eliade also calls these phenomena "kratophanies."[18] More than Van der Leeuw, Eliade tends to ascribe an ontological status to the "sacred."[19]

Although one of the tasks of this kind of religious studies is to name, describe, and classify religious phenomena, this is only a beginning. The goal is to understand religious phenomena not in the sense of their historical and social significance but as an expression of a "structure," a context of meaning, an attitude toward the world. Every religious phenomenon, every hierophany, thus represents a part that refers to a whole. However, according to Van der Leeuw, the goal is above all to decipher them as an appearance of an ultimately atemporal existential problem and—in addition—to testify to the latter.[20] Eliade picks up on this notion and speaks of the continuity of the sacred, which leads from the most elementary to the highest appearances of the sacred, or he identifies authentic religious experience as a demand for the revelation of an ultimate reality transcending time and history.[21] And even Van der Leeuw's call for testimony is followed by his proclamation of the phenomenology of religion as a new religion—his "new humanism."

Finally, Van der Leeuw and Eliade share the assumption of a religious a priori. For them, the human is *homo religiosus*; Van der Leeuw used this concept before Eliade did.[22] It is the existence of nonreligious persons that needs to be explained, not the existence of religious ones. Both Van der Leeuw and Eliade combine this assumption with a cultural critique of modernity. What Eliade adds to Van der Leeuw's phenomenology is an idealization of "archaic man" as the embodiment of *homo religiosus* and the opposite of modern man. And he further critiques historical thinking and the belief in progress and enlightenment.[23]

What are the strengths and weaknesses, the advantages and disadvantages, of this approach? In recent decades it has become fashionable to discredit politically the Romantic or phenomenological approach as a whole by branding it a mere forerunner of fascist thinking, if not an early expression of it. In my view that is too simple, historically inaccurate, and not particularly helpful as a method of analysis. For someone examining only Eliade and his political past, it may be tempting to suspect all hermeneutic interpretations of religion of being fascistic.[24] Yet if we examine the historical evolution of this approach, it becomes clear that it cannot be directly identified with specific political positions.

The Romantic and phenomenological approaches are still of interest to us insofar as they made an enormous contribution to comparative research and the interpretation of religious phenomena. Above all, with their insistence on religious experience and on the study of religious objects and actors, they represent a counterweight to functionalist or Marxist interpretations that ultimately don't care about religious phenomena. But from a sociological perspective such approaches are highly problematic. For one thing, in these approaches the phenomenological return to "things themselves," while in itself welcome, is overlaid with a subjectivist interpretation in which the "true" meaning of religious phenomena always lies in some sense beyond their historical, social, and pragmatic contexts. The model of religion as revelation leads to a constant overinterpretation of religious phenomena while simultaneously neglecting the meaning of religious action as it arises out of institutional realities and concrete life. At the same time, this approach gives priority to the study of virtuoso practices and neglects religion in everyday life, thus excessively narrowing the range of religious studies.

Second, the assumption of a religious a priori cannot be justified. Man is not "by nature" religious. What is considered religious experience is not given a priori but first learned through socialization and practice. What one culture understands as religious experience may in another be seen as deviant behavior. In addition, there is the empirical inaccessibility of subjective experiences of revelation.[25] In many societies, religious experience does not consist in a "taste" for the infinite but, rather, in contact with definite powers to which very specific potentials are attributed.

This approach suffers above all from its apologetic intentions. It attempts to immunize religion against criticism. The separation of religion from society and its internalization as a "province in the soul" seems to put it beyond the reach of criticism. Ultimately, only a religious person knows what religion is. Those who criticize religion have "no ear for religion" and should be pitied for their banality. The approach is thus ultimately subjectivist. Existential empathy and the interpretation of religious phenomena cross the boundary between "understanding" and "bearing testimony," to adopt Van der Leeuw's terminology. The religious scholar commonly appears here in the guise of a virtuoso, an illuminator, a mystagogue, or a prophet. The understanding of religious phenomena becomes a matter of a mystical empathy through religiously sensitive people. At the same time, this "experience" is understood quite ethnocentrically. It is always a variant of Romantic "experience" [Erfahrung] that has been smuggled in and claims universality.

Moreover, this approach offers no method that makes the cultural diversity of religious experiences truly accessible to analysis. To that extent it fails both to understand, because its stereotypes narrow its range, and to explain, because it short-circuits explanation by assuming religious experience to be an anthropological given. The central concern of this approach, which is to reclaim absolute autonomy for religion, cannot be maintained empirically; instead, it is a theological postulate.

Religion as Projection

Theories of projection are generally critical theories of religion. The concept of projection can be used narrowly or broadly. We can subsume the theories of Ludwig Feuerbach, Karl Marx, and Sigmund Freud under the narrower variety. This approach always implies the assumption of a misunderstanding. Feuerbach's anthropocentric critique of religion sees religion as a projection of ideals of human perfection onto a metaphysical authority that operates as a superhuman god, dominating and paralyzing its inventors. Freud views religion as an illusion, as wishful thinking, and sees it as indicating the lack of a strong ego and an insufficient acceptance of reality.[26] I will return to the psychoanalytical approach in chapter 8, in discussing the explanation of the universality of religion. Here, since neither Freud nor Feuerbach is primarily guided by a sociological perspective, I will concentrate on Marx, who further develops Feuerbach's approach and at least partially anticipates Freud's.

Like Feuerbach, Marx sees religion as an expression of false consciousness.[27] Marx follows Hegel in assuming that the history of humanity leads from the realm of necessity to that of freedom. But he views the development of human consciousness not as a relatively independent process, but rather as the manifestation and consequence of the development of the material conditions of human existence. According to Marx, humans create themselves as a species by producing and reproducing their concrete lives. In other words, humans transform nature by cooperating with each other; and, by means of the technology they have developed, they shape themselves as a species, increase their elevation over nature, and thereby realize their freedom as creative activity.

In Marx's view, the role of religion as an expression of social consciousness changes in the course of this socioeconomic development. In societies that have little control over nature and are organized in a relatively egalitarian way, the material environment is the great riddle. In earlier times, humans mythified nature, which seemed to them to be dominated by invisible powers, and at that stage religion expressed primarily a misunderstanding of nature's "true" ways of functioning. An increasing mastery over nature resulted from the division of labor, which produced class differences, especially between intellectual and manual labor, and led to the development of private property. In the course of this social development, knowledge was acquired about nature and how to control it through technology. Nature was demystified and seen increasingly as a rationally ordered whole, governed by laws that required no religious explanation. Whereas this development of the natural sciences and technology led to the demythification of nature, social relations were becoming steadily more complex. Social development created growing social differences, and modern capitalism increasingly reified and depersonalized social relations. It now seemed that society, not nature, was getting more and more difficult to understand.

For one thing, consciousness is falsified by alienation, which manifests itself in the organization of labor and in the resulting social relations among members of different classes and within the same classes. In other words, human existence is stunted by being reduced to purely economic relations. Labor as creative, sensuous, meaningful activity is seen as no more than a means of physical survival or of maximizing profits. People come to see themselves primarily as self-centered actors in the economic process, treating their peers as competitors for jobs or profits. Interpersonal relations take on an instrumental character. The production and exchange of commodities characterizes the social. People encounter each other not as human beings in all their complexity but as "one-dimensional." In addition there are the interests of those who benefit from these alienated structures and, in order to justify their privileges, develop a legitimating ideology that alternates between illusion and deliberate deception.

With this socioeconomic development, religion too changes from an expression of the failure to understand nature to an expression of alienated social relations and social structures. It can assume a series of different functions and forms. It can serve to justify the existing form of society and domination, urging acceptance of this form, for example, by referring to God's will or to a better future in the afterlife. Occasionally, religion can also articulate protests against unjust relations, but because of its illusory ideas it is incapable of formulating a realistic proposal for transforming society. Furthermore, religion embodies alienation, since it is always particularist. As Feuerbach had already put it, Christian brotherly love is obviously not universalist but is restricted to particularism by the very attribute "Christian."[28] Thus religion always represents a restrictive qualification of human existence and thus implies domination, oppression, and alienation.

Since religion, for Marx, is ultimately little more than an expression of alienated social relations—that is, an illusion and a form of escapism in the Freudian sense, on the one hand, and a justifying ideology, on the other—the study and criticism of religion is already largely concluded. Criticism of religion becomes criticism of society. As soon as humans have learned to understand society as being just as rational and controllable as nature, religion will disappear on its own. Whereas for the Romantic approach, subjective understanding ultimately involves explanation, from Marx's point of view the "subjectively intended meaning" is quite insignificant and uninteresting. In Marx's work, explaining religion consists in criticizing it as a false consciousness, but one that arises not out of religion itself but out of alienated social relations.

Thus Marx's view of religion, which in itself is quite consistent and sociologically interesting, has led to the wide neglect of the study of religious phenomena or to their being interpreted in a merely formulaic way. The Marxist approach nevertheless deserves to be better exploited, because it offers many possibilities for a complex analysis of the links between religion, social structure, and history. Recently, this approach has been revived, especially in analyses of the connections between neoliberal globalization and renewed belief in miracles, witchcraft, and the devil.[29]

On the other hand, the Marxist approach also has implications that are problematic from my point of view. For one thing, it is tied to a philosophy of history whose Enlightenment-style optimism is now rather questionable. Even if alienation in the Marxist sense of the term could be overcome, that would not necessarily entail the disappearance of religion. For another, the approach is based on a tendency to closely link class with religion—a tendency that derives from the Marxist deductive procedure with regard to religious phenomena. Class and religion are far less closely connected than Marx seems to assume. Naturally, there are class-specific religious groups and movements, but there are also groups that integrate different classes. Moreover, the class point of view neglects the role played by the self-image of religious groups. Religion always turns out to be false metaphysics, false morality, and false experience in the interest of or as an expression of a false social order. Hence, for Marx the analysis of religion means essentially the critique of ideology. To be sure, this perspective offers many interesting insights. But because of its connection to a teleological philosophy of history, the relation between understanding and explaining is not satisfactorily resolved, and the privileged status accorded the critic is insufficiently justified.

Religion as Protoscience

The idea that religion is an early form of science is found in many Enlightenment authors, usually with the implication that it has now been replaced by science. Moderate versions of this thesis are found in Auguste Comte and Émile Durkheim. Primarily, however, it was the British anthropologists of religion Edward B. Tylor and James Frazer who defended this view. On the basis of a cognitively oriented associationist psychology, they identified religion with early forms of rational and, especially, scientific thought. For them, religion represented an insufficient answer to cognitive problems such as the explanation of dreams or death.[30] Religion and magic were related in the same way as theory and practice or science and technology. This tradition is represented today by anthropologists such as Robin Horton, who maintains that "primitive" religion is primarily a rational attempt to interpret the world. Horton develops this approach further by emphasizing the cognitive and intentional dimensions as opposed to symbolic interpretations. Traditional religious systems in Africa are thus theoretical models comparable to Western scientific models.[31] The grounds for the emergence and reproduction of religion thus lie in the need to control the world around us.

The weakness of this approach, I think, lies in its one-sided intellectualism, in its emphasis on religious ideas as an explanation of the world at the expense of religious practices and the emotional dimension. To be sure, one can argue that where religion and science are not differentiated, religion does offer an explanation of the world. But this is a very narrow perspective. Moreover, the approach seems to me connected to evolutionary models according to which religion is replaced by science. This has led, for instance in the work of Frazer, to a neglect of other aspects of religion that cannot be replaced by science. Durkheim was right to point out that religion may continue to exist even when science has assumed a major role in explaining the world.

Continuing these early attempts, Pascal Boyer has developed an extremely interesting cognitive-evolutionary theory of religion.[32] For Boyer, religious thinking does not represent a specific kind of thinking that can be localized somewhere in the human brain; instead, religious ideas arise out of a combination of general concepts. Thus, for instance, ideas of supernatural agents do not appear solely in religious thinking proper, but also in dreams, fantasies, fairy tales, and legends.[33] Such concepts are not implanted in the brain, innate or genetically inherited, but rather learned.[34] According to Boyer, from an evolutionary point of view, ideas of superhuman actors have spread because of their utility as an aid to thought. Although many points in Boyer's explanations remain somewhat vague and captive to an evolutionary utilitarianism, his approach seems very promising.

Religion as Affect

In contradistinction to the cognitive and rationalist approaches represented by Tylor and Frazer, on the one hand, and by Durkheim and his school, on the other, a view of religion developed around 1900, especially in British anthropology, that identified it chiefly with emotionality and the control of affects. Authors such as William McDougall, Robert R. Marett, and Bronislaw Malinowski can be counted among those adopting this approach, whose earliest predecessor was David Hume. Hume located the origin of religion in the context of everyday life. As he wrote in his *Natural History of Religion*, the first polytheistic religious ideas evolved not from the observation of nature but from concern about the imponderables of life, from hope and fear.[35]

Marett, and then Malinowski, developed this position most clearly. Since Marett came first, I will focus on him. His contribution to the theory of religion belongs to the context of the debates about the theory of evolution that took place around the turn of the twentieth century, which were concerned with the elementary or rudimentary forms of religion. Marett's theoretical argument to these debates was initially directed against Edward Tylor's animism thesis. Tylor had proposed a minimal definition of religion as belief in the continuing life of the soul after death and also the belief in spirits, including powerful gods; he subsumed these beliefs under the concept of animism. Animism for him represented an attempt to explain the world and its riddles rationally. Marett objected that elementary religion could not have been based on rationalist speculation, since such speculation itself is a product of evolution. According to Marett, religion is initially an emotional, affective reaction to the experience of awe-inspiring powers that may be not only animate but also impersonal forces, such as storms and earthquakes. "Primitive" religion was danced rather than thought. Moreover, "primitive" societies are for the most part governed by custom and tradition. In other words, what is lacking here too is reflection. The religion and morality of "savages" are collectively and traditionally set, sanctioned, and grounded. They are "mobbish."[36] Marett also criticizes Frazer's revisions of Tylor's thesis because they retain its intellectualist perspective. A sharp distinction between magic and religion cannot be maintained. And certainly one cannot claim that magic represents a stage in the evolution of thought that precedes religion, which is supposed to have emerged from the falsification of magic as a pseudoscience. This view of magic is based on an anachronistic confusion of the observer's standpoint with that of the object observed.

Marett also distinguishes his position from that of Durkheim and his school, though he generally approves of the latter. Whereas he regards Tylor and Frazer as representing an old-fashioned paradigm, he sees the scholars associated with the journal *L'Année sociologique* as allies in the search for a new approach. Marett's affinity with Durkheim is not surprising insofar as both of them were significantly influenced by Robertson Smith and his emphasis on the social character of sacrifice and on the priority of ritual over belief, of practice over theological explanation. Nevertheless, Marett was not an uncritical supporter of the Durkheim school, to which he clearly took a contrary position on central issues. Thus he criticizes the socio-morphological approach for its determinism, which cancels the dialectic of freedom and determinism in human action and ignores individuality. Whereas British anthropology gives individual psychology too much attention, the Durkheim school has fallen into the opposite extreme. It is not only excessively deterministic but also proceeds unrealistically in assuming a very high degree of social homogeneity and integration. Social communication is a largely incomplete, contradictory, and heterogeneous process that oscillates between publicly staged norms and a Babel-like confusion of languages. For Marett, the concept of a collective consciousness should be rejected.

Marett's own theory of religion seeks to achieve a synthesis of British and Durkheimian social anthropology, as well as to reconcile sociology with social psychology. In this regard, his writings represent a transition from classical evolutionism to functionalism as later represented by Malinowski and others. According to Marett, two dimensions of human experience can be distinguished: everyday and non-everyday. Everyday experience is familiar, normal, predictable, and controllable; non-everyday experience consists in crises like hunger, illness, war, birth, and death—in short, in what is unexpected, unknown, dangerous, life threatening. For Marett, the psychological basis of religion lies in experiences of crisis.[37] Non-everyday experience, which escapes "normal" control by humans, is attributed to superior, superhuman, or even supernatural powers and is experienced as an encounter with such powers. The existential dimension of the non-everyday can be conceived by means of the "mana-taboo formula." The non-everyday as an experience of or encounter with a superhuman power is expressed in the concept *mana*; and the aspect of awe, fear, and the need to avoid contact because of the danger involved is expressed in the concept *taboo*. For Marett, the dual concept of mana-taboo most adequately expresses the heart of religion.

The process of religious experience, for Marett, can be divided psychologically into two stages. First, the experience of a superhuman power leads to humility and humiliation. But this encounter also guides human beings out of depression and to revival. To that extent, religion serves ultimately to overcome emotional crises and results in an affirmation of life. Here Marett is closely following William McDougall's social psychology.[38] Ways of coping with crises are not, however, something that each individual invents anew; rather, in all societies such coping strategies are organized, regulated, and conventionalized or traditionalized. In other words, the "existential situation" and its overcoming are always pre-shaped culturally and socially. This conventionalizing of religious experience has two interconnected aspects. First, successful practices of communication with superhuman powers are ritualized. Second, certain persons acquire privileged positions in these rituals. The exercise of such functions often requires the actors themselves to have superhuman abilities that allow them to expose themselves to what is otherwise a generally fatal encounter with those powers. To that extent, political domination is based, at least in "primitive" societies, on the belief that certain exceptional individuals or categories of people possess superhuman abilities.

Religion and magic are not grounded in different psychological experiences; neither can they be distinguished on the basis of cognitive categories. For Marett, the essential difference lies instead in the social and moral evaluation of various practices. All societies distinguish between socially beneficial, legitimate practices, on the one hand, and antisocial, illegitimate practices, on the other. In the first case we are speaking of religion; in the second, of magic.

In the course of religious evolution, a far-reaching ethicization of religion takes place. In earlier stages of development, this dimension is not wholly lacking, being ultimately based on a universal experience of humiliation. Nonetheless, according to Marett, religious ethics in the true sense first emerges with increasing freedom of thought and greater individualization. For this to happen, the bonds of tradition and convention must be broken along with their religious sanctions. This argument represents a clear parallel to Max Weber's theory of religion and the process of disenchantment.

Marett's theory is interesting for its intermediate position. While still largely captive to colonial and evolutionary stereotypes, it pursues Hume's crisis-oriented interpretation of religion, formulates a position mediating among Durkheim, Weber, and Malinowski, and—more than most of its predecessors—takes the emotional dimension of religion into account.

Religion as a Function of the Brain

In recent decades, neurologists have increasingly concerned themselves with religion. Since I am no expert in this area, I will limit myself here to a few central aspects of their explanations and offer my critical objections to them. First, I will try to determine which conception of religion underlies these neurological approaches, for it is according to their preconceptions that neurologists look for religion in different areas of the brain.

Andrew Newberg and his collaborators associate religion largely with mysticism. Although they also deal with myth and ritual, they arrive at the following conclusion: "Evidence suggests that the deepest origins of religion are based in mystical experience, and that religions persist because the wiring of the human brain continues to provide believers with a range of unitary experiences that are often interpreted as assurances that God exists."[39] Or, in another passage: "All the great scriptures make the same point: Fundamental truth has been revealed to human beings through a mystical encounter with a higher spiritual reality; mysticism, in other words, is the source of the essential wisdom and truth upon which all religions are founded. But before religions can begin, mystical experiences must be interpreted in rational terms, and the ineffable insights they bestow must be translated into specific beliefs."[40]

These authors' conception of religion is thus very close to the Romantic one. They also maintain that religious ideas persisted and spread because of their evolutionary utility. They then refer very broadly to the allegedly healthful effects of religion, such as reduced frequency of strokes and heart attacks, a better immune system, and so on, as well as to its potential for producing social integration.

What contribution does this approach make to understanding or explaining religion? From my point of view, very little. Its essential contribution consists in proving that mystical states are "neurologically real."[41] In other words, mystical experiences are not deceptions produced by religious charlatans, but can be shown, through neurological investigations, to be associated with real changes in brain activities. This insight may indeed be helpful, but I am not sure whether anyone ever doubted that lengthy mystical contemplation had a material correlate in the brain.

The major problem with this approach, however, is that the authors cannot distinguish between religious and nonreligious phenomena, as they themselves admit. They are unable to differentiate religious rituals or mystical experiences from nonreligious rituals or experiences.[42] A Stone Age hunter concentrating on his prey "is setting in motion the same biological chain of events triggered by contemplative techniques of religious mystics."[43] I don't doubt that these neurologists can also make the pleasure of eating desserts visible in their SPECT images.[44] But can a SPECT image show whether a bricklayer is tucking into an apple pie or a pietist mystic is receiving nourishment from the sweet wounds of Jesus? In other words, the approach proves only that all practices, including religious practices, have correlates in the brain, whether one is meditating or running a marathon. Neurologists do not seem capable of using their images to distinguish between religious and nonreligious activities, and their grab bag of views regarding the utility of religion is taken from outdated evolutionary biology and functionalism.

The neurologist V. S. Ramachandran has also studied religion and attempted to localize God in the limbic system.[45] The limbic system is an area of the brain that functions chiefly to regulate the experience and expression of emotions.[46] Like his colleagues discussed above, Ramachandran assumes that religion is primarily an emotional experience. Hence he mainly examines epileptics, and claims that during seizures they frequently have religious experiences. Most remarkable are the cases in which patients are said to have had deeply moving spiritual experiences, including a feeling of divine presence and direct communication with God, everything around them filled with cosmic significance.[47]

Here, too, a vague, Romantic conception of religion underlies the discussion, and I have my doubts whether the path leading to an explanation of religion passes by way of epilepsy. The central problem of the neurological approach to research on religion is that it understands religion one-sidedly as the emotion and experience of virtuosos. For Newberg and his colleagues, the model is the mystic, and for Ramachandran, the shaman. These researchers may be very competent as neurologists, but they are somewhat naïve and simplistic as researchers in the field of religion.

Religion as Sacralized Society

For Durkheim and his school, religion and society are inseparable from one another. On the one hand, Durkheim argues that religion is an eminently social phenomenon; on the other, he argues that almost all mental categories and institutions developed out of religion. In other words, neither religion nor society has priority over the other; instead, they mutually produce each other. Likewise, Durkheim equates religion with the sacred. The social can develop only on the basis of the distinction between the sacred and the profane. Without distinguishing between the sacred and the profane, what is commanded and what is forbidden, what is sanctioned and what is not sanctioned, society cannot be formed. For Durkheim, religion is equivalent to the sacred insofar as it founds and maintains community. Religion refers to the sacralized central cognitive, moral, and aesthetic principles and classifications without which cooperation and coordination would not be possible.

For Durkheim, human beings and society have two dimensions, a profane and a sacred. Man is profane in his bodily needs and desires, in his egotism and self-centeredness. He is sacred as a moral, social being who is able to transcend these limitations. Society is profane in its everyday economic life, which primarily serves the needs of physical reproduction. Even though Durkheim shows that economic orders are regulated morally, everyday life is still very distant from high religious festivals and rituals, in which the central symbols of social principles and ideals are invoked and people's hearts are moved. For Durkheim, a society based on utilitarian self-interest, that is, a fully profane society, cannot exist and represents a contradiction in terms. Society always has a sacred dimension and thus a religion. Society constantly creates ideals, and the ideal society is a necessary component of real society—and not a sort of accidental addition.[48]

This sacred dimension finds visible expression in non-everyday rituals in which social norms and ideals are periodically reinforced and even renewed. In ecstatic group experience, people overcome their particularist interests and carry out new acts of sacralization. Thus, if in his analysis of religion Durkheim identifies God with society, he should not be understood as endorsing existing conditions. He is referring here not to society as it actually is, but rather to its moral principles, ideas of order, and ideals. God symbolizes society's self-transcendence. Moreover, in ritual, religion provides another means of surmounting social crises.

At first glance, Durkheim's version of religion seems to represent the opposite of Marx's. For Durkheim, all religions are true; for Marx, all are false. For Marx, religion becomes superfluous through science and the overcoming of alienation; for Durkheim, religion remains an indispensable component of society, even if partially replaced by science. What we must not overlook in this opposition, however, is Durkheim's alteration of the very concept of religion. Marx was thinking of the concrete religious institutions of his time, which he correctly regarded as instruments of domination. At the same time, Marx, and even more Engels and Kautsky, emphasized religion's potential as a form of protest. In contrast, Durkheim's concept of religion has very little in common with the conventional one. His approach does not distinguish between religious society and political society. According to him, society's "basic law" is anchored in religion, so to speak, a position close to Rousseau's concept of a civil religion.

Durkheim's theory of religion has proved fruitful in several respects. His interpretation of religion by way of symbols and his contribution to the analysis and interpretation of rituals have enduring value. Nevertheless, his unique understanding of religion, with its fusion of religious and politico-social orders, is problematic, especially historically. For one thing, it ignores all forms of religion and historical phases in which religious and political communities are not identical. Wherever religious diversity or religious pluralism are predominant, or where orthodoxy and heterodoxy are opposed, this approach encounters difficulties in mediating between subgroups and the society as a whole. Either religion is related to segments of the society's membership, in which case the integration of the various religious communities into the whole society remains unexplained, and religion even proves to be dysfunctional, or else religion is related to the society as a whole, in which case the particularist religious practices and ideas are not accounted for or are depicted as successful integrations at various levels of social aggregation that are themselves in harmony.

With due respect for Durkheim's magnificent outline, I consider his theory of religion generalizable only to a limited extent. It offers, above all, a brilliant reflection on the structural and institutional problems of the modern nation-state. First, it infers from an analysis of Australian totemism, which is primarily a social classification scheme, a general theory of religion as the guiding center of society as a whole. Second, the theory serves as a foundation for a civil religion for the modern state, traditional salvation religions having lost their earlier integrational potential. Just as totemism overcame the particularism of specific groups, so civil religion overcomes the particularism of specific vocational groups and of modern individualism. In other words, the whole operation serves to resolve a specifically modern problem that has less to do with "religion" than with "nation." Hence the concept of religion is defined not only idiosyncratically but also in a way that restricts it very narrowly to social and public functions. Many religious phenomena (in the conventional sense) are thus ignored or marginalized, or even relegated to the category of "magic." Third, the dimension of domination is lacking in Durkheim's conception of religion. What Hobbes clearly characterizes and justifies as an act of domination appears in Durkheim as a miraculously produced, self-creating consensus.[49]

The problematic nature of Durkheim's approach is also manifested in the way his work was received by later social scientists, who tended to further narrow its perspective. On the one hand, anthropology in particular drew heavily on his concept of religion, since it found very congenial his identification of the religious and political orders as applied to the societies it studied. But this led, for example, in British structuralism, to seeing religious powers as nothing more than symbolizations of social categories.[50] On the other hand, sociology used Durkheim chiefly for investigating political religion, nationalism, and the cult of the state. The "civil religion" debate and studies of political rituals provide examples.[51]

Thomas Luckmann's thesis regarding the privatization of religion picks up on Durkheim's theory but combines it with Georg Simmel's analysis of religiousness.[52] According to Luckmann, in modern industrial societies religion has withdrawn from society to the individual. There, however, it does for the individual exactly what it did for society according to Durkheim. In Luckmann's view, every form of self-transcendence is a religion. But since he regards self-transcendence as an indispensable presupposition for the formation of the person, for him all people are religious in the same sense that for Durkheim all societies are religious.

Systems theory also goes back partially to Durkheim's approach, insofar as it further develops his view into a general analysis of social directive processes and of the role that religion plays in them.[53] Niklas Luhmann, for example, analyzes social phenomena from the point of view of problem solving. For him, religion deals with the problem of contingency, which he defines as the fact that something is not necessarily the way it is, that it could be otherwise. Here I will forgo more detailed discussion of Luhmann, since it is impossible to do justice to his theory in a limited space. A good critique of his approach has been made by Detlef Pollack, and a fruitful, empirically oriented application of his theory can be found in the work of Peter Beyer.[54]

Religion as an Interest in Salvation

Max Weber's action-oriented, interpretative sociology examines religion primarily under the aspect of its contribution to the shaping of a specific habitus of typical social actors and its formative influence on culture in general. It puts more emphasis on the development of classes, domination, and ethos than on order, integration, and social equilibrium. It has become commonplace to object that at the beginning of his unfinished manuscript "Religious Communities" Weber fails to offer a definition of religion—indeed, that he explicitly refuses to do so. This interpretation seems to me to be based on a misunderstanding. Here, Weber does not reject the possibility of a scholarly definition of the object, but rather—as he expressly states—a definition of the "essence" of religion. Clearly referring to such attempts in the contemporary literature, he notes critically that an "essential definition" cannot be achieved through a priori definitions. On the contrary, it would require the study of many different religions in the forms in which they appeared historically. In other words, a definition of religion cannot be achieved a priori, but—if at all—only a posteriori. No one seems to have noticed that Durkheim is saying essentially the same thing when he argues that the initial definition can only be preliminary and does not capture the essence of religion: "It is not that I hope to arrive straightaway at the deep and truly explanatory features of religion, for these can be determined only at the end of the research."[55]

Weber, however, does not seek to define the "essence" of religion; he pursues the sociology of religion by investigating the "conditions and effects" of religiously motivated action. In his view, this can be done only in terms of content, not in terms of form. Only through "subjectively intended meaning" can an analytical unity of the object be created, since religions in their "external course" manifest such diversity that a coherent definition of the object is not possible. And even if one were to discover formal parallels between religions, these same forms could have very different meanings.

For Weber, religion concerns the "conditions and effects of a specific kind of social action."[56] Generally speaking, religion represents the formation of a sphere of interest, namely, interest in salvation. What changes in the course of social and cultural developments are the definitions of "salvation" along with ways and means of achieving the goal of salvation.[57] In "primitive" societies, salvation interests are understood in a purely immanent, this-worldly way. Since the goal—that "it may be well with you and that you may live long on the earth" (Ephesians 6:3)—often cannot be achieved on one's own, the aid of extraordinary personal or impersonal powers may be needed. But access to these powers is reserved for especially—usually ecstatically—gifted persons, on whose mediation ordinary persons are therefore dependent. A differentiation between religion and other spheres of action cannot be discerned here on the basis of the goals pursued, but only on that of the means used and the specific actors involved.

According to Weber, in the development of "religions of salvation" and their rejection of "the world," a special religious interest is formulated and institutionalized, namely, the goal of being saved from the world, which may conflict with everyday interests or at least be in a tense relationship with them. The rigorous pursuit of this peculiar religious interest is often an activity for specially qualified individuals. Only in exceptional cases, such as that of ascetic Protestantism, is it extended to all laypersons. Weber is primarily interested in how and to what degree religious goals of salvation and paths to salvation have helped shape the behavior of the laity. He starts from the assumption that—depending on the salvation goals and paths to salvation, as well as the corresponding religious demands on the various social groups—different tensions, conflicts, and contradictions resulted, which in turn led to different processes of rationalization. He pays special attention to the development of different types of rationalism as an often unintended effect of incentives to religious action. His guiding interest here is to explain the unique development in the West of a mass ethic focused on this-worldly, rationalized, and disciplined action.

In addition to long-term religious developments and their effects on secular ethics, which Weber discusses in *The Protestant Ethic and the "Spirit" of Capitalism* and in *The Economic Ethics of the World Religions*, he proposes an analysis of religious institution-building with his conception of "charisma." According to Weber, the "religious experience" of especially gifted persons is the origin of every religion. But he is not interested in whether this "experience" is genuine. Neither does he declare it to be the "essence" of religion. Instead, he is concerned with its social effects, and above all whether this "experience" is believed in by others, and what consequences this might have for social action. Thus Weber adopts the Romantic idea of religion but at the same time transforms it into a sociological question.

Since religious experience is transitory, it has to be institutionalized. The purely personal, charismatic power relationship between the religiously gifted person and his followers is transformed into a regulated, enduring relationship, made routine, and converted into a permanent power relationship on traditional or bureaucratic foundations. Hence, in religions of salvation there is an increasing adaptation of salvation interests to secular interests. In other words, in his theory of religion Weber is concerned chiefly with the role of religion in defining and transforming ideal and material interests in their mutual relations, as well as in the elaboration of a specific ethos or habitus and the resulting differences in status and power relationships.

Pierre Bourdieu adopted the Weberian approach but narrowed it considerably.[58] The tensions and dynamics among prophecy, the clergy, and lay rationalism that Weber had described are transformed by Bourdieu into a theory of the "religious field." For Weber, the question was how this situation, in the context of congregational religions, contributes to an ethical rationalization of broad strata of the population. For Bourdieu, religion in general represents another arena of the battle for power, in which a specific capital can be acquired and exchanged for other kinds of capital. Thus, as in the cases of science or art, religion is ultimately a matter of acquiring symbolic capital. Whereas for Weber the particular meaning in the form of salvation interests and the religious shaping of the person plays a central role, Bourdieu reduces religion to an instrument for pursuing this-worldly power interests and social advancement. Thus he concentrates on a dimension of religions that is certainly present but not specific to religion.

Religion as a Commodity

For the past thirty years or so, utilitarianism has undergone a revival in the social sciences, and it has also entered the sociology of religion in the form of "rational choice" theory. This perspective includes many approaches, which differ from one another chiefly in the way they deal with cultural factors. In principle, the theory is based on the assumption of rational actors and stable preferences. Whereas Weber, for example, had shown that material and ideal interests are culturally determined and may often be in conflict, rational choice theory, by assuming that preferences are constant, seeks to exclude culture as a variable. As ever more cultural factors are built into the concept of rational choice, the more it is watered down and overloaded with assumptions that are basically alien to it.

Rational choice theory can be applied both to individual action and to religious market research. In relation to individual action, maximization of utility is the key element, utility in the case of religion being described as compensation for goals that cannot be achieved.[59] In this respect, the approach shows similarities to Freud's theory of compensation and projection, but without offering an explanation for the deep psychic level. According to this view, religion holds out the prospect of a satisfaction of needs that are not met in normal life, such as immortality. Surprisingly enough, even this religious commodity is not offered by all religions, which undermines the thesis that the preferences of religious consumers are constant.

The rational choice approach has yielded highly interesting results in its religious market research, producing interesting hypotheses regarding the growth and diminution of religious groups, secularization, and schisms within religious groups.[60] Such research is less relevant, however, to a theory of religion.

From my point of view, the rational choice approach is problematic in several respects. For one thing, preferences are not constant. Different societies, classes, and groups have different preferences. The theory uses various counterarguments to deal with this objection. Some proponents maintain that this is primarily a question of methodology, and that variations in preferences should be attributed to different conditions in the social environment, not to inaccessible subjective factors. Others argue that what matters is not the actual preference or actual rational choice, but only that these assumptions in the model have proved themselves prognostically. As a whole, however, this approach cannot make up its mind whether its argument is intended methodologically or ontologically, and thus it remains inconsistent.

Second, the theory is tautological. Whatever people do, it implies, expresses their preference. In the event this assumption proves clearly absurd, then the actors must have lacked sufficient information.[61] Martyrdom can be declared just as much a rational decision as hedonism can.[62] If one of three siblings has himself transformed into a human bomb and kills dozens of people in addition to himself, another goes to Japan as an itinerant worker, and a third becomes a bobsled driver, all three of them have obviously made rational decisions! In each case, of course, motives and socio-structural conditions for such decisions can be identified; but these can no longer be meaningfully explained within the framework of stable preferences.

The rational choice approach suffers from a simplistic modeling of human action. Weber distinguished four types of action: means-end-oriented, value-oriented, traditional, and affective. According to him, the reality of social action is composed of combinations of these four types, which are not determined by goal-oriented rationality alone. The construction of an actor guided by interests may be a useful methodological tool, but rationalism should not lead us to discount deviations from the model.

Furthermore, the rational choice approach contains a fundamental contradiction. The theory is based on the pleasure principle, that is, on the premise that human beings calculate rationally in order to avoid pain and maximize pleasure. But rational calculation itself is often not a pleasure—think of filling out an income tax form. If the theory took its premises seriously, it should count on rational calculation only when the stakes are relatively high, that is, when the punishment for not calculating is greater than the unpleasantness of calculating. Here too, however, preferences are not constant. Some people go to great lengths to get items on sale, while others buy what they see without comparing prices.

The theory is most appropriate for analyzing situations in which rational calculation is institutionalized. It is unsuitable as a foundation for a universal theory of religion. Even for market research it is of limited use, for it is based on the model of a Protestant sect. The claim that religion remains vital only as a voluntary association—in Weber's terminology, as a "rational compulsory association" based on a shared ultimate conviction—with strict boundaries and high demands on its members reveals an astonishing historical and cultural ignorance.[63] East Asian religions represent a diametrically opposed model; there are hardly any strict boundaries between one and another, and exclusive membership is characteristic only of monks. And while religious practice is often tradition-bound and community-oriented, it is not lacking in vitality.

Outlook

This survey has shown that there is more than one legitimate perspective on religion. All the various approaches, whether we accept or reject them, contribute to a more complex understanding of religion, if only because they express such a diversity of points of view. Religion is conceptualized anthropologically (Romanticism, phenomenology), psychologically (Tylor, Frazer, Marett, Freud, Malinowski, rational choice theory), and sociologically (Marx, Durkheim, Weber). All these concepts have certain weaknesses. For example, the Romantic and phenomenological approaches imply judgments of the religious and give priority to virtuoso practices. Many approaches lean toward functionalist explanations of religion in the sense of its "contribution" to the establishment of a social equilibrium. Others reduce religion to an individual phenomenon that resolves intellectual problems or satisfies subjective wishes. Nearly all tend to proceed in a highly deductive manner and make a priori assumptions regarding "humankind," "society," or "modernity." The studies of religion that are the most theoretically and empirically differentiated are those of Max Weber, though he is interested chiefly in the differences among religious traditions and in the contribution made by religions to the development of a specific ethos. My recognition and criticism of these theories will allow me to present my own approach more clearly.

CHAPTER FOUR

Religious Practice and
the Promise of Salvation:
Outline of a Theory of Religion

It is now time to draw conclusions from the preceding discussions and sketch the outlines of my theory of religion. To that end, I will discuss three elements in the construction of the theory: defining religion, understanding it, and explaining it. I begin by formulating my position in the manner of a thesis, which I then proceed to explain in greater detail in the course of this chapter.

First, I note that only a content-oriented definition based on the meaning of religious action allows us adequately to delimit religion as a universal social phenomenon. Like other social phenomena, religion cannot be satisfactorily explained without its meaning being understood. Reference to its actual or presumed effects on society does not represent a definition of religion, since such reference infers the origin from the function and thus argues metaphysically, as if everything were arranged by an "invisible hand." Religion can be grasped theoretically only if its specific meaning clearly distinguishes it from other types of social action. This specific meaning lies in its relation to personal or impersonal superhuman powers, that is, to powers that control or influence what escapes human control.[1]

Only an interpretive, that is, a meaning-oriented theory of action, is capable of bridging the gap between religious internal perspectives and scientific external perspectives. Explanations that ignore internal perspectives have to justify the outside point of view they adopt. In contrast, interpretive explanations arrive at their external perspective by abstracting and systematizing internal perspectives, and thus claim no privileged or even objective status for themselves. Instead, they transform internal perspectives into an external perspective, which differs from the internal perspectives but does not contradict them.

Religion is a complex of meaningful practices—that is, of actions—that are situated in a relatively systematic web of meaning.[2] From a sociological point of view, each religion is thus an empirically given system rather than a theologically constructed "tradition." Hence Christianity or Buddhism are not religions but traditions that contain, or (in the case of "syncretic" systems) participate in, diverse religions.

The meaning of religious practices cannot be adequately understood either on the level of intellectual discourses or "theologies" in the broad sense of the word, or on that of subjective interpretations, including the Romantic or phenomenological variants. They can be properly understood only on the level of institutionalized practices or "liturgies," under which concept I subsume rules and meanings for human intercourse with super-human powers.[3]

All religious liturgies contain promises regarding what religions are capable of doing. In their liturgies, religions usually claim the ability to ward off misfortune, surmount crises, and provide blessings and salvation by communicating with superhuman powers.[4] If we systematize the self-images that religions produce, we see that they contain a sufficient foundation for explaining religion in general. They illuminate the institutionalized meaning of religious practices and allow us to conclude that although this meaning is not identical with the meaning that practitioners attribute to their actions, it nonetheless corresponds to it. These self-images explain the origin and reproduction of religion without conflating them functionalistically. And they explain the power of religious institutions as mediators or gatekeepers of access to superhuman powers.

Defining Religion

The primary distinction to be drawn in developing a theory of religion is that between a content-based and a formal or functional determination of the concept of religion. The debate between representatives of a content-based and a functional concept of religion is very old. It reached an apex when Peter Berger discussed the difference between his theory of religion and that of his friend Thomas Luckmann, which they had bracketed in the book on the foundations of a phenomenological sociology they wrote together.[5]

I will not summarize this debate here, but only set forth my reasons for rejecting a functional definition of religion. Functional definitions explain the alleged contribution of religion to the constitution and reproduction of society. This appears meaningful from the point of view of organicist social theories, which work with models of equilibrium, or from that of theories that consider religion in relation to power and domination. But it misses the meaning of religion from the point of view of religious practitioners and thus also from that of the theory of action. It is unlikely that anyone would seriously attempt to define and explain other institutions—such as music, literature, theater, or sports—solely in relation to their actual or alleged social function. By analyzing, for instance, the social function of soccer, one thereby neither understands the game nor explains it. Since functional definitions ignore the meaning of action, they are generally quite unspecific.

Moreover, the concept of function is in no way unambiguous, as Robert Merton has already shown.[6] He points out that function is often confused with motive. His distinction between manifest and latent functions serves to distinguish between conscious and unconscious consequences, not between motives and effects. The functional concept of religion is usually concerned with latent functions, that is, with effects that are objective but usually unconscious. Logically, a functional definition consists in describing as X everything that fulfills function F. Functionalist theories of religion commonly argue that everything that fulfills the function of "integration"—the latter term normally referring either to "social integration" or to the integration of the person through the creation of "identity"—is "religion."[7]

As Merton has noted, religion is often dogmatically credited with functions that it fails to fulfill, either constantly or universally.[8] Furthermore, functional definitions differentiate religion from other phenomena in a nonsensical way, are unspecific, and include too many phenomena that can hardly be subsumed under the concept of religion. All kinds of activities can be interpreted as socially integrative or identity creating—for instance, forming associations or temporary relationships, or devotion to a hobby. The sociology of religion would therefore have to concern itself with alpinists, nudists, vegetarians, philatelists, golfers, and rabbit breeders. In this definition, barbecues with guitar music, soccer games, or group sex are at least potentially religious phenomena. Surprisingly, however, the representatives of such broad definitions of religion for the most part study only phenomena that correspond to a much narrower concept of religion. In addition, the functional definition of religion proves to be particularly nonsensical from the point of view of the comparative study of cultures, since it lumps together phenomena that are perceived by those concerned as being extremely different.

All this is based on a superficial interpretation of Durkheim's theory of religion, which clearly distinguishes between a content-based definition and a functional explanation of religion.[9] Those who trivialize his theory transform his explanation into a definition. Moreover, Durkheim does not characterize every ecstatic group experience as religious. His work is concerned with the construction of community on the highest level of social aggregation in every instance, not with sociability or clubbiness. Durkheim's theory of religion is a theory of the demands for social integration in the age of the modern nation-state, to which he attempts, through his study of "totemism," to give a status comparable to that of the law of evolution. The functional concept of religion, however, is too broad but also too narrow, and it excludes—if it is consistently applied—certain forms of religious practice insofar as no integrative function can be attributed to them; such practices include consulting oracles, proclaiming curses, or making amulets. For that reason, Durkheim himself tried, with doubtful success, to distinguish between magic and religion.

Luckmann once argued that the content-based concept of religion was too theological. In fact, this objection is far more cogent when directed against his own functional concept of religion. According to his concept, religion is a necessary condition for society or the self and has a necessary function in maintaining them. Thus it becomes by definition an indispensable presupposition for human and social existence. This claim seems to me far more theologically oriented than the content-based definition.

My criticism of functional *definitions* of religion does not mean that functional *explanations* are absurd. But the latter too ignore the meaning of religious action and explain not religion but society, as Spiro has convincingly shown.[10] Moreover, I think postmodern critics of the concept of religion are correct in saying that religion does not have the same function (in the sense of objective effects) in all social systems.

What does my alternative look like? As an initial step, I suggest that religious practices should be differentiated as clearly and unambiguously as possible from other kinds of practices. First, this differentiation should be made in such a way that our everyday understanding of religion is not stood on its head; instead, phenomena that are commonly considered religious should fall under the definition given. Second, the definition should not already contain the explanation of the phenomena, as is the case in the phenomenological and functionalist approaches; instead, phenomena should be analytically isolated in such a way that they can be explained by systematic comparative analysis. Third, the definition should be compatible with religions' self-understandings as expressed in their practices.

The definition that seems to me the most appropriate is content-based and widely accepted. It is based on what William James called an "ontological imagination," and it draws on Melford Spiro's definition but modifies it to include impersonal powers.[11] According to this definition, religion is a complex of practices that are based on the premise of the existence of superhuman powers, whether personal or impersonal, that are generally invisible.[12] I call this the religious premise. The "superhumanness" of these powers consists in the fact that influence or control over dimensions of individual or social human life and the natural environment is attributed to them—dimensions that are usually beyond direct human control. Religious practices normally consist in using culturally prescribed means to establish contact with these powers or to gain access to them. What contact or access means depends on the religious imagination concerned and on the social and cultural forms of accessibility. This cultural learning of religious practices was clearly expressed by Augustine when he wrote, concerning his childhood,

> But, Lord, we found that men called upon Thee, and we learnt from them to think of Thee (according to our powers) as of some great One, who, though hidden from our senses, couldst hear and help us. For so I began, as a boy, to pray to Thee, my aid and refuge; and broke the fetters of my tongue to call on Thee, praying Thee, though small, yet with no small earnestness.[13]

There are at least four types of contact with or access to superhuman powers. Establishing contact can mean—in Spiro's sense—interaction through symbolic actions such as prayers, chants, gestures, formulas, sacrifices, vows, or divination. Second, establishing contact in the sense of manipulation may take place, for example, by wearing amulets or performing "magical" acts. Establishing contact can also mean temporary interaction or even fusion with superhuman powers, as experienced in mystical trance and ascetic ecstasy. Finally, establishing contact can mean activating superhuman potential that slumbers within a person; it includes practices of self-empowerment through contemplation and the "enlightenment" experienced thereby. The last two ways of establishing contact are usually reserved for religious virtuosos. All such practices, which aim at establishing contact with superhuman powers, I call interventionist practices. Many concern what has long been called "cult."[14]

Interventionist practices are closely connected with two further types: discursive and behavior-regulating practices. By "discursive practices" I mean interpersonal communication regarding the nature, status, or accessibility of superhuman powers, their manipulability, and their will, as well as techniques of self-empowerment. Discursive practices hand down and revise religious knowledge concerning interventionist practices and stand in a dialectical relationship to that knowledge. They are the foundation of religious interpretive cultures. Theology also falls under this rubric and should not be seen as limited to an academic discipline and intellectuals. Theologies also make an important contribution to the reproduction of religion in the socialization process.

"Behavior-regulating practices" pertain to the religious reshaping of everyday life with respect to superhuman powers. These usually concern the avoidance of sanctions or the accumulation of merits. They deal with such matters as how people should treat one another; what, when, and with whom they may eat; whom they may marry; what clothing and hairstyle they should adopt; at what times and places they should carry out, or avoid, certain actions; how they should bury their dead. Such regulations regarding behavior are, however, valid as religious practices only when they occur in accord with the will, the principles, or the sanctions of superhuman powers. In an intensified form, behavior-regulating practices can also assume the meaning of interventionist practices, for example, when they are interpreted as communication with superhuman powers or as a strategy of self-empowerment. Ethical behavior or the intensive study of sacred texts can be interpreted as a form of religious service and thus take on the quality of an interventionist practice. It is as if the limits were constantly in flux. As I will argue later, interventionist practices are the key to explaining religion.

From these definitions we can derive further terminological refinements. "Religious" actions are those whose meaning is defined by their reference to personal or impersonal superhuman powers. Religion denotes a complex of religious practices that should be distinguished from the concept of religious tradition. "Religiousness" refers to the subjective appropriation and interpretation of religion. No one practices religion without appropriating forms and contents. Whereas religion can be theoretically conceived primarily on the level of institutional practices and their meaning, religiousness is best understood as the result of a dialectic of institutionalized practices and subjective appropriation and interpretation. These definitions imply, then, that people can act religiously without practicing a religion. Someone who practices Zen meditation on Mondays, turns tables on Tuesdays, lays out Tarot cards on Thursdays, and goes to mass on Sundays is performing religious acts, but the systematic connection among them is lacking. If this connection is produced only subjectively, if it is not shared with and confirmed by others, then these practices lack the social character of a religion.

Further, these definitions imply that religion, as a complex of practices, is marked by a certain interpretive systematicity. It need not be a theologically "pure" system. Its systemic character emerges from the context of meaning that has been institutionalized and is bound to various practices. It may well have "syncretic" traits. Religion denotes the institutionalized complex of practices in each case, not a theologically normative system.

This view also makes superfluous the question of whether Hinduism or Buddhism are religions. To the extent that Hinduism and Buddhism represent complexes of religious practices, they are religions. At the same time, we must not reduce them to the concept of religion. They may even be far more than religions or, in part, something other than religions. To be precise, all religions in the traditional sense of the concept are actually religious traditions that have produced or contributed to a multiplicity of religions in the empirical, historical sense of given complexes of practices.

The concept of religious tradition can mean at least three different things. First, tradition can refer to a theological category that constructs religion as a symbolic historical continuity in order to differentiate it from internal deviations or external competitors. When, for instance, a pope determines what is allowed or forbidden according to Catholic tradition, or what leads to excommunication, he is acting in accord with a theological concept of tradition. Second, tradition can be a classificatory concept that distinguishes among religious practices or complexes of practices on the basis of their key symbols and self-classifications. If, for example, a ritual is described as Christian because it contains the symbol of a cross, this concept of tradition is being used. Finally, tradition can be an empirical category describing spatially and temporally delimited practices and structures of meaning that were "always already" performed in this way. In contrast to the theological concept, this concept of tradition can be syncretic. These three different meanings of tradition should be kept distinct from one another.

What has motivated me to propose this definition of religion, and what do I see as its advantages? First, the definition is applicable to all the phenomena that are commonly understood as religious. It does not associate religion exclusively with personalistic or monotheistic ideas of God, but also includes beliefs in polytheistic and nonpersonal powers. Thus structures of meaning such as are widespread in Asian religions, for instance, as well as contemplative and ascetic practices of self-empowerment, are given appropriate consideration.

The definition also avoids the absurd, overly broad understandings of religion according to which soccer games, shopping at a supermarket, or barbecues are religious phenomena. Not every community experience involving a certain amount of sentiment or excitement becomes an object of the sociology of religion. Even "spirituality" is subsumed under the concept of "religion" only if it does not remain slumbering within an individual but, rather, leads to contact with superhuman powers, on the one hand, and becomes something social, on the other.

Neither does my definition involve any compromise with nebulous expansions of the concept of religion, according to which every person must be "somehow" religious, or aesthetics is raised to a quasi-religious status. This expansion of the concept of religion seems to serve the repression of subjective processes of disenchantment rather than the pursuit of analytical goals. Some people find it easier to broaden the concept of religion to the point of meaninglessness than to admit to themselves and others that they no longer believe in superhuman powers and their accessibility. In contrast, my definition restricts the concept of religion to a "realistic" belief in superhuman powers, which leads to a communication that is subjectively believed in. Metaphorical references to superhuman powers, such as the "power of history" or the "power of money," are subsumed under the concept of religion only if they result in interventionist practices.

A further advantage of my definition is that the extremely problematic distinction between magic and religion falls away. I know of no convincing distinction between these two phenomena. Neither Durkheim's distinction between religion as social and magic as asocial nor Weber's distinction between religious supplication and magical coercion, nor that between morally oriented religion and scientifically or technically oriented magic, are confirmed in the interpretation of religious practices. The distinction is probably based primarily on value judgments. In any case, fixation on this distinction leads to modes of investigation that are more theological than sociological.

My definition also clearly differentiates religion from philosophy. It is not reflection or discourse that characterize religious practice, but rather the establishment of contact with superhuman powers. Insofar as reflection and discourse are not based on the presupposition of a belief in such powers and communication with them, they do not constitute religion in the sense defined. To choose one example, it is not necessary to classify under the rubric of religion every reflection made by a Buddhist regarding human existence and its meaninglessness simply because someone has decided a priori that Buddhism is a religion. In general, it is the speculations of intellectuals within different religious traditions that occasionally exceed the framework of religion as I have defined it here. I see no disadvantage in treating their thought as philosophy.[15] Otherwise one would have to broaden the definition of religion so enormously that its object would become incoherent and no longer manageable sociologically.

Finally, my approach leads to a revision of the priorities of the sociology of religion. In classical sociology, the ethical-moral and power dimensions of religion were foregrounded. It was a matter of determining the influence of religion on the conduct of life, the role of religion in the production of belief in legitimacy, or its contribution to the maintenance of the social system. Recently, these perspectives have been broadened through discourse analysis. But what is still neglected is the analysis of individuals and group intercourse with superhuman powers—powers that from the point of view of religious practitioners clearly represent the very core of religion. To that extent, the sociology of religion has shown mainly an instrumental interest in religion; it has given little attention to religion itself. In that respect, it resembles current sociology of culture, which likewise is not really interested in culture but only seeks to demonstrate that any given body of data can be run through the shredder of a certain conceptual apparatus. Thus, my approach constitutes a plea for taking an interest in religious phenomena themselves, qua religious phenomena, but for doing so empirically, as an investigation into their institutionalized and appropriated meaning, not, in the manner of phenomenology, as an "intuition of essences."

Understanding Religion

I have offered a content-based definition of religion and thus made the meaning of religious practices central. The next question is how the meaning of religion as a complex of practices can actually be discovered. What sources are to be used? In principle, there are three possible interpretations: intellectualist or "theological" (broadly understood), subjectivist, and liturgical. I will first discuss the problem of intellectualist and subjectivist explanations of religion, and then outline my liturgical alternative and its advantages. It is not at all my intent to deter researchers on religion from engaging in subjective interpretations of religions or theologies. As subjects of research, such interpretations are and will remain of great interest. I simply argue that on purely methodological grounds they are unsuitable as sources for a theory of religions.

Intellectualism

Intellectualist interpretations of religious action usually begin with the construction of complex religious ideas. Religious intellectuals create world images. They transform the chaos of the world into a holy cosmos and thus produce certainty and objectivity.[16] If we assume with Peter Berger that religion is best understood through the world image that is reproduced and transformed through processes of internalization, externalization, and objectification, then along with this assumption we have to accept certain theoretical and methodological problems. For one thing, societies would be expected to have a high degree of homogeneity and to largely exclude religious pluralism. In Berger's work, this expectation led to the assumption that pluralization inevitably ends up in secularization, a position that he has ceased to defend.[17] Second, this approach privileges the cognitive side of religion and attributes a secondary role to practices, as if the latter were simply the implementation of a worldview or a theology. Naturally, every theory of religion confronts the problem of the relations between religious ideas and practices. This problem can be seen as a question of factual priority or as a question of methodology. Factually, the question is whether religious belief founds practices or whether it expresses the constantly renewed and changing meaning of existing practices. But this question seems to me wrongly framed. In essence, it continues the old debate about the priority of myth or ritual, in which the chief issue is which one is "more original." Empirically, it can probably be said that both content (myth) and form (ritual) change historically, and it is usually assumed that form is more resistant to innovation than is content. Ultimately, however, only in concrete cases can we decide what has changed in each instance and on what grounds.

As a methodological problem, the relationship between belief and action is far more interesting. A proponent of an intellectualist approach begins by constructing a worldview, a system of symbols and beliefs, which, it is then claimed, inspires or underlies religious practices—possibly "unconsciously." This kind of procedure has problematic implications. At the beginning of the analysis stands a systematized body of knowledge that is as a rule reserved for intellectuals. The practitioners—laypersons and clergy—are unfamiliar with this knowledge, at least in its complexity, systematicity, and entirety. Thus religion is constructed primarily as "belief," knowledge of which is ultimately limited to religious intellectuals or, in the absence of such a group, to ersatz theologians. Anthropologists are fond of playing this role for societies that neither have nor need theologians. Geoffrey Lienhardt's studies on the Shilluk people provide a rather good illustration. According to Lienhardt, the Shilluk have not systematized their cosmological ideas; instead, they simply reveal them in their behavior and in their proverbs. The ideas must be abstracted from this reality and given a certain degree of coherence. Thus a system of thought is created of which there is no shred of in the thinking of the Shilluk themselves.[18]

This way of proceeding may be of some interest for a comparative theology, but for an analysis of religious practices oriented toward the sociology of knowledge it has unacceptable consequences. At the outset, religion is defined as theology and so intellectualized that the religious practices of the laity seem almost without meaning. As a rule, laypersons have at most a rudimentary knowledge of worldview, symbols, or doctrines. A typical example of this kind of intellectualist approach is represented by Marcel Griaule's *Conversations with Ogotemmeli*. Griaule explains that the full range of the doctrine is known only to the aged and a few initiates; but he claims that it is not esoteric because all have access to it when they grow old. Furthermore, totemistic priests of any age are entrusted with the parts of the doctrine that particularly concern them, whereas the whole population performs its ritual duties as they are prescribed in these religious ideas. Naturally, Griaule tells us, the common people do not understand the deep meaning of their actions and prayers; but this is true in all societies.[19]

However, if systematized religious ideas are quite unknown to religious practitioners, how helpful are they then in explaining religious action, and how much is our understanding of religion distorted by reducing religion essentially to "theology"? If we begin with an intellectualist analysis of complex systems of belief and symbols, then we are left with four options for determining the meaning of religious practices.

First, we can maintain that religious laypersons are aware of the meaning of their action in its full "theological" scope. This interpretation is so obviously false that we can immediately set it aside.

Second, we can—with Marcel Griaule, for example—maintain that religious laypersons "unconsciously" express complex religious and theological knowledge in their practices, making use of deeply significant symbols and actualizing their meaning, although they themselves do not understand them. A metaphysical reality is thus attributed to these symbols, which express a timeless meaning, even if this meaning is unknown to those involved. They do not have the meaning that is attributed to them in various instances; instead, inherent in the symbols is an objective meaning that is not accessible to everyone in the same degree. This option also privileges the point of view of religious intellectuals, by whose standard other people's interpretations are judged. They decide what practices "really" mean. Here the intellectualist interpretation intersects with the subjectivist interpretation. Instead of taking into account the multilayered nature of symbolic representations, an elitist orthodoxy is established. From the standpoint of empirical social science, this solution too is unacceptable.

Third, we can juxtapose the "folk religion" of the laity with the religion of the intellectuals. But this simply reformulates the distinction between the "true" religion of the educated and the "superstition" of the common people, or even between orthodoxy and heterodoxy.

Fourth, we can try to justify the procedure historically by maintaining, for example, that intellectuals preserve the original meaning of religious practices, which was involved in the institutionalization of those practices but was later forgotten. Even if this were true, it includes the value judgment that this original meaning should be preserved and is of greater value than later interpretations. Once again, this view merely expresses the interests of religious intellectuals, whose privileged status is connected with the maintenance of the "original" knowledge.

All four options that follow from a methodological priority accorded to religious ideas strongly privilege the perspective of intellectuals. Hence they tend toward a theological overinterpretation of religious action, making covert or overt value judgments regarding the rationality or appropriateness of religious laypersons' actions. More importantly in such approaches, belief systems and religious action are simply juxtaposed, for the most part unrelated to each other. An adequate theory of religion would require a better connection between belief and practice.

Subjectivism

The second possibility of conveying the meaning of religion is represented by subjectivism. In order to know what Christian, Jewish, or Buddhist practices mean, one simply asks people who belong to one of those religions and practice it. This strategy has become popular chiefly because of the thesis regarding the privatization of religion. The model of "Sheilaism"[20] makes every Tom, Dick, and Harry into founders of their own "religions." Such investigations not only promote narcissism but also have methodological disadvantages that disqualify them as the foundation for a theory of religion.

It is generally acknowledged that many of our actions proceed in an unreflective way, and anyone who observes him- or herself knows this is true. We are not constantly accounting to ourselves for our action, nor are we constantly reflecting on its meaning. Instead, we often act intuitively on the basis of learned behaviors, the internalized expectations of others, habits, conventions, or incorporated experiential knowledge. We also change our opinions from time to time and believe today something that we will consider nonsense a day, a month, or a year later. We interact with others on the basis of a certain trust, as, for example, the assumption when we are driving a car that other drivers are familiar with traffic laws. All this points to the problematic character of subjective explanations of religious action.

Only selected dimensions of religious action, if any, are subject to reflection. Subjective explanations, therefore, are usually extremely unsystematic, unstable, and incomplete. Moreover, they are frequently situation-specific, ad hoc. Individuals offer quite different interpretations of their action, depending on their whims and moods; today's interpretation of an action may differ from yesterday's or tomorrow's. People express themselves regarding matters on which they are presently reflecting, but take other central aspects for granted.

Furthermore, subjective statements or investigations commonly do not reveal a meaning of which the actor was aware before or in the course of an action; instead, they result from an ex post facto reflection, that is, of a subsequent effort of rationalization. Most actors also lack the ability to articulate adequately the motivations of their action, insofar as they are aware of them. Intellectuals may have a certain skill in doing so, and it is not least for that reason that they are often the objects of questioning, whereas average practitioners cannot give adequate answers.

Although research into the concrete, subjectively intended significance of religious action is indispensable for ethnographic study or for understanding and explaining personal religiousness, it is neither possible nor helpful for a theory of religion. For one thing, even if we want to, we are fundamentally incapable of understanding the religious practices of earlier periods because we can neither ask the actors nor deduce their subjective interpretations from other sources. For another, in attempting to understand the meaning of a ritual in which hundreds or thousands of people participate, we cannot ask each one of them about his or her understanding of the event. At most, we could try to find out which basic assumptions are shared by many of the participants and which are not. After all, we understand a play or an opera not by interviewing the actors, singers, musicians, or spectators but by grasping the meaning of the action. This meaning is expressed above all in the texts spoken or sung, in the sets and the staging, in the actors' gestures and mimicry. It is also determined primarily by the author, composer, and director, not by scholars or critics. In other words, the "subjectively intended meaning" of religious action should not be interpreted subjectivistically. Rather, it is constituted in each case in the context of an institutionalized social and cultural meaning and can be deciphered only in relation to that meaning.

A variant of subjectivism is represented by Romantic and phenomenological approaches, which strive to anchor subjectivism objectively. Here *homo religiosus* is constructed as the bearer of a certain experience that is laid out a priori, usually derived from the repertoire of mystical virtuosos. The procedure is, as I have already explained, not only theoretically but also methodologically untenable, for sources of entirely different statuses are used in a highly selective way and interpreted arbitrarily. "Religious experiences" are seen as the center of religion, and are then read into all kinds of texts and actions. This is in no way an "interpretive" procedure as it claims to be but, rather, a dogmatic, deductive one, which ignores the intended meaning in each case in favor of an a priori understanding of "authentic" religion.

Worship and Liturgy

As an alternative to intellectualistic and subjectivistic interpretations of the meaning of religious practices, I propose to privilege worship (or cult) and its liturgies as sources for the investigation of the meaning of religious practices. By "liturgies" I refer to any kind of institutionalized rules and scripts that guide humans' intercourse with superhuman powers, express its meanings, and are enacted in interventionist practices or in worship. Such rules and scripts may be codified in writing or transmitted orally; they may be generally acknowledged and accessible, or secret and reserved for special persons. To make this procedure and my use of the concept of practice plausible in the framework of a theory of religion based on action theory, I begin with an excursus on the method of interpretive sociology.

The concept of practice has come into wide use partly as a result of the postmodern decentering of the subject, and partly through the influence of Michel Foucault and Pierre Bourdieu in the humanities and social sciences. It has been both unreflectively adopted and subjected to criticism.[21] Here, however, I would like to show that it is entirely compatible with the Weberian concept of action. Weber defines the task of sociology as interpreting and explaining social action, which he describes as meaningful interaction. He mentions three methods for deciphering the "subjectively intended meaning." First, this can be done empirically by questioning actors directly. Second, one can proceed statistically by making use of opinion surveys and trying to determine "the average intended meaning." Third, one can proceed in terms of ideal types and construct the meaning of action through typical interests and motivations of typical actors in typical situations. In almost all his studies on the sociology of religion and cultural history, Weber uses the third method simply because subjective questioning and statistics are not available for use as sources in historical studies.

Constructing meaning on the basis of ideal types, however, leads to other questions and problems. First, we have to deal with the fact that most actions are performed unconsciously or semiconsciously. For the actor, the meaning in any instance thus tends to be unclear or, at best, vague. So we have to try to infer this meaning indirectly. This takes place with the help of ideal-type constructions. On the basis of material and ideal interests, types of action are constructed that can then be compared with actual behavior. If they essentially coincide, then we can assume that the posited ideal-typical meaning is in accord with the implicit meaning of the actors themselves. If a discrepancy between these meanings is discovered, then the reasons for the deviation must be explained, and we must try to identify the meaning actually intended. Therefore, so long as we remain within ideal-typical construction and do not analyze concrete personal actors, we are still not dealing with the subjectively intended meaning of actions, in the strict sense, but rather with the construction of typical models of action of typical actors in typical situations.

This kind of construction is close to the concept of practice. Weber's assumption that ideal-type construction of meaning may be assumed "as if" this meaning were intended by the actor can be combined with Bourdieu's assumptions regarding "habitus." But Weber's conception of "praxis" as the ideal-type construction of the "subjectively intended meaning" of social action proves considerably more flexible than Bourdieu's. In Weber, deviation from expectation and innovation are taken into account from the outset by comparing ideal type with action. In Bourdieu, on the other hand, social action is usually subsumed under the concept of habitus, as if there were a kind of class-specific "collective unconscious." Bourdieu conceives habitus as a factually internalized standard of action that is internalized by the actor, and not, like Weber, as a methodological aid to approaching subjective meaning. These reflections may be applied to the interpretation of religion as a complex of religious practices.

Earlier, I distinguished among three types of religious practices: interventionist, discursive, and behavior regulating. Sociology and religious studies have always privileged certain practices analytically, which has produced different perspectives and consequences. If behavior-regulating practices are made central, religion appears to be primarily a matter of morality or ethics. If discursive practices are made central, religion appears to be primarily a medium for the linguistic establishment of a worldview and the authority structure connected with it. If interventionist practices are made central, we can—as I will show in the following chapters—arrive at a self-interpretation of religion as a system of warding off misfortune, overcoming crises, and providing blessings and salvation. Whereas the sociology of religion has been chiefly interested in behavior-regulating and discursive practices or, at best, in the effects of interventionist practices on everyday action, power relationships, or the social order, I put interventionist practices at the center of my analysis of religion. What justifies such an emphasis?

Logically, systematically, and pragmatically, behavior-regulating and discursive practices presuppose the existence of interventionist practices. Just to believe in the abstract that superhuman powers exist does not make them a reality that holds the whole human being in its grip. Only the fact that one not merely "believes" in the existence of superhuman powers but also communicates with them justifies all the other practices. What Clifford Geertz, in his well-known definition of religion, has called the "aura of factuality"[22] is certainly not produced solely through interventionist practices, but it is produced primarily through them. They not only express the "religious premise" of the existence of superhuman powers and their accessibility, but also dramatize it. Interventionist practices such as sacrifices, prayers, formulas, and chants that are addressed directly to such powers—as well as religious objects such as architecture, pictorial representations, sacred fragrances, and sounds in which interventionist practices are embedded—both ground and strengthen the experience of religious reality emotionally and cognitively. Belief and action, symbolization and ritualization, go hand in hand.

The different types of religious practices, of course, are interconnected. Discursive and derived practices are an important part of religious socialization. Discursive practices interpret the "religious premise" underlying changing social and political conditions. Religious discourses explain interventionist practices, reflect on their nature and on the will of superhuman powers, and teach new generations to believe in them. They explain how contact can be established with these powers, who controls access to them, and what behavior-regulating practices are expected of the practitioners.

Discursive practices are thus to be accorded a major albeit derivative significance; they are meaningful chiefly in relation to interventionist practices. Only because interventionist practices provide protection against misfortune, means of overcoming crises, and the promise of salvation do discursive practices become important. Behavior-regulating practices are also dependent upon the "religious premise." Without belief in the possibility of establishing contact with superhuman powers, religious discourses are relatively insignificant and behavior-regulating practices lack a foundation. The meaning of discursive and behavior-regulating practices becomes accessible through the analysis of interventionist practices, not the other way around. The privileging of discursive and behavior-regulating practices has systematically treated interventionist practices as an embarrassing, left-over category, without assigning it a clear value within the religious system as a whole. In contrast, the privileging of interventionist practices gives other practices a place in the system.

Methodologically, interventionist practices also offer the clearest and strongest basis for a comparative analysis of the meaning of practices over the millennia and across cultural boundaries. Whereas discursive and behavior-regulating practices largely underlie intellectualist and subjectivist inter-pretations, interventionist practices are much more strictly regulated and fixed in their liturgical meaning. This has crucial methodological advan-tages for research on the meaning of religious practices.

Since it is impossible to formulate a universal theory of religion on the basis of subjective appropriations of institutionalized ways of giving mean-ing, the meaning of religious action must be sought on the level of the in-stitutionalized meaning of religious practices or liturgies. In other words, liturgies serve as ideal-type constructions of the meaning of religious prac-tices, though this does not imply that all acting subjects have appropriated and want to express this meaning in exactly this way. Liturgies express the meaning of religion, not of religiousness. Focusing on liturgies relieves us of the need to speculate about subjective meanings. Of course we know that religious practitioners are not robots that have simply internalized the in-stitutionalized meaning. Neither do they constantly question the meaning of their religious action, or obsessively carry out meaningless actions. How-ever, they all have a "religious competence," insofar as they know enough to carry out practices themselves or to participate in their performance. This knowledge can be deduced not from theologies but from religion's promises as inscribed in interventionist practices.

What is the outcome of this strategy? First of all, the source materials change. The meaning of religious action is no longer derived from subjectiv-ist interpretations, "worldviews," the interpretations of religious intellectu-als, or political discourses. Rather, it is derived from liturgies, that is, from the meaning of practices as expressed in spoken words, symbolic actions, formulas, gestures, or songs. Religion is thus no longer identical with intel-lectual "high religion" but is expressed primarily in the concrete, practiced religion in question. It is a matter no longer of idealized structures of mean-ing but of institutionalized ones. Intellectual interpretive cultures are no longer privileged as the bearers of "genuine" meaning and opposed to the philistine superstition of the masses. Religion is not a theologically "pure" tradition but a factual system of religious practices that combines theory and practice.

This methodological priority accorded to the meaning of religious practices allows us to avoid reified debates over religion. Whether Buddhism, Confucianism, Judaism, and Christianity are "religions" becomes a meaningful question only if one is arguing on the level of worldviews and religious traditions. If we start out from religious practices, then empirically observable complexes of practices replace idealized theological systems. Such complexes may certainly be syncretic and contradict intellectual doctrinal traditions. Here, tradition refers not to a dogmatic claim but rather to long-term religious practices.

Whereas on the empirical level the specific degree of appropriation or deviation from institutionalized structures of meaning must be determined in each case, the meaning inscribed in liturgies is fully sufficient for religion to be conceived theoretically. Concretely, the meaning of religious practices can consist in the actor's considering them a necessary or useful part of his life. To be sure, in almost every case they bring along with them more than this rudimentary meaning, but added meaning is not absolutely necessary for practice. For example, one can go to the synagogue, church, mosque, or temple every week because one has done so since childhood. One may also harbor a vague fear of sanctions if this habitual duty is neglected. Or, to take another example, one may light a candle in front of a saint's image in the hope of being healed of a disease. For this purpose, one does not need to know the saint's specific status in the celestial hierarchy, how canonization works, or how the saint actually heals. For practice, belief in the possibility of healing is quite enough. Additional religious knowledge can be useful, however; for example, knowing which saint is responsible for what allows the supplicant to direct his or her appeals more precisely.

But these examples concern empirical research on religiousness, not theory construction. On the theoretical level, one can make do with the analysis of liturgies, for liturgical language dominates all subjective interpretations made both by the laity and by theologians. All my friends who are pastors, rabbis, or priests and at the same time liberal theologians read to their congregations texts that are not in agreement with their own theological positions. As participants in worship, even unbelievers, agnostics, and doubters give thanks to "God" and sing his praises. Intellectuals and uneducated people read the same texts and go through the motions of submission to the "Lord." Only such supra-individual, objective levels of religion enable us to determine the meaning of religious practices for the purpose of formulating, in a methodologically clean way, a universal theory that transcends historical and cultural boundaries. Neither intellectualist constructions of worldviews nor subjectivist interpretations that lack both stability and practical relevance allow us to do that. This concentration on liturgy also has far-reaching implications for the explanation of religion.

Explaining Religion

How do we advance from understanding religion to explaining it? Here I want to describe how I have actually proceeded. First of all, I worked out a typology of practices that is supposed to cover the range of possible practices in a relatively complete way. Then, after spot-checking, I formulated the hypothesis that the meaning of religious practices is connected with averting crises or overcoming them. This hypothesis later proved too narrow and one-sided because it gave insufficient recognition to the promise of salvation offered by religions. The next step consisted in analyzing and comparing calendrical, life-cycle, and variable practices, as well as the virtuoso practices of various traditions. The true interpretation of meaning occurs first on a concrete, culture-specific level. No religion speaks abstractly about superhuman powers; instead, it names them concretely. On the basis of this cultural interpretation of meaning, a sociological interpretation of meaning is worked out that, by means of a one-sided theoretical interest in certain aspects of the cultural meaning, transposes interpretation to a more abstract level. Thus the sociological interpretation of meaning represents an abstraction and selective systematization of concrete cultural meanings, but does not break with them.

As I will show in the following chapters through an investigation of general practices and virtuoso practices, all religions claim to have the ability to avert misfortune, overcome crises, and provide salvation. On this view, religion is primarily a promise of salvation. It is the promise of salvation offered by religions and their ability to engender belief in their control of the means of salvation and the paths toward it that constitute their potential to exert authority. The promise of salvation is not a latent function of religious practices; it is the meaning inscribed within those practices. This explanation of religion is not already contained within its definition, and it has the advantage of being falsifiable.

To be sure, great cultural differences exist between religions regarding the way superhuman powers are imagined, their accessibility, the paths to salvation, and the benefits of salvation. But structures of meaning can be elaborated through abstraction and systematization that totally respect these cultural peculiarities. Thus religious practices everywhere are addressed to superhuman powers that influence or control something beyond human control. All religions claim the ability to address misfortune, crises, and salvation.

Blessings and misfortune can be found in three domains: nature, the human body, and social relations.[23] With regard to nature, the focus is on such forces as thunderstorms, earthquakes, floods, droughts, volcanic eruptions, invasions of locusts, disappearing game herds, or epidemics. With regard to the human body, the themes of reproduction and mortality—fertility and birth, disease and death—are dominant. Social crises that become the object of religious practices are often closely connected with questions of social superiority or inferiority and with changes in social status. Such crises may concern domination, conflict and sanction, initiation, marriage, and death. They are often causally attributed to superhuman powers. In monotheistic systems, they frequently appear as punishments sent by God that can be avoided only by reaffirming submission to his will. In dualistic, polytheistic, or polycratic systems, good gods are called upon to provide protection against evil powers. As already noted, all religions promise salvation, sometimes in this world and sometimes in the next. Herman Oldenberg puts it this way: "Man's activity vis-à-vis gods and spirits is directed towards seeking their blessings and help and warding off their malice influence."[24]

In order to organize the analysis and explanation of interventionist practices more clearly, I distinguish between general practices that tend to be performed by or for the religious "laity"—namely, calendrical, life-cycle, and variable practices—from virtuoso practices. Calendrical practices are prescribed and routinely performed on a daily, weekly, monthly, yearly, or other regular schedule. As a rule, they serve to maintain good relations between social actors and the superhuman powers with which they are in contact. They prevent crises, not least by averting possible punishments by the superhuman powers, express gratitude for past favors and hope for future ones, and remind people of important events when blessings were granted or salvation was commemorated. Calendrical practices, however, may be heavily influenced by the risk one runs in dealing with such powers. Depending on the idea formed of the religious powers, many attitudes are conceivable, ranging from fear and tension to serenity and good cheer.

Life-cycle practices follow the individual life rhythm and are located between calendrical and variable practices. On the one hand, they are less predictable than regular practices, but they are nonetheless planned and expected, even if the precise point in time when they are to be carried out remains open. Birth and death, initiation and marriage, are among such events. They are often characterized by ambivalence, since they involve a restructuring of social relationships. Both joy and concern, both hope and danger, enter into a mixed relationship that is specific to each case.

Variable practices react to unforeseen events. By nature, they can be both pleasant and anguishing, and their result can be uncertain. Correspondingly, they either express gratitude or seek the help of superhuman powers in order to produce a good outcome from some impending event or to deal with problems, losses, dangers, and crises. Risky enterprises, diseases, natural catastrophes, lovesickness, murder and sudden death, political crises, and poor harvests are events to which variable practices react.

All three types of general practices are based on the anticipation or experience of misfortune, as well as on the hope of blessings and salvation. Whereas regular and life-cycle practices tend to remain the same, variable practices react to external influences. They are therefore particularly suited to demonstrate the connection between religion and the fear or experience of misfortune. In crisis situations they dramatically increase in number and emotional intensity.

Virtuoso practices represent a radicalization of general practices. For one thing, misfortune is relativized and reevaluated insofar as it is consciously sought out. Mystics and ascetics usually bring forms of suffering such as pain, poverty, loneliness, or hunger upon themselves deliberately, so as to achieve a higher religious benefit. Union with the absolute, the immutable, and the eternal is often possible only if one detaches oneself from everything that is temporally bound, changeable, and mortal. Someone who succeeds in doing so not only attains a temporary or lasting state of salvation but may also acquire the status of a superhuman power as a mediator or savior.

In the following chapters I hope to show that my interpretation of religious practices is compatible with the self-interpretation of various religions and transcends historical and cultural boundaries. My explanation of religion is not based on an interpretation of religious practices that is imposed from without, but is found in the respective meanings of religious practices and their liturgies themselves. In other words, I argue that the threefold theme of averting misfortune, overcoming crises, and providing salvation appears in all types of religious practices in the most diverse religions, regardless of time, place, or specific cultural form. My argument does not imply that religions deal with no other themes or could not be explained in terms of them. Religions are extremely complex social and cultural structures. But anyone offering an alternative explanation of religion would have to show that other themes are equally universal and central.

CHAPTER FIVE

Averting Misfortune:
General Religious Practices

Oni va soto! Fuku va ushi!
· Demons out! Happiness in!*[1]*

As I made clear in chapter 4, I place worship—or interventionist practices, that is, human communication with superhuman powers—at
the center of my analysis of religion. I do so for several reasons. First, these
practices form the logical and psychological precondition for discursive and
behavior-regulating practices. Without the possibility and practice of communication with superhuman powers, discursive and behavior-regulating
practices lack both authority and relevance. Second, interaction between
social actors and superhuman powers is a significant area of activity that
can be isolated without interfering in specific cultural interpretive patterns.
This fact further justifies the universal use of an analytical concept of religion. Third, interventionist practices constitute a large part of everyday
religious life. Whatever religious intellectuals may present as the "essence"
of their respective religions, the center of every religion lies in the practice
of communication with superhuman powers. It is there that religious life
is primarily played out. Fourth, interventionist practices combine religious
theory and practice. Unlike analyses of ritual as quasi-mechanical, traditionalist behavior that lacks meaning, on the one hand, and unlike analyses
of worldviews, theologies, or subjective interpretations as meaningful in
the absence of practice, on the other, in my analysis, meaning and action
are united.

In this chapter I analyze the meaning of general practices, by which I
mean interventionist practices in which virtually all members of a religious
community can or should participate. They are practices performed for the
religious laity or by them, communally or individually. In the interest of

clarity, I will distinguish between calendrical, life-cycle, and variable practices. In actual religious life, all three may overlap both temporally and spatially. All religions contain a complex repertoire of practices in which the meaning of religion, beyond subjective idiosyncrasies or theological speculation, is liturgically inscribed, whether transmitted orally or in writing. To make claims regarding religion, we must first come to grips with these repertoires and bring our interpretation of religion into harmony with them.

The identification of such repertoires has turned out to be more difficult than anticipated. Normally one would assume that the literature would contain plenty of factual descriptions of religious practices and of their meaning. Which practices are regularly performed by whom and on what occasions? What does the everyday religious life of social communities, families, men, women, children, and the elderly look like? Which practices require the help of religious specialists, and which can be performed by laypersons themselves? How is the religious calendar structured in any given case? What regularly recurring festivals and holidays are there? How are successive practices meaningfully linked with each other? What unforeseen events motivate people to perform religious rituals?

So long as we are dealing with relatively systematized and codified religions, or with a lay-oriented communal religiousness, we rarely find such information in the scholarly literature, but we do find it in religious manuals of the various traditions. Liturgical writings record the correct procedure for religious practices, and usually also their historically fixed meaning. This information enables specialists to perform rituals correctly and thus effectively. Such knowledge may also be communicated to laypersons, so that they can be sufficiently informed about religious actions to be able to participate in them and pass their meaning on to their children.[2] These codifications are historically variable, of course, and are revised from time to time.

Not all religious traditions have written codifications. Liturgical knowledge is often part of the oral tradition and is considered secret lore that requires special initiation. It does not follow, however, either that the performance of rituals in such a case is more loosely determined or even arbitrary, or that the laity does not understand the pragmatic meaning of such practices. For example, even if the text recited or the formula spoken by laypersons or priests is incomprehensible, participants still know enough about the ritual to expect that an incorrect performance or even its omission could yield negative results.[3] Conversely, they know what positive results religious practices are supposed to have in a given case. While laypersons obviously lack all the knowledge enjoyed by religious specialists, they can certainly participate in or perform such practices in a way that has meaning for them.

In doing research on the liturgies of nonliterate cultures, it is often extremely difficult to find source materials. When it comes to the description and interpretation of religious rituals and practices, ethnographic reports usually prove inadequate. There are probably two reasons for this: the fixation on worldviews, and functionalist or structuralist theoretical approaches. Functionalism and structuralism generally lead to analyzing rituals on the basis of examples. The investigator picks out a few rituals, assuming that they can be explained even while their content is ignored. Their specific meaning and their setting—which are often seen as abstruse—are not taken into account, so that fertility rituals, burials, or inaugurations are reduced in an undifferentiated way to aspects of social integration, legitimation of authority, or symbolization of the social structure.[4]

In investigating and describing "primitive" religions, many scholars have been guided consciously or unconsciously by the criteria of Christian theology. Ignoring religious practices, they have systematized religious ideas and seen practices only from the point of view of their performance.[5] Yet practices do not lend expression to intellectuals' speculative interpretations; rather, they express the institutionalized "theologies" of liturgies. Moreover, they usually follow a religious logic. In order to understand a religion and explain it, neither constructions of worldviews nor the selective analysis of a randomly chosen ritual—on the basis of which the whole society is then explained in symbolico-theoretical, structuralist, or functionalist terms—are adequate methods. Instead, systems of practices and their own structures of meaning must be investigated in their mutual relationship.

The approach proposed here also has consequences with regard to sources, in that liturgical instructions and detailed descriptions of religious practices and sequences of practices are of central importance. Who is allowed to participate in a ritual, and how are the participants positioned with respect to each other? How closely do participants stand to one another, and what individual or collective movements of bodies can be observed? How are the participants involved practically and emotionally? Which words or texts are spoken, read, or sung, and by whom? What do the rituals promise, and what do the participants hope for?

If we begin our analysis of religion with religious practices, and if we focus on religious calendars, life-cycle practices, and variable practices, the plausibility of my definition of religion immediately becomes clear. All these practices relate to superhuman powers, which are believed to have influence on those dimensions of human life that escape direct human control. People turn to these powers for protection, help, and blessings. What counts as a blessing or a misfortune is interpreted in specific cultural terms, but there are also constants, transcending historical and cultural boundaries. Dimensions of salvation and misfortune are the natural environment of humans, the human body, and interpersonal relations.[6] Thus, for instance, disease and hunger, suffering and pain, need and repression, persecution and expulsion, flood and drought, war and annihilation are generally seen as misfortune, whereas health and abundance, successful hunts, fertility and large harvests, peace and social harmony are seen as blessings. In addition, there are transcendent expectations of salvation that transpose earthly blessings and misfortune to another level. Here, for the saved there is no disaster, no crisis, no misfortune. They enjoy an eternal state of bliss. In contrast, for the damned or the souls that find no peace, a temporary or eternal state of suffering, pain, and torment is expected. Even when heavenly salvation is not described with much precision, there is usually no lack of detailed and often crude descriptions and pictorial representations of the suffering in hell that awaits those who fail to subject themselves to supernatural powers and their will.[7]

As a rule, religious calendars are determined by three cycles in different combinations: vegetative, astrological-cosmic, and salvation-historical. The third of these is related to superhuman powers as well as to traditional deeds and events that are attributed to them. Virtually all calendars combine all three. Whereas the calendars of East Asian religions are structured more by the astrological-cosmic and vegetative cycles, in Abrahamic religions the principle of salvation history is dominant, though that of the cycle of nature is sometimes clearly visible. We can probably assume that the vegetative cycle is the oldest principle. For my conception, however, questions of antiquity or originality play no role, and the development of a salvation-history cycle does not represent a "higher development." Calendrical practices represent the core of what is commonly called worship.[8]

In these practices, the constitutive importance for religion of the relationship between social actors and superhuman powers becomes clear. As I have already emphasized, the kind of relationship depends on the characteristics of the superhuman powers, the methods of access to them, and the salvation goals involved. For Judaism, Christianity, and Islam, these are relatively easy to describe. All three Abrahamic religions define themselves through their relationship to a supreme god, to whom they subject themselves. This god is generally seen as all-powerful. Insofar as relations to other powers or mediators are established, their power is borrowed or derived from the supreme god, from whom all power ultimately comes. This is essentially a monocratic system. All forms of religious practice finally consist in cultivating this relation to power, and the way the relationship is imagined may be influenced by familial and political structures of power that have been actually experienced or merely desired. The religious community as a whole, or at least the individual person, is a subject and requires the protection of this god, who determines blessings and salvation as well as misfortune and damnation for humans on earth and in the beyond. Humans, often incapable of understanding the god's decisions, subject themselves, make supplications, and offer thanks, even though they may sometimes doubt or rebel. Since the god controls everything, he also stands behind the cycle of the regeneration of nature, the change in the constellations, and history. All this is expressed in the liturgies of the religious calendars of Judaism, Christianity, and Islam.

In East Asian religions as well, superhuman powers are central. But here ideas vary considerably regarding the personal or impersonal nature of these powers. The differences are often status specific. Whereas ideas of impersonal powers are widespread chiefly among the educated and the virtuosos, the same ideas are interpreted in a personal way by the mass of believers. In Buddhism, this personal interpretation ranges from belief in the possibility of saving oneself to veneration of monks or belief in salvation through a bodhisattva. Similar variations are found in Daoism and Shinto.

Joseph Kitagawa explains the Shinto conception as a combination of two words, *shin* (Chinese *shen*) and *to* (Chinese *tao* or, today, *dao*). *Shin* means superhuman power, and *to* means path or teaching.[9] The concept of *kami* is a Japanese variant of the Chinese *shen*. *Shin* or *kami* can be interpreted as a multiplicity of powers or a multiplicity of forms in which the same power appears.[10] The same goes for Daoism as the autochthonous religion of China. For some people, *dao* represents the original principle of being, out of which the world proceeded through differentiation. Human beings can put this original principle to work within themselves by means of certain practices. For other people, veneration for the bearer of the *dao* is central to their religious practices. In its function as a lay religion, Daoism is a kind of mystery religion.[11] In East Asian religions, the specific relations between humans and superhuman powers have also been brought into the liturgies of the religious calendar.

In varying degrees, general religious practices express fundamental structures of meaning. As a rule, they are characterized by two major elements: affirmation of the reality of superhuman powers and, expressed in different ways, attribution to them of the power to avert misfortune, overcome crises, and provide salvation. To be considered religious, practices must be addressed to superhuman powers and affirm their existence. To that extent, not every festival should be considered religious. In general religious practices, affirmation of the existence of superhuman powers takes many different forms, such as calling a power by name, directing prayer to a power, making an offering or sacrifice, bowing or kneeling before a pictorial or symbolic representation. Such representations are commonly not regarded as symbolic but are identified with the superhuman power itself. Practices of this kind usually involve requests, expressions of respect or gratitude, or gestures of submission. The affirmation of the existence of superhuman powers as well as their power of intervention is then staged, with reference to various temporal levels, as remembrance and thanks for past favors or as a request for present and future salvation and protection from misfortune. Frequently, however, superhuman powers also inflict suffering and have to be appeased by material or symbolic bribery in the form of sacrifices and vows, or neutralized by invoking opposing powers.

Obviously I cannot deal with all the world's religions throughout history in order to illustrate my thesis. Since I maintain that the basic models I have identified are transhistorical and transcultural, I have selected my materials from traditions and periods that are as different as possible, without wandering through history and geography too arbitrarily. Thus, I draw materials from the Abrahamic religions of Judaism, Christianity, and Islam, on the one hand, and, on the other, from the (East) Asian traditions of Buddhism, Daoism, and Shinto. My choice was based on several grounds. First, the examples include a variety of religious types, such as universalist and ethnic or national religions, more strongly "ethical" religions, and "magical" religions. Second, I place religions of Asian origin on an equal footing with religions that emerged in the eastern Mediterranean region and that today are considered, at least in part, specifically Western. This selection should ensure that my theory of religion is more than a disguised theory of Christianity but represents a wide range of religions. In particular, the attention given to East Asian religions provides both instruction and a fine corrective for apparently self-evident assumptions.

An important difference between the Abrahamic religions and East Asian religions lies in the formers' claim to exclusivity. Whereas Judaism, Christianity, and Islam expect their adherents to respect the boundaries between the traditions, East Asian religions, with the exception of Nichiren Buddhism, make no such claim. No Japanese is forced to choose between Shinto and Buddhism; no Chinese must choose between Daoist, Buddhist, or "popular religious" practices. On the contrary: for the most part, even Chinese and Japanese rulers cultivated a variety of religious traditions at their courts, and sometimes practiced these various forms privately. Thus, for example, at a Qing dynasty court, state rituals were performed from five traditions: Confucian, Chinese and Tibetan Buddhist, Daoist, and Shamanistic; and the rulers' private rituals showed similar diversity.[12] The same holds true for the mass of religious laypersons. This inclusiveness is particularly impressive in general practices, and already appears in the religious calendar.

Whereas Judaism, Christianity, and Islam each have a religious calendar of their own that is binding on their respective adherents, one cannot speak of a purely Buddhist, Daoist, or Shintoist calendar, but only of a Chinese or a Japanese one. In addition, the liturgies of the festivals are frequently based on oral traditions and bear a local stamp.[13] Such distinctions as exist among religious traditions in the East Asian realm relate to virtuoso practices. Religious laypersons usually see in Buddhist, Daoist, Shamanist, or Shintoist practices various ways of interacting with superhuman powers that in no way mutually exclude each other. In Japan, for instance, a person may choose a Shinto marriage ritual and a Buddhist burial ritual. In recent times, Christian weddings have become fashionable. The laity both perform rituals and consult specialists who may be shamans or Daoist, Shinto, or Buddhist priests.[14]

Chinese holidays are a mixture of different religious traditions that have been combined into a new synthesis. No one finds it self-contradictory to celebrate both Buddha's birthday and Lao-tzu's. On holidays, shamans or Daoist or Buddhist priests perform rituals that generally serve the same purpose, and—at least for the laity—are often interchangeable.[15] Michael Saso reports that in Taiwan, the rituals commissioned by pious laypersons in Buddhist monasteries hardly differ from those in Daoist temples.[16] At the same time, a Daoist priest, for example, may explain the same ritual differently in addressing two different audiences. Thus, for initiates an annual rebirth ritual is an inner meditation, whereas for the laity it is a petition directed to the heavenly bureaucracy.[17]

Wolfram Eberhard has shown that the average Chinese would not describe him- or herself as either Buddhist or Daoist. A farmer goes to the village temple, whether it is dedicated to the Dragon King and is therefore Daoist, or to Kuan-yi and is therefore Buddhist. For the farmer, the difference lies less in the religious tradition than in the function. In this case, one deity is responsible for rain, the other for children.[18] Stephen Teiser, in his study of ghost festivals, notes that for a minority the sacrificial offerings made by Buddhist priests were distinct from those made by Daoist priests, but that the majority of the population always used the closest temple and altars, and made offerings in a way that did not distinguish between Daoist and Buddhist elements.[19]

This attitude in the religions of East Asia made it clear to me that a religion should be defined not as a theologically delimited tradition but as a particular system of practices. Whether practices can be attributed to one or more religiously or theologically defined traditions is insignificant from a sociological point of view. East Asian religions can best be described as systems that combine practices that were originally Buddhist, Daoist, Confucian, Shintoist, or connected with "popular religion." A similar complexity can also be observed in other religions, so that it makes little sense to try to separate doctrinally "pure" elements from others. With such an approach, even the study of Abrahamic religions would be de-dogmatized.

Here I make no pretense to offer a representative description of the Abrahamic and East Asian religious traditions. That would not only exceed my competence but would also be a hopeless undertaking, given the internal variety of forms and historical variations. In what follows, I will therefore not present the religious practices *of* Judaism or Buddhism, but rather certain religious practices *in* Judaism or Buddhism. I intend only to suggest that the structures of meaning I present can be found in all traditions and in all times.

I do not claim that the practices of all religions are exhausted by the structures of meaning I have identified, that they are therefore "somehow the same" or "ultimately identical," or that other structures of meaning might not be identified in them, whether more universal or more particular. Nor do I attempt to detail the structures of meaning in individual practices. Given the multitude of traditions, holidays, and rituals, as well as their historical and regional variations, such a description would be excessively long, let alone tedious. I have therefore selected examples to show the tenability of my thesis. While I would gladly have included other religions, I believe that a larger number of examples would not increase the persuasiveness of my argument.

Religious Calendars

Abrahamic Religions

Since the religious calendars of the Abrahamic religions are presumably more familiar to my readers than those of East Asian religions, my description of them will be extremely brief. The calendrical practices of Abrahamic religions essentially dramatize their respective salvation histories, sometimes with embellishments and expansions. In a certain respect, all their religious practices are based on this dramatization. They define the origin of salvation, the paths to salvation, and the goal of salvation. These practices affirm the reality of a single god, demonstrate his power, and instruct people regarding their relationship to him. Liturgy shows what this god can do, how one can gain access to him, and how one must approach him. It defines the meaning of salvation and how one can achieve it. At the same time, it opens up areas in which one can individually request the granting of everyday salvation goods, protection from disaster, or help in overcoming a misfortune.

It is often argued that all this may be true of premodern forms of religion, but not of enlightened versions such as modern Protestantism. However, even a contemporary Lutheran hymnal characterizes worship as an encounter with God and asserts his reality and presence among the faithful. In it we read: "Worship—gathered together in the presence of God. Secure in our nearness to him, guided by his Word, strengthened by his power, encouraged to action."[20] The assumption of the existence and presence of God runs through the whole of the church service: prayers, hymns, sermon, and blessing. Above all, the creed, whether in the Apostolic or the Nicene form, is an attempt to affirm the reality of the Christian God in his threefold form as Father, Son, and Holy Spirit.[21] The same holds for the Sanctus.[22]

Whether in a synagogue, a church, or a mosque, in the worship of all Abrahamic religions, praising God and emphasizing his sovereignty, submission (in very different degrees) to his majesty and will, and prayers of thankfulness and supplication are central.[23] No matter how many doubts an individual believer might carry around, in religious practice the existence of God is presupposed and confirmed in word and deed. This structure of meaning is public, observable, and reproduced over long periods of time. In contrast, subjective doubts remain for the most part internal, inaccessible to outsiders, and specific to the individual in question.

In liturgy, believers call upon God, pray to him, and humble themselves before him through gestures of submission, bowing down before his pictorial or symbolic representations, kneeling or throwing themselves on the ground. In readings of the scriptures, people listen to the words attributed to God, or they sing in his honor. The religious calendar structures human life as a relationship to God and to salvation history.

In themselves, Judaism, Christianity, and Islam are manifold, complex phenomena that have gone through historical changes and cultural diversification. It is not surprising that their religious calendars vary. I therefore limit myself here to relatively uncontroversial and generally acknowledged characteristics that make no claim to originality or completeness. Judaism,

Christianity, and Islam all have weekly holidays that serve essentially to honor God. The Jewish Sabbath commemorates God's rest on the seventh day of the Creation. At the same time, it represents a radical separation between profane, everyday life and the holiness of the holiday, when everything is focused on God. The Christian Sunday combines the Jewish Sabbath and the Roman *dies dominica*. It serves to commemorate God's rest on the seventh day of the Creation, and thus is not a workday; but it is also considered the first day of the week. Nonetheless, its interpretation was reshaped Christologically, in that every Sunday represents a small Easter holiday, on which the Last Supper or the Eucharist is celebrated. In Islam, the Friday prayer replaces the prescribed midday prayer as one of the five daily obligatory prayers and is supplemented by a two-part sermon. The first part of the sermon consists of a reading of the first chapter of the Qur'an, the Sura al-Fatiha. The second part praises Allah and asks for help and protection.[24] However, Friday is not generally a work-free day.

The religious holidays of the Abrahamic tradition can be subdivided thematically as follows. First, some are devoted to the commemoration of God's gift of salvation and serve to renew and strengthen it. Second, there are periods of penance and fasting, as well as days commemorating the dead, in which repentance, penance, forgiveness, and divine judgment of humans are central. Third, some holidays are devoted to specific expressions of gratitude and intercessions. The meaning of many of these calendrical practices is linked not only to each individual holiday but to the whole liturgical sequence.

In the Jewish calendar, Purim and Passover, in particular, commemorate God's intervention in history. Purim commemorates the deliverance of the Jews from genocide in their Babylonian exile, while Passover commemorates the exodus out of Egypt and the deliverance from the Pharaoh's soldiers on the Sea of Reeds. Shavuot, which was originally a harvest festival, commemorates God's revelation of his commands to Moses on Mount Sinai. Sukkot, originally the conclusion of the harvest, commemorates the Jews' forty years of wandering in the desert. Hannukah commemorates the rededication of the Temple in Jerusalem and the rebellion of the Maccabees. All these holidays, then, are related to salvation history.

Among the days of penance and fasting are Rosh Hashanah, the Jewish New Year festival, as well as Yom Kippur, the day of atonement and the highest holiday. It commemorates the divine tribunal before which humans are called to do penance, repent their sins, and ask for forgiveness. In the context of Jewish holidays, salvation means essentially saving the entire people from repression and destruction; misfortune means the threat of this fate.

The Christian calendar has essentially two salvation-history cycles: the Christmas cycle, from Advent to Epiphany, and the Easter cycle, from Ash Wednesday to Pentecost.[25] In the Catholic Church, in addition to the "Lord's year" a sequence of holidays is devoted to St. Mary and the saints, which, however, derive their meaning only from the former. The Christmas cycle turns around the birth of Christ, the Easter cycle around the Crucifixion, the resurrection, and redemption. In Christianity, salvation consists chiefly in the overcoming of sin, death, and the devil, as well as in the achievement of eternal life through Christ; misfortune consists—from a liturgical point of view—in sinfulness and the threatened divine judgment. The Islamic religious calendar also varies depending on the region and the group, for instance, between Sunnis and Shiites.[26] In essence, the Islamic calendar has six major holidays pertaining to God's intervention and revelation as well as to humans' duties with regard to God. The year begins with the New Year's festival on 1 Muharram, which commemorates the Prophet Muhammad's flight from Mecca to Medina in 622 CE. Ashura, the holiday on 10 Muharram, has various meanings, including the creation of Adam and the date of divine judgment. In Shiite Islam, it commemorates the death of the imam Hussein. One of the most important holidays is the sacrifice festival, which commemorates Abraham's readiness to sacrifice one of his sons, and God's intervention to replace this sacrificial victim with the slaughter of a sheep instead. It is assumed that the site of this sacrifice is identical with the Kaaba in Mecca. The month of Ramadan is a month of fasting and penance. Both the beginning of the fast and its end are celebrated. Another holiday is the birthday of the Prophet. In Islam, salvation lies in Allah's revelation to Muhammad as the seal of the prophet and obedience to God's commands, while misfortune consists in the impending judgment of God.

In all three Abrahamic traditions, the weekly and calendrical holiday liturgy does not consist solely in great themes; a considerable amount of time is also devoted to gaining blessings and avoiding misfortune in this world. Prayers and intercession for healing, peace, consolation, protection, and well-being for oneself and for others are embedded in holiday rituals. Later, I will analyze such practices in greater detail later under the rubric of variable practices.

East Asian Religions

The Chinese calendar is shaped primarily by astrological changes and vegetative regeneration. It combines the solar and lunar calendars, thus representing the principles of yin and yang.[27] The solar calendar is structured by the solstices and equinoxes and divides the year into twenty-four periods, which are described as nodes of energy. The lunar calendar divides the year into twelve months of twenty-nine or thirty days, each of which begins with a new moon. The fifteenth day of each month is a full moon. In addition, there are ominous astrological signs and a division of days and years into units of sixty apiece. Numerous religious festivals are based on this calendar, some with the solar calendar, but most with the lunar. The solar-calendar festivals tend to center on the family, whereas the lunar-calendar festivals are usually communal. There are also annual festivals, in which local gods and saints are venerated.

Festivals take place not only in local temples, but also at the household altars that are part of every typically Chinese house. The altar has two parts. The left half contains a shrine for the local gods, a Buddha, the earth god (Tudigong), or local heroes, while the right half is devoted to ancestors. Many life-cycle and calendrical practices are carried out there, but it is also the place where individual problems, requests, and duties that do not require the aid of a religious specialist find expression.[28] Then there are divinatory rituals, such as those that are supposed to predict how large the harvest will be. Many of these festivals have been celebrated for nearly two thousand years, though their form and content may have changed somewhat.[29] Mu-chou Poo has proposed an excellent interpretation of the religion of ancient China that is compatible with my perspective.[30]

If we analyze the Chinese calendar with regard to the typical festivals and the rituals connected with them, we see that generally speaking they serve to avert evil and promote a good life, including the life of the dead.[31] There are various typologies of Chinese festivals, but all of them confirm this interpretation. In his study of the Han period, Derk Bodde distinguishes five kinds of festivals: rituals of sacrifice and pacification, which are devoted to ancestors, household gods, or heroes; rituals of exorcism and purification, which seek to drive out evil powers and demons; fertility festivals for land, people, and animals; cosmological festivals, which restore and preserve the balance between yin and yang; and state ceremonies, which serve to maintain order and morality as well as to legitimate the state.[32]

John Lagerwey distinguishes between liturgies for the living and liturgies for the dead.[33] Alvin Cohen identifies six categories of festivals, four of which concern the world of the living, and two that of the dead. These seek to provide protection for life and property, health, a long life, and to avoid misfortunes and drive out evil spirits. They also promote the balance of the natural order, such as the control of rain and aridity, the correct placing of buildings and tombs so that they do not interrupt the natural flow of energy,

and protection for the fields and cities. They seek to provide peace and harmony in domestic life: protection for the hearth and entrance to the house,
easy childbirth, protection for children, and the well-being of the ancestors.
During festivals, prayers are offered for the means to support oneself and
one's family, the blessing of the gods of agriculture and fertility, of crafts
and well-being. In relation to the world of the dead, people ask for deliverance from punishment in hell, for the forgiveness of sins, and to be spared
suffering. Finally, they strive for a privileged rebirth, in the form of reincar-
nation in a prosperous family or in the Buddhist or Daoist heaven.[34]

Some rituals and festivals are connected with the natural cycle and astrologically important dates; others are related to the family's ancestors and
the dead; and still others are devoted to gods and heroes, or Buddhist or Daoist saints. These areas often overlap. Major festivals such as the New Year's
festival, the birthday of the Jade Emperor (Yuhuang Shangdi), of Lao-tzu,
and of the "Celestial Empress" (Tianhou) Mazu follow the lunar calendar.
As in the Abrahamic religions, there is a sequence of festival days and fes-
tive activities. Naturally, there are local and regional variations of all these
festivals, as might be expected, given the lack of a central religious authority. The following few examples indicate their range.

The New Year's festival (Xinnian) begins on the first day of the first
month, and is the most colorful and joyful festival of the year. People do
everything they can to ensure that they will have good luck in the coming year. Evil spirits are driven out with noisemakers; gods, spirits, and
ancestors are venerated. The god of the family hearth, dispatched on the
twenty-third day of the twelfth month to render account to the Jade Emperor, is provided with delicacies to enhance his report on the family, and
he is welcomed back again on the fourth day of the new year.[35] Doorways
are decorated with pictures of the gods and good-luck scrolls containing
such formulas as "Blessing and prosperity for the new year."[36] It is also high
season for fortune-tellers.[37]

The Dragon Boat festival takes place on the fifth day of the fifth moon,
around the time of the summer solstice, when the yang phase of nature's
growth passes over into the yin phase of decline and retreat. This is the beginning of the rainy season after the rice planting has been completed.[38] At
the same time, this day commemorates Qu Yuan, a minister in the Chou
dynasty, who warned against a military campaign and was exiled. When
he learned of the capital's fall, he wrote a famous elegy; he finally drowned
himself in a river.[39]

Among festivals commemorating the dead is Qingming, which is devoted to one's own ancestors and provides an interesting example of overlap

between an old spring festival and Buddhism.[40] The name of the festival, which means "bright and clear" or "clear brightness," still shows its relation to the seasons and the regeneration of nature. In ancient times it was a festival of pairing and fertility, in which young people flirted, cooked, painted, and cracked eggs, and trees were planted.[41] Just as the ancient spring festival was overlaid with Christianity to become Easter, so Qingming was transformed into a festival for the dead. It takes place on the 106th day after the winter solstice. Nowadays, the tombs of the ancestors are visited, cleaned, and decorated on that day. The ancestors are offered sacrifices of meat, wine, vegetables, and flowers, either at the tomb or in the family's ancestor room, and paper money is burned for them.

A festival of the dead with a somewhat different character is the ghost festival, which also goes under a variety of other names, but is always celebrated at the end of the seventh month. A source from the eighteenth century already describes its multiple meanings.[42] More recent descriptions also recognize its local peculiarities. But all the variants share in the festival's basic idea: the redemption of the dead who are wandering or suffering. On this day, the gates of hell are opened for thirty days. The spirits languishing in hell—those whose descendants have not cared for them properly—now beleaguer the living. Some are maleficent, and these have to be pacified and bribed. They are not allowed to enter the house; the offerings take place outside.[43] From a Buddhist point of view, this festival is about the transfer of merits (Sanskrit *punya*) to a dead person. Helen Hardacre explains this as follows:

> Based on a canonical story, the All Souls Festival, or Avalambana, is observed throughout Southeast and East Asia. The story concerns one of the Buddha's disciples, Maudgalyayana, known for skill in meditation and supranormal powers. The mother of Maudgalyayana appeared to her son in a dream and revealed to him that she was suffering innumerable tortures in the blackest hell because of her *karman*. Through magic Maudgalyayana visited his mother in hell, but his power was of no avail in securing her release. Eventually the Buddha instructed him to convene an assembly of the priesthood which then would recite *sutras* and transfer the merit of those rites to ancestors. In other words, descendants must utilize the mediation of the priesthood in order to benefit ancestors. The result is annual festival, traditionally observed on the day of the full moon of the eighth lunar month. At this festival special *sutra* recitations and offering rites for the ancestors are held in Buddhist temples, and domestic rites differing in each country are performed. In

addition to rites for ancestors, observances for the "hungry ghosts" and
for spirits who have died leaving no descendants are performed.[44]

In addition, there are holidays on which gods and heroes, saints, Buddhas,
and bodhisattvas are venerated, and prayers for protection or help are said.
These holidays include, among others, the birthdays of the Jade Emperor,
Lord Lao, Lord Buddha, Confucius, and Mazu. Festivals and rituals on the
occasion of the birthdays of gods, heroes, or Buddhas generally express the
recognition of special powers and forces. At the same time, specific capa-
bilities are often attributed to them that have little to do with their original
roles. These powers used to be called "functional gods."

The birth of the Jade Emperor is celebrated on the ninth day of the first
moon. "Jade Emperor" is not a name but a title attributed to the ruler of
heaven. Hence he is also called Tiangong, "Master of Heaven." The Jade
Emperor's court consists of all the gods that rule on or under the Earth, the
gods of the stars, the winds, the rain or thunder, the mountains and the
seas.[45] The Jade Emperor is frequently said to be the ruler of the universe.
On his birthday, five different kinds of meat are brought to him, along with
prayers, women being excluded from the ceremony. The Jade Emperor is
considered particularly important for the production of male children.[46]

The sixteenth day of the second month is Lord Lao's birthday,[47] and the
nineteenth day of the second moon is the birthday of Guan Yin, in Japan
called Kannon. The latter is a goddess of sympathy and mercy, who is derived from the Indian bodhisattva Avalokitesvara but who in East Asia took
on female traits. Daoists call upon Guan Yin in a ritual that is supposed to
protect the soul from punishment in hell after the body is buried. Her image is commonly found over the family altar, or a statue of her stands in the
center of the family shrine.[48]

As in China, Buddhist household altars are widespread in Japan. Representations of Buddha and tables of ancestors are venerated side by side.
Although the Japanese often describe themselves as nonreligious, 59 percent of households in 1995 contained an altar.[49] The old Japanese calendar
is related to the Chinese. It is also a lunar calendar, in which the numbering
of the years begins over with each new dynasty. The Meiji dynasty introduced the Gregorian calendar. It is one of the peculiar features of calendrical practices that they are either handed down by tradition or codified by
hierocratic regulation and then traditionalized. In early times, this held true
mainly for court rituals, such as we find in the eighth book of the *Engishiki*,
a tenth-century codex originally in fifty books.[50] This codex was based on
the earlier codifications of the *Koninshiki* and *Joganshiki*. The *Engishiki*

contains twenty-seven prayer texts for rituals fixed by the calendar.[51] At the same time, new practices developed out of more recent codifications and traditions. In the course of historical development, Buddhist and Shinto festivals were largely integrated into a Japanese calendar. The Meiji reforms established a new division between Buddhism and Shinto, but after World War II it was attenuated again. It is probably fair to say that the Japanese religious calendar represents a fusion of Shinto's vegetative-cosmological principles with Buddhism's salvation-history principles. Not only do the first two books of the *Engishiki* deal with the celebrations of the four seasons, but many present-day Shinto practices still follow a seasonal logic.[52]

The eighth book of the *Engishiki* describes the most important festivals in Japanese antiquity. The Toshigoi festival takes place at the beginning of the sowing period. In addition to more general praise and prayers for the preservation of power, peace, and prosperity, people pray especially to the relevant *kami* for a good harvest. "Before the presence of the *kami* who govern the crops we do humbly speak, praying that the mighty *kami* may vouchsafe to us the late-ripening harvest of grain."[53]

Other festivals include prayers for good harvests, thanks for the harvest expressed by presenting its first fruits, and a general prayer for protection by day and by night. Further regular festivities are connected with matters such as the general purification from all offenses and protection from wrongs, evil spirits, storms, and fire in the ruler's palace.[54] The *minaduki tugomori no oho-harahe* is a major purification ritual, an exorcism at the end of the sixth month in which heavenly and earthly crimes are eliminated and disaster thereby averted.[55] Many of these festivals combine ceremonies of supplication and gratitude with intercession on behalf of the ruler, who in the ideology of state Shinto is descended from the gods and will become a god after his death.[56] As in Daoism, many of Shinto's rituals are organized on the model of such court ceremonies as audiences or petitions. This is well illustrated by the ritual performed on the occasion of the presentation of a golden sword to the ruler by representatives of two Korean immigrant families: they ask for protection from all disasters and the expansion of the ruler's power and thus of peace.[57]

Descriptions of present-day Shinto confirm the persistence of earlier rituals based on agricultural cycles and their pragmatic character.[58] The series of ritual acts is divided into purification, presentation of a gift in kind or in money, and prayer. In conclusion, there may also be a common get-together of all participants. Although the gift is important, an almost "magic" significance is attributed to the words spoken.[59] Many shrines in Japan venerate *kami*, who have special responsibilities. The beloved god Inari, for example, is responsible for the harvest. All shrines, however, are used for prayers for good fortune and the prevention of misfortune, whether with regard to health, an examination, or personal relationships.[60]

The Japanese year-cycle begins in January with *Ganjitsu*, the New Year's festival, in which Shinto and Buddhist practices are combined. Temples, shrines, and houses are decorated with symbols representing long life, fertility, and virtues. Paper talismans are thought to ward off bad luck.[61] *Setsubun*, in early February, marks the beginning of spring. During festivals in temples and shrines, beans are thrown on those present in order to drive out evil spirits. Other festivals are similarly shaped by the seasons and are supposed to prevent misfortune or provide blessings.

Two ancient local festivals are worth mentioning here: the *Omizutori Matsuri* in Nara and the *Aoi Matsuri* in Kyoto. The former is connected with the Todaiji temple complex, the oldest Buddhist temple in Japan. In the fire ceremony on March 12, young monks purify the temple with burning torches to protect it against harm.[62] The following day comes the water-drawing ceremony, in which the Buddha is presented with the first water drawn in the year. This festival ends with the monks performing a fire dance. In the middle of May, the Aoi Matsuri, or mallow festival, is held in Kyoto. According to legend, during the Heian period (792–1185), after severe storms the ruler sent messengers to the Shimogamo and Kamigamo shrines in Kyoto, whose gods are responsible for floods and droughts. Participants' costumes are decorated with mallow, which is traditionally considered a reliable way of protecting against catastrophes such as storms and earthquakes.

This brief outline has, I hope, sufficiently shown that the liturgies of calendrical practices in both the Abrahamic and East Asian religions promise to provide blessings and salvation, to ward off misfortune and disaster, or to help humans in overcoming crises. In the cultural interpretations of the idea and goals of salvation, there are, of course, differences, which are closely connected with how superhuman powers are imagined and function. But there are also common features insofar as all religions also include salvation in this world as part of the goal of these practices. This holds true both for life-cycle and for variable practices.

Life-Cycle Practices

As their name indicates, life-cycle practices concern transitions in humans' social status. They are performed on occasions such as birth, entry into the religious community, the affirmation of the latter by young adults (initiation, complete membership), marriage, dying, and death. Such transitions are usually accompanied by religious practices through which blessings and salvation are supposed to be won and misfortune and disaster averted. Not all take place as community rituals in houses of worship; some are performed at home, among family and friends. Informal prayers and appeals for blessing may be substituted for official rites.

Abrahamic Religions

In Judaism and Christianity, life-cycle practices tend to assume the character of official actions, whereas in Islam they are less formally conceived, because of the lack of religious officials. In both Judaism and Christianity, children are inducted into the community through a religious ceremony. In Judaism, induction takes place through circumcision and is therefore limited to male children. In this ceremony, the bond with God is strengthened and the protection of the Prophet Elijah, who is considered to be present, is requested. In Christianity, baptism symbolizes admission into the religious community. Here, sponsors act as the child's representatives in expressing the desire to belong to the community. In the baptism ceremony, the child is called God's creature and by the act of baptism is put under God's protection. In Islam, the newborn's membership in the religious community is not performed symbolically, although here the child is also considered a gift from Allah. In some Muslim countries, it is customary to celebrate the naming of the child and to distribute gifts to the poor on this occasion. Circumcision is usual, but is carried out at differing ages.

Coming-of-age ceremonies exist chiefly in Judaism and Christianity. In Judaism, boys reach religious majority on their thirteenth birthdays. The occasion, known as Bar Mitzvah, is celebrated. In the twentieth century, a similar ceremony for girls, known as Bat Mitzvah, was developed, but is not universally accepted. In Christianity, confirmation corresponds to these ceremonies on the occasion of reaching religious majority. In confirmation, the earlier baptism is now confirmed by the young person him- or herself. Those who have been confirmed henceforth have a right to take communion. A few Protestant groups reject infant baptism and recognize only adult baptism. In Judaism and Christianity, marriage also involves a religious ceremony, whereas in Islam it is a civil ceremony.

Dying and death are universal occasions for religious practices. All societies accompany death and dying with religious rituals in which the dying or deceased person is entrusted to superhuman powers. Religious practices seek to cleanse the deceased as they make the transition from this life to another, to protect them or provide for them materially, to dispose of their sins, to pray for them, or to transfer merits to them. In some religions, an attempt is made to pacify deceased persons themselves, so that they pose no threat to the living.

In the Abrahamic religions, rituals connected with death and dying serve to produce reconciliation with God, repentance, penance, and exoneration from sins. In Judaism, for instance, it is important that dying persons meet all their social obligations and still do as much good as they can, in order to earn merits. At the deathbed, prayers are said for the forgiveness of sins, for the protection of the family, and for salvation. In an ideal case the dying person should say: "Hear, Israel, the Lord is our God, the Lord alone. Blessed be the Name of His glorious kingdom for ever and ever."[63] After death comes, the body is washed and clothed. The burial must follow soon thereafter.

In Catholic Christianity there is the institution of "extreme unction," earlier called the "last unction." A priest anoints the dying person's forehead, saying, "Through this holy anointing, may the Lord in his love and mercy help you with the grace of the Holy Spirit." He then anoints the hands, saying, "May the Lord who frees you from sin save you and raise you up." Extreme unction is also practiced in Lutheran Christianity, though it is not considered a sacrament. Prayers are said for the dying, especially for the forgiveness of sins. Communion is often given. At death, the deceased is commended to God. This condition is described as "eternal rest," a peaceful and happy existence without cares or suffering.[64]

In Islam, death is accompanied by a simple ceremony. The dying person is positioned with face or feet toward Mecca and asked to recite the confession of faith and other prayers. After death, the body is laid out again facing Mecca. Family and friends meet at the deceased's home, where they recite from the Qur'an and say prayers. Prayer is a communal duty.[65] The burial takes place soon afterward. The body is washed, clothed, taken to the mosque or directly to the place of burial, and interred while the whole assembled community prays.

In all Abrahamic religions, intercession on behalf of the deceased may continue for months or even years. In addition, days are set aside for the general commemoration of the dead.

East Asian Religions

Among religious life-cycle practices in China, the most important are those associated with birth and death. These are performed in connection with pregnancy, birth, early childhood, weddings, family separations, death, and the transition to the status of ancestors.[66] Most involve rituals of protection.

When a woman becomes pregnant, a fetus spirit emerges that must not be offended if one wants to prevent damage to the child. After the birth, the woman and the room in which she has given birth are considered unclean and must be purified in order to avoid harm. For the most part, marriages are scheduled for astrologically favorable days. When a son marries and brings his bride home, space may be inadequate, and the household has to be divided. In this event, a new hearth and a hearth god are dedicated, some of the ashes from the family hearth always being placed in the new one. However, the most important ritual concerns death. Geomancers are called upon to find the right place for the grave. If ancestors have been buried in the wrong spot, they are moved to a new resting place. The correct placing of the graves of ancestors brings their descendants health, prosperity, and well-being.[67]

A document from the Sung period reports that during the first forty-nine days after death—a phase in which the deceased is between his previous and his future existence—sutra readings take place that are supposed to transfer good karma to him.[68] A hundred days after death, a ritual (probably borrowed from Confucian practices) is performed in which the end of the period of mourning is celebrated and the deceased is interred in his final resting place. On the next day, a memorial plaque for the deceased is put in the ancestors' room. Henceforth it is no longer a matter of protecting the deceased from harm, but rather of asking his or her help, as an official ancestor of the family. This practice is also reported in more recent times.[69]

Among the life-cycle practices in Japan, those connected with births, weddings, and deaths are of the greatest importance. The newborn child's first visit to a shrine and the tutelary god residing there takes place within the first three months of the child's life. When a boy reaches the age of five, or a girl the age of three or seven, a further ceremony takes place. The children thank the *kami* and ask for continued healthy growth. The wedding ritual is also supposed to ensure that the gods will protect the couple. In Japan, burial rituals are usually carried out in accord with Buddhist practices.[70] They are extremely elaborate, and performing them is largely the responsibility of the family, with the help of a Buddhist priest to recite the sutras.[71] In addition, prayers are said and joss sticks burned. The goal of the ceremony is to enable the deceased to make the transition to his or her future status.[72]

Variable Practices

Calendrical and life-cycle practices in no way cover all potential threats to human beings. Thus all religions have a series of practices that seek either to avert impending misfortune and produce future blessings, or to give

thanks for blessings already provided and cope with misfortunes already suffered. Proactive means of salvation traditionally include talismans, amulets,
divination, consultation of oracles, vows and formulas, praise, intercession,
prayers, and a correct way of life. In Abrahamic religions, especially Judaism,
Islam, and Protestant Christianity, prayers and a pious lifestyle are generally regarded as major ways of seeking blessings and salvation and gaining
protection against misfortune. "Magical" practices, while usually scorned,
are nonetheless found in these traditions, in which case they are frequently
described as heterodox or connected with "popular religion." For my purposes such descriptions are irrelevant, because I am concerned with actual
practices, not with questions of dogmatic correctness. Furthermore, people's
reactions to crises and misfortunes clearly show their expectation that religion represents a means of acquiring safety and coping with difficulty.[73]

Abrahamic Religions

In Judaism, Christianity, and Islam, numerous prayers serve to avert disaster and achieve salvation. The prayer books of all three traditions provide a
very rich body of material for observation. A typical example is the Jewish
evening prayer (Ma'ariv), which consists of the Jewish confession of faith
(Shema Yisrael) and the Amidah (the central prayer of the Jewish liturgy).[74]
In both, God is praised, thanked, and asked for protection. Jewish prayer
books consist primarily of prayers of praise, request, and thanks associated
with calendrical or life-cycle festivals. But special occasions are also sometimes mentioned. A mid-nineteenth-century German siddur (Jewish prayer
book) contains a prayer to be said by a woman who is attending the synagogue for the first time after giving birth to a child, as well as prayers to be
said by the sick and by newlyweds.[75]

In addition, there is a collection of German prayers and hymns that can
be used on many occasions, such as the hymn "Der Herr unsre Burg," which
is based on Psalm 46.[76] The choir sings:

> God is our refuge and stronghold,
> a help in trouble, very near.

And the cantor continues:

> Therefore we are not afraid
> though the earth reels,
> though mountains topple into the sea—

its waters rage and foam;
in its swell mountains quake.[77]

In a prayer for "general troubles," we read: "Have mercy, Lord of our life, for salvation comes from you alone; if you do not help us, then we must strive and battle in vain. You become wrathful—and worlds bow down; Lord, our God, have mercy! Have mercy on us!"[78] A twentieth-century American prayer book is structured in a similar way. In addition to prayers and praises connected with calendrical and life-cycle festivals, it also includes prayers to be said before taking a trip, prayers for the sick, a prayer for rain, a night prayer, a prayer for the state of Israel, and various blessings.[79]

Christian prayer books, like Jewish ones, include prayers connected with the religious calendar and life-cycle festivals; but they devote more space to prayers for other occasions. A Protestant prayer book from the early eighteenth century, composed by the Frankfurt preacher Johann Friedrich Stark (1680–1726), sums up its content in an almost endless title: "Daily Handbook in Good and Bad Days, that is: Encouragements, Prayers, and Hymns, (1) For the Healthy; (2) For the Sad; (3) For the Sick; (4) For the Dying; Also How to Say Proverbs, Lamentations, and Prayers for the Dying, in Addition to Ceremonial Prayers. Many Fine Prayers for Repentance, Confession, Communion, and Weather; Morning and Evening Prayers for Every Day of the Week; Prayers of Consolation and Refreshment; Together with Hymns, and also Prayers Relating to War, Inflation, Plague, and Peace, Useful on All Occasions, and Adorned with Copper Engravings; Also Supplied: a Daily Booklet for Women who are Pregnant, Giving Birth, and Infertile, as the Fifth and Sixth Parts of this Handbook, by Johann Friedrich Stark, formerly Evangelical Preacher in Frankfurt am Main."[80]

A Protestant prayer book from the nineteenth century mentions, in addition to morning and evening prayers for all weekdays, festivals, and holidays, "Confession and Communion Prayers," "Prayers for Particular Times and Situations," "Travel Prayers," "Seasonal Prayers," "Prayers in Times of Suffering, Grief, and Need," as well as "Prayers for the Sick and Dying."[81] An American prayer book from the same period is similarly constructed.[82] All these prayers ask for blessings, help in time of need, protection from misfortune, or thanks for rescue and salvation.

A similar repertory is found in Islam. Many of the prayers have a direct connection with Qur'anic texts.[83] One collection of prayers mentions over eighty different occasions.[84] This multitude of themes, which puts the whole of life in relation to God, is also found on a contemporary Internet site, where we read:

Nothing is too unimportant to be presented before God: ask for proper
guidance, help in illness, intercession, trust, hope for the forgiveness of
sins [. . .] In addition, there are also prayers of supplication on special
occasions, such as lunar or solar eclipses, long droughts, natural catastrophes, and so on. Further subjects for prayers of supplication exist in
plenty: the bodily and psychological health, happiness in this world and
the next, individual and communal security, undesired and dreaded
events, illness, poverty, deceptive wealth, base cravings, fear of the Devil
and Hell, debts, mourning, and worries, tyranny and enmity, powerlessness, scandal, suffering in the grave, birth, death, travels, worship, eating, drinking, sleep, dreams, awakening, bathing, shopping; protection
from bad things caused by ignorance, useless knowledge, bodily lusts,
hatred, jealousy or hard-heartedness; love, sympathy, good morals, etc.
Prayers from books in which prayers for all these occasions are collected
should be recited at all times.[85]

Another prayer book mentions solar and lunar eclipses as well as droughts
as special occasions for prayers.[86] In other words, in Islam as well, all crisis
situations in nature, the human body, and social relationships are occasions
for religious practices.

In Abrahamic religions, variable practices are not confined to prayers.
There are also practices that are either considered heterodox or whose original "magical" character has later been reinterpreted as "antimagical." A
practice exists in Judaism of invoking the name of God or the names of an-
gels and demons.[87] The Library of Congress has the manuscript of a Hebrew
Bible written in such a way that it can be used as a set of instructions for
producing amulets.[88] In ancient Israel there was silver jewelry with priestly
blessings. The hexagram, pentagram, and metal plates in the form of the
hand of God also served as amulets. The *mezuzah* attached to the front
door was originally supposed to keep demons away from the house.[89] A Jewish website notes that according to the Talmud, obeying the commands of
the *mezuzah* results in a long life and protects the household. It is further
believed that every *mezuzah* helps increase God's protection for humans in
general.[90]

In general, Christianity is described as if such practices belonged to the
past or were peculiar to Catholicism, which is in fact so rich in "magical" practices that one could write a whole book about them.[91] But in both
pre-Reformation Christianity and Protestantism, a multitude of alternative
practices can be found. For instance, a cross is commonly used as an amulet.
Certain charismatic groups use sanctified oil with which to anoint affected

parts of the body in case of illness and which may also be applied to one's billfold in the event of financial problems.[92] Miracle healing is believed to take place on television when a preacher calls upon the name of Jesus; donations to such preachers or their institutions are thought to be redeeming, because God pays them back with interest.[93]

In Islam as well there are variable practices, such as the veneration of saints and the use of amulets as protection against demons, the evil eye, illness, or financial losses. Amulets are also regarded as positive forces promising success in love or in business, or protection while traveling.[94] An Indian prayer book contains not only prayers for forty-three different occasions but also instructions on increasing one's partner's love by putting a piece of paper with special writing on it under the pillow, or on easing childbirth by tying a similar piece of paper to the mother's right leg.[95] In Islam, calling out God's name is also considered powerful.[96] And newborn children are often given a protective amulet.[97]

Finally, in Abrahamic religions we find the belief that a pious lifestyle promotes salvation not only in the beyond, but also in this world. The fulfillment of religious duties leads to blessings, whereas their neglect leads to divine punishment. Ethical conduct is seen as pleasing to God and therefore has a salvation-promoting and disaster-averting function. In the *Shema Yisrael*, Deuteronomy 11:13–15, we read: "If then, you obey the commandments that I enjoin upon you this day, loving the LORD your God and serving Him with all your heart and soul, I will grant the rain for your land in season, the early rain and the late. You shall gather in your new grain and wine and oil—I will also provide grass in the fields for your cattle—and thus you shall eat your fill."[98]

Many Hebrew and Christian scriptures, as well as various suras in the Qur'an (especially sura 17) expressly mention the connection between ethical conduct and well-being in this world. That connection also comes into play when the suffering of innocent or virtuous people is lamented.[99] It is here that the problem of evil arises in all Abrahamic religions.

Religions struggle with this problem at both the individual and the collective levels. Unforeseen good or ill fortune, sudden perils or deliverance from fears, generally provide occasions for religious practices. Uncertainty regarding the future, shaped by hope or by worry, is also associated with rituals such as divination, consulting oracles, interpreting Tarot cards, praying that a sign be given. Whereas the reaction to positive events seems to consist simply in thanking God for them and perhaps fulfilling a specific vow, threatening events or catastrophes confront people with the problem of evil, particularly in the Abrahamic religions. Why must a young man die in a traffic accident? Why does a tidal wave leave one person alive and another dead? Why does an all-powerful God allow misfortune and disaster to occur? Has he sent it himself, as a punishment, or is he not as powerful as we think?

Whether they are epidemics, erupting volcanoes, or wars, catastrophes have always led to religious reactions.[100] Furthermore, natural catastrophes also often entail social and economic ones. The Black Plague in 1347–52 killed a large part of the population of Italy and destroyed the social and economic structures of whole cities and their surrounding areas. There was a widespread idea that a vengeful God was responsible for these disasters and had to be appeased. People scourged themselves, and special plague chapels were erected.[101] Jews were often blamed for this misfortune.[102]

The Lisbon earthquake on All Saints' Day 1755 destroyed a large part of that city. Particularly worthy of notice was the fact that the prostitutes' quarter was spared, whereas many churches filled with believers collapsed. The contemporary report of a Protestant merchant describes the chaos. A merchant hurried into the house to save his sick wife and three children. He found his wife praying in bed, but succeeded in getting her and the shrieking children out of the house. In the crowd outside, he found his relatives. Each aftershock increased the panic. The merchant writes: "Everyone wanted to confess and be absolved. The priests were therefore excessively pestered by the common people. They all ran around with their saints' images, and this made us even more fearful and terrified than we already were. We had to kiss these images if we didn't want to be stoned to death by the crowd."[103]

The catastrophe led to a lively discussion regarding the problem of evil. A Jesuit by the name of Gabriel Malagrida interpreted the earthquake as a punishment sent by God. "Learn, O Lisbon, that the forces that destroyed houses, palaces, churches, and cloisters, that caused the death of so many people, and the flames that have destroyed so many treasures were your damnable sins, not natural phenomena."[104] Voltaire used the earthquake as an occasion to challenge Leibniz's notion of the "best of all possible worlds." Why did it hit Lisbon, and not London or Paris, where there were just as many sins?[105]

The 1906 Azusa Street revival in Los Angeles—often considered the starting point for the Pentecostal movement in the United States—was also connected with an earthquake. The first report on the revival was printed in the *Los Angeles Daily Times* on April 18, 1906, the day of the devastating earthquake in San Francisco. One day later, an aftershock hit Los Angeles. These events significantly increased attendance at Pentecostal worship services.[106] Frank Bartleman, a publicist for the movements and participant in this revival, wrote in his memoirs that his pamphlet *The Last Call* subsequently met with a much larger response.[107]

After the September 11 attacks in New York, altars and memorials were spontaneously set up in the streets around the World Trade Center, where people prayed and mourned the dead. The Sumatra-Andaman earthquake, which launched the devastating tsunami of December 2004, inevitably raised the problem of evil. Mohamed Faizeen, the head of the Center for Islamic Studies in Colombo, Sri Lanka, interpreted the tidal wave as God's punishment for the violation of his commandments.[108] Hurricane Katrina also produced a widespread religious response.[109] And the Protestant television preacher Pat Robertson even interpreted Ariel Sharon's stroke as God's punishing him for having given up the Jewish settlements in Gaza.[110] All these examples show that over centuries the experience of disaster has been connected with the operation of superhuman powers. In Abrahamic religions, it is connected with the operation of either a vengeful God who has sent the disaster in order to force humans to adhere to his commandments, or a helping God who aids them in overcoming the disaster.

On the whole, we can probably maintain that in the Abrahamic religions, general religious practices are seen as interactions with a God who controls salvation and can both avert and cause disaster. God is praised. He is thanked for favors granted and asked for his protection so that a disaster may be prevented. In an emergency, he is called upon for consolation and help. People try to give difficult living situations a meaning and to determine God's will. God's laws and regulations are followed in order to achieve eternal salvation and avoid punishment. That is the core of the calendrical, life-cycle, and variable practices institutionalized in the Abrahamic religions.

How theologians will interpret or reinterpret these practices remains to be seen. The meaning of religion, as expressed in the language of liturgies and prayer books, is clear, however. And it is this language, not the language of the discourse of intellectuals, that religious practitioners speak. When a liberal theologian leads a worship service or celebrates a mass, he speaks the language not of his own theology but of liturgy. It is the language of liturgy that unites priests and laymen, intellectuals and farmers, workers and officials, and even doubters and unbelievers. Liturgies overlie subjective meanings in order to produce a generally binding symbolism and language that is recited, preached, and sung. And this language of liturgy is not the least of the things that every generation learns anew.

East Asian Religions

East Asian religions include an immense number of variable practices, as anyone who was ever in China, Korea, or Japan, or has visited a temple in an American Chinatown, can confirm. The room is full of the smoke of burning joss sticks. Priests recite sutras, people pray and bow down. Talismans and lucky charms for all possible occasions are available for sale. They are thought to help achieve success in love or on an examination, or to acquire riches and have good health. All these practices have a long tradition. A few bear specifically Buddhist or Daoist traits, but most are characteristic of Chinese culture in general.[111] Divination in particular has existed in China for a very long time. Royal divinations concerned the success of the crops, the outcome of battles, the best time for sacrifices, and even the causes of royal toothache.[112] The common people made use of divination to realize the hopes and wishes and to avoid sufferings. Divination used to be an integral part of the everyday life of all Chinese, whether their status was high or low, whether they were rich or poor, Daoist or Buddhist.[113]

Among Chinese informal religious practices is the consultation of mediums and shamans, usually in connection with such misfortunes as illness in the family, nightmares, or demonic possession.[114] When a house is being built, a geomancer is consulted in order to determine the most favorable site. In the event that despite precautions the house lacks harmony, a shaman or a Daoist priest may perform an exorcism that drives out the spirits responsible for the unrest.[115] The lord of the foundation stone (Ti-chi-chu) is offered gifts in order to preserve harmony in the house.[116] Purification rituals may be performed to provide protection from evil forces.[117]

Contrary to the widespread assumption that Theravada Buddhism has fewer "magical and popular religious" traits than Mahayana Buddhism, we find even in the former the tradition of reciting Paritta verses.[118] These are protective texts that both avert disasters and help overcome them. They are recited not only on public occasions, when, for example, they are supposed to favor the success of an undertaking or to provide protection and blessings for a new building, but also on private occasions such as births, healings, or exorcisms.[119] Another collection for novices contains a prayer asking for the Buddha's protection.[120] An idea we have already noted in the Abrahamic religions, that ethical conduct results in worldly blessings, is also found in these Buddhist texts. Anyone who cultivates true friendship is promised hospitality, honor, victory over enemies, high social standing, fame, wealth, invincibility, and protection.[121]

In addition to these individualized practices, communal rituals such as *jiao* provide protection from dangers. John Lagerwey distinguishes between liturgies for the living and liturgies for the dead. The former are called "gifts" (*jiao*), while the latter serve to accumulate "merits" and are called "fasting."[122] *Jiao* is performed regularly in some communities and only on specific occasions in others. Thus it could also be considered a calendrical or variable practice. According to Lagerwey, it is performed in modern Taiwan, either after the completion or total renovation of a temple, or to ward off catastrophes.[123] Thompson reports that the four most common occasions for *jiao* are the desire for peace and security, the prevention of epidemics, general blessings, and protection from fire.[124] Schipper describes *jiao* as a genuine sacrifice to heaven, comparable to the sacrifice made by the ruler.[125] Michael Saso describes it as a village festival that takes place about every sixty years. Its participants include both mortals and immortals, the living, the dead, and the gods. It is a festival of purification, fasting, penance, and the earning of merits, with the goal of renewing protection for the village and its inhabitants.[126]

The public is excluded from the actual sacrifice in the temple, and only selected dignitaries take part in the ritual.[127] The sacrifice is carried out by a grand master, that is, a high-ranking Daoist priest. His profession is not without risks, for any error in the liturgy leads to misfortune. The grand master must know the complicated and tedious liturgy by heart: the text, the movements, the secret formulas. Should he deviate in the slightest way from the liturgy, he loses the right to celebrate a *jiao*, and many stories tell of terrible consequences, such as the loss of memory, madness, or possession.[128]

Schipper's description well illustrates the question of the ritual's meaning. The dignitaries present perform various sacrificial acts in accord with precise instructions given by the ritual helper, but as a rule they do not understand a word of the clerical liturgy, since it is spoken in classical Chinese. Moreover, the meaning of many gestures and symbolic acts is known only to initiates.[129] Thus, although the text of the liturgy is not understood, the meaning and goal of the ritual is quite clear both to the dignitaries present and to the excluded public: thanks for past favors and the prevention of future disasters. How do they know that? The priest has told them; he puts a plaque on the outside wall of the temple that is essentially identical with the memorial plaques that are read out during all the major rites.

A plaque used for the dedication of a temple invokes the majesty of the temple, which is as solid "as the mountains and the rivers." Because the people to whom this temple belongs have always enjoyed the protection that their collected merits have earned, the plaque says, they constantly think about how they might show their gratitude. It is further explained that rituals will now be performed for three days and three nights. At given times a drum will be beaten and oil burned in order to drive out misfortune.[130]

Although the complete text of the liturgy is known at most to the priest alone, the plaques explain the ritual and its pragmatic meaning in a way that the public can understand. Furthermore, such festivals are not confined to the central ritual; the public is included in the preparations. Stephan Feuchtwang describes in detail the "external order" of such a festival.[131] Houses are cleaned, and additional temples erected, in which the people deposit sacrifices. The gods are ceremonially invited and taken to the temple. A period of fasting is observed, during which no meat or alcohol is consumed. The gods are thanked, the souls of orphans are fed, and vows are made. There is theater, music, and spectacle.[132]

In Japanese religion, occasions for variable practices resemble those in China. Anyone visiting a large Buddhist temple or a Shinto shrine can find stands where talismans are for sale. The themes range from health to love to examinations. In present-day Japan, fortune-telling is widespread, and the Japanese resort to various religious measures that are supposed to protect against disaster and bring good luck.[133] Even Japanese garden architecture has precautionary rules. The *Sakuteiki*, the oldest book on garden architecture, which dates from the Heian period, lists a series of taboos whose violation will lead to disaster. If stones are wrongly placed, the master of the house will fall ill and ultimately die, and his land will go to ruin and become the residence of devils.[134]

In the Japanese context, as elsewhere, catastrophes are often interpreted in religious terms and used by prophets as an occasion for calling the people to religious revival. Nichiren Buddhism emerged in the thirteenth century as a reaction to disasters such as earthquakes, poor harvests, and epidemics. In a dialogue between Nichiren and a guest, we read that the beneficent gods and the wise men had left the land because of the people's immorality. Devils and demons had taken their places and brought one misfortune after another upon the people.[135] Nichiren further opines that only the Lotus Sutra is authoritative, and blames other Buddhist sects for the decline.

The great Kanto earthquake of 1923 also invited religious interpretations and practices.[136] The problem of evil—that bad things happen to good people—is also discussed in East Asian religions. In Japan, the blame for such things is often put on wandering spirits, that is, dead people who for various reasons are not at rest.[137] Such examples could be endlessly multiplied.

Thus we can say in summary that in both Abrahamic and East Asian religions, calendrical, life-cycle, and variable practices seek to protect people from misfortune, to help them overcome crises, and provide blessings and salvation. Of course, in the cultural interpretations of salvation and the paths that lead to it, we find differences that are closely connected with the way superhuman powers and their functions are imagined. But all religions include this-worldly salvation in these practices. Well-being on earth is a central theme even in "salvation religions," which—from a theological point of view—ultimately strive for transcendental salvation. The meaning of general practices can be most precisely understood as a response to the promise made by religions that claim for themselves the ability to avert misfortune and provide blessings. To what extent the people who carry out these practices do so because of this promise is hard to tell. But we can surely assume a degree of correspondence between the content of the promise and the basis for the practice, since general practices are geared to the mass of religious laypersons and their needs. If we turn to the practices of virtuosos, however, our interpretation requires radical revision, for virtuosos seem hell-bent on seeking out misfortune and crises.

CHAPTER SIX

The Radical Quest for Salvation:
The Practices of Religious Virtuosos

The calendrical, life-cycle, and variable practices described in chapter 5 serve to illustrate the interpretive model I have postulated for the central thesis of my theory of religion: that such practices have the threefold goal of averting misfortune, overcoming crises, and providing salvation. The present chapter will analyze the practices of virtuosos, that is, of men and women who, superficially regarded, seem to court misfortune. They intentionally and systematically set conditions for themselves that most mortals try to avoid by religious means. What average laypersons consider a horror, virtuosos voluntarily accept and make the basis of their way of life. They seek poverty and dirt, pain and privation, homelessness and loneliness, humiliation and social contempt, sexual abstinence and sleep deprivation, malnourishment and self-denial.

This would seem to contradict my thesis. I will show, however, that the practices of virtuosos follow, on a "higher" level, the same logic as those of laypersons. The laity and virtuosos have different ambitions. Whereas most laypersons are content to be protected from misfortune, virtuosos seek salvation, whatever the cost. If the price of achieving eternal salvation is putting up with temporary suffering, virtuosos accept it. Salvation and misfortune are reinterpreted and revaluated. Athanasius aptly describes this price from an early Christian perspective when in his *Vita Antonii* he writes:

> For the entire life span of men is very brief when measured against the ages to come, so that all our time is nothing in comparison with eternal life. Everything in the world is sold for what it is worth, and someone trades an item for its equivalent. But the promise of eternal life is purchased for very little. [. . .] When, therefore, we live the whole eighty years, or even a hundred in the discipline, these hundred are not equal to

the years we shall reign, for instead of a hundred we shall reign forever and ever.[1]

This logic of the quest for salvation also holds true for virtuosos in other traditions, even if expressed in terms of a different set of concepts. At the same time, as I will show, virtuosos' practices reveal the secret of charisma, the genesis and logic of superhuman power.

On the Concept of Virtuosity

Let me begin by offering a more detailed definition of virtuosity. Both Émile Durkheim and Sigmund Freud pointed out that an ascetic drive is inherent in society; for without asceticism, without the repression and regulation of individual desires, society would not be possible. Thus ascetic virtuosity represents only the extreme form of a general necessity. Virtuosos show in an exaggerated form what society expects of everyone.[2] This explanation may provide an interesting insight into the requirements of society, but it is not very helpful in understanding or defining religious virtuosity. We can speak of virtuosity only when there is an extreme difference between ordinary and extraordinary expectations, forms, and achievements of ascetic discipline, contemplative concentration, or ethical rigor.

Of course, intermediate levels between ordinary people and virtuosos exist everywhere. Laypersons can also subject themselves to ascetic practices, have ecstatic experiences, or form virtuoso communities. And nominal virtuosos can lower their standards so much that they no longer represent virtuosity. There is no sharp line between laity and virtuosos. As Peter Brown points out in his remarkable study on early Christianity, even the pious Christian paterfamilias had to be prepared to suffer martyrdom for his faith. And in Augustine's time, conversion to Christianity still implied sexual abstinence even in marriage.[3] Moreover, there have been lay communities of religious virtuosos in both Judaism and Christianity.[4]

Thus virtuosity cannot be identified with asceticism or mysticism, or with being a monk or a nun. This view is reflected in the literature, in which the concepts of asceticism and mysticism are so broadly defined that the practices of virtuosity are subsumed under them, but virtuosos are not credited with a monopoly on asceticism or mysticism. A foundation for the broad definition is found, for example, in Bernhard McGinn's discussion and definition of the concept of mysticism in the Christian tradition: "This goal, essential characteristic, or defining note has most often been seen as the experience of some form of union with god, particularly a union of absorption or identity in which the individual personality is lost. If we define mysticism in this sense, there are actually so few mystics in the history of Christianity that one wonders why Christians used the qualifier 'mystical' so often."[5]

For this reason, McGinn argues for a broader determination of the concept and defines mysticism as the experience of the immediate presence of God.[6] Ascetic and mystical practices alone are thus insufficient to distinguish virtuosos from the laity. One alternative would be to limit virtuosity to its institutionalized monastic forms, where life is devoted especially to asceticism or contemplation. But here, too, we must be careful. Monastic communities are institutions whose goal is to standardize asceticism and contemplation and make them an ongoing activity. Hence, over time such communities have reduced their demands, in contrast to individual virtuosos or spontaneously formed communities of virtuosos. The organization of monastic communities, as well as the implied equality among their members, required a standardization of the performances expected of monks and nuns. This is particularly true in times when the majority of the members no longer join a monastery out of a sense of individual vocation. The expectations formulated in monastic rules, while usually set higher than those for the laity, generally allow for compromises with everyday needs. For example, "poverty" is a precondition for membership in Christian monastic communities, but at the same time the individual is cared for by the monastery and often enjoys a relatively comfortable economic situation, compared with those who live in real poverty.[7]

We encounter similar leveling phenomena in Buddhism. The *Visuddhi-Magga*, a systematic handbook of Theravada Buddhism that describes the way to enlightenment, is full of definitions that close loopholes that might be used by monks seeking to escape strict asceticism. For "forest dweller's practice," for instance, it defines precisely what "forest" means, namely, a place that is at least five hundred bow-lengths outside the village.[8] Apparently, some monks had to be told that the "forest" did not begin right in front of their own huts. The *Visuddhi-Magga* also distinguishes between "strict," "medium," and "mild" ascetics.[9] The mention of "mild" ascetics suggests that being a monk did not automatically imply virtuosity. Similar distinctions are found in Mahayana Buddhism, as John Kieschnick's very informative work shows.[10] In analyzing the logic of virtuoso practices, therefore, I will refer to particularly strict ascetic and contemplative rules or codifications. To be sure, in these cases as well, one must assume that norm and reality are often poles apart.

For my theoretically oriented approach, focusing on extreme virtuosity allows the logic of the relevant practices to emerge with special clarity. To that extent it is useful to discuss the category of virtuosity once again in the context of Weber's sociology of religion, in which it plays a central role. Weber uses the concept to express people's different religious qualifications. According to him, almost all cultures distinguish between religiously gifted and ordinary people:

> The empirical fact, important for us, that men are *differently qualified* in a religious way stands at the beginning of the history of religion. [. . .] The sacred values that have been most cherished, the ecstatic and visionary capacities of shamans, sorcerers, ascetics, and pneumatics of all sorts, could not be attained by everyone. The possession of such faculties is a "charisma," which, to be sure, might be awakened in some but not in all. It follows from this that all intensive religiosity has a tendency toward a sort of *status stratification*, in accordance with differences in the charismatic qualifications.[11]

Although such differences are often considered innate, they nonetheless require confirmation and verification. This means that religiously qualified persons must test and confirm their qualification by a special way of life and by carrying out certain practices. However, Weber distinguishes these charismatically gifted individuals not only from the religiously "tone deaf" and the religious "masses," but also from the officials of hierocratic organizations who owe their charisma solely to the institution and thus need not be personally qualified. These ecclesiastical organizations tend to be monopolistic, hierarchical, and "democratic"; that is, they promise salvation to anyone who submits to them. This opposition necessarily leads to the competition between virtuosos and hierocratic officeholders that Pierre Bourdieu, drawing on Weber, made the center of his theory of religion.[12] According to Weber, virtuosos are neither normal laypersons nor priests attached to hierocratic organizations; rather, they are bearers of personal charisma, such as shamans, hermits, monks, ecstatics, visionaries, mystics, and prophets.

I adopt Weber's distinctions but frame the question differently. What interests me here is not how the dynamics of competition between virtuosos and priests influences communal religiousness and shapes the ethos of the laity. I am concerned chiefly with virtuosos—what religious practices make them virtuosos, how their religious action and its meaning differs from that of the laity, and what effects it has on their religious status and their relation to the laity. How does one become a shaman, an ascetic, or a mystic? What kinds of discipline lead to ecstasy, enlightenment, visions, or the attainment of superhuman power? What services can virtuosos perform for the laity, and how do these services shape their mutual relations? What services are expected from "living saints," and what kinds of virtuosity does their status presuppose?

To avoid drowning in the abundance of the material, I will concentrate here on the forms of virtuosity that are based on intentionality and discipline. Thus I am concerned with virtuosos who have to earn their virtuosity by systematic self-discipline and have not simply inherited it. Virtuoso discipline can take various forms, which need not be mutually exclusive. I distinguish, in ideal-typical terms, among ascetic, contemplative, and ethical disciplines. Ethical discipline represents a special case, not found everywhere. It is a specific, rationalized, and disenchanted form of asceticism that produces not "living saints" but "models" for all others to emulate. In this case, the gap between the laity and virtuosos is not as wide as it is in the case of the ascetic or contemplative disciplines. Therefore, I will limit my examples to ascetic practices, which serve as means to achieving extraordinary states that are not expected of the laity.

Not only are the practices of religious virtuosos manifold, but their subjectively intended meaning and their cultural and institutional acceptance vary considerably. Extreme virtuosity may indeed be frowned upon, contested, or even lead to persecution.[13] Although it occurs in nearly all religions, it seems to encounter the greatest obstacles in the strictest monotheistic religions: Judaism, Islam, and Protestant Christianity. This is probably connected with the fact that in these religions the distance between humans and God is seen as particularly great, so that a virtuoso approach to God seems especially problematic. On the other hand, the structures of religious communities play a role, mainly with respect to the emphasis put on all people's fundamental equality before God. And finally, with the help of political authorities, dominant religious institutions can marginalize or even repress virtuosity.[14]

All virtuosos seek to approach the "holy" or even to merge with it, the "holy" being characterized as something eternal, uncreated, immutable, undifferentiated, unified, or atemporal. The holy represents a state of eternal salvation or at least the absence of misfortune. For virtuosos, misfortune consists primarily in being separated from the holy. At the same time, everything that is time-bound and thus mutable tends to be regarded as not really existing, as appearance or a lower form of existence, by contrast with the timeless, which is the only reality.[15] For almost all virtuosos, one can approach the holy only by distancing oneself from the profane. This distancing can range from indifference to strict rejection. Accordingly, it leads to practices that range from the neglect of worldly interests to the most rigorous bodily and mental discipline.

Unlike the laity, who in their interactions with superhuman powers strive for protection against misfortune as well as a little happiness in this world, virtuosos are radical salvation seekers who voluntarily accept suffering in order to approach the holy or to merge with it, in order to move, first temporarily and later eternally, into a state of salvation.[16]

In the course of this radical quest, seekers relativize and reinterpret suffering by defying what laypersons consider misfortune. Through this voluntary acceptance of suffering, virtuosos willingly or unwillingly increase their power and themselves become, as dispensers or mediators of salvation, objects of religious veneration. These two dimensions of suffering and power are very closely connected and provide the key to an understanding of the genesis and logic of superhuman power. To present this relationship as clearly as possible, I will focus on extreme forms of virtuosity.

Virtuosity's path to salvation has certain typical characteristics that persist over time and cultural boundaries. In principle, it consists in the creation of a new person. This self-transformation has bodily, social, and spiritual dimensions. First, the bodily self is transformed by subjecting itself to misfortune either voluntarily or on command by a higher power. Through discipline, privation, suffering, and pain, the body is reshaped in accord with the goals of salvation and the paths that lead to it, in such a way that it differs in appearance from that of an ordinary person. The ability to conform to such a bodily discipline requires an extraordinary psychological attitude, which is further developed by means of ascetic practices.

Second, the social self is transformed. Bodily discipline alone separates virtuosos from the laity socially. In addition, virtuosos deliberately change their system of social relations by means of spatial or symbolic separation. They restructure their social relations by refusing to conform to certain role expectations, taking refuge in illness or in mental anomalies. Virtuosos separate themselves at least partially or temporarily from family and friends, from co-workers and other members of their class. Instead, they associate with like-minded people and avoid others, or seek solitude in deserts, forests, or mountains. Frequently they live abroad and lead a nomadic life.

Third, virtuosos transform themselves spiritually. For them, the most important social relations consist not in everyday interaction with other people but in extraordinary relations with gods, spirits, the dead, saints, or mythical animals that they encounter in ecstatic states, visions, revelations, or daydreams. In their spiritual lives, virtuosos interact with invisible powers that seem to them more real than the social world in which they live.

As a result of this threefold transformation, a new, powerful self develops. Precisely because a religious virtuoso has braved misfortune and suffering and overcome it, he or she becomes a bearer of charisma, of super-human power. Virtuosos are often thought to be capable of performing mir-acle cures, awakening the dead, or being present at several places at once. They are deemed able to read people's thoughts, to prophesy, to determine the moment that will bring victory in battles, to resolve social conflicts, and to avert dangers. Virtuosos are powerful as dispensers and mediators of salvation, and they serve as mediums through whom the gods communicate with humans.[17] It depends largely on the specific religious tradition whether this empowerment is consciously and systematically sought, simply "hap-pens" to the virtuoso (perhaps only because he has not consciously sought it), or is lent as a gift of grace from a higher power, which the latter could also take back again. However that may be, virtuosos are venerated as living saints and providers of salvation, and in many religions even their remains, in the form of relics, are still thought to have superhuman power.

This basic model of self-transformation tends to be universal, found in all periods and cultures. That does not mean that all virtuosos in all times have followed this same model. Virtuoso practices are diverse, and their forms and specific cultural meanings vary not only from one religious tradi-tion to another but also historically within the same tradition. It is not my intention to play down these differences. Nonetheless, I want to show that beneath this diversity lies a structural principle that allows us to determine cultural peculiarities more specifically and to compare them transculturally. Differences are, after all, of interest mainly insofar as they can be related to underlying commonalities.

In order to avoid misunderstandings, I will once again briefly explain my use of the sources. If I appear to take religious legends and myths liter-ally, I am doing so methodologically, not naïvely. I take the sources at their word because the logic of religions is revealed in these self-expressions. The sources used seek to affirm or create belief, not to convey scientifically provable facts. But precisely for that reason they clearly express what the various religions in general, and the different forms of virtuosity in par-ticular, claim to provide. It is the "promise" of religions that concerns me here. For the purpose of theory building, I avoid a "critical" perspective that "unmasks" religious ideologies and their involvement in power interests; rather, I adopt an interpretive perspective that arrives at an explanation of religion by systematizing religious self-representations. In this way I hope to explain how religion comes to be capable of constituting authority and power. What promises does it extend that allow relations of domination to be created and maintained? That religion grounds and legitimates authority is beyond doubt and therefore requires no special emphasis.

Shamans

From a certain point of view, shamanism is a prototype of religious virtuosity.[18] Shamans are often people who have already been predisposed for
their task by illness and suffering. Moreover, severe bodily ordeals are an
essential part of a shaman's initiation. Mircea Eliade describes the initiation
schema as a sequence of suffering, death, and resurrection. Connected with
this schema are ecstatic states and the learning of techniques and special
terminology (Eliade, *Shamanism*).

Eliade reports that Caribbean shamans' apprenticeship is "extremely
rigorous" (128). The initiation course lasts twenty-four days and nights. A
group of six neophytes lives in total isolation in a hut, works during the day,
and receives instruction from the master at night. Throughout, the group
largely fasts, though much tobacco is smoked, chewed, or drunk in the form
of juice. The goal of the first stage of instruction is to call forth trance states
that are ended when the master presses a braided mat crawling with large
poisonous ants onto the pupil's skin (129).

Among the Yakuts, a person who is to become a shaman begins to rave,
loses consciousness, and withdraws into the forest, where he eats bark,
jumps into water and fire, and lacerates himself with a knife (16–17). The
actual initiation, concerning which we have various reports by shamans,
takes place afterward. The dismembering ceremony is of special interest,
because it probably represents the most extreme and graphic transformation of the bodily self and thus also the social self. It is a trance experience
that follows a specific script. One report of what was seen in a trance goes
as follows: "The candidate's limbs are removed and disjointed with an iron
hook; the bones are cleaned the flesh scraped, the body fluids thrown away,
and the eyes torn from their sockets. After this operation all the bones are
gathered up and fastened together with iron" (36). Other reports say that
the candidate's body is cut up into small pieces and distributed among the
evil spirits of disease and death, which devour the parts they like. This later
gives the shaman the power to heal the corresponding diseases (36).

These practices lead to the shaman's acquiring superhuman powers and
being able to act as a mediator between humans and superhuman powers.
Eliade describes shamans as healers and spiritual guides:

> Healer and psychopomp, the shaman is these because he commands the
> techniques of ecstasy—that is, because his soul can safely abandon his
> body and roam at vast distances, can penetrate the underworld and rise
> to the sky. Through his own ecstatic experiences he knows the roads

of the extraterrestrial regions. He can go below and above because he has already been there. The danger of losing his way in these forbidden regions is still great; but sanctified by his initiation and furnished with guardian spirits, the shaman is the only human being able to challenge the danger and venture into a mystical geography. (182)

In Siberia and Central Asia, the classic areas of shamanism, the shaman is chiefly a healer. The most widespread cause of illness is the loss of the soul, and the cure consists in finding it again and putting it back in its proper place in the body.[19]

It is interesting to compare Eliade's account with Carmen Blacker's description of Japanese shamanism. According to Blacker, the starting point for understanding shamanism is the belief in the existence of two worlds, one inhabited by humans and the other by nonhuman powers. The nonhuman powers not only have free, unhindered access to the human world but also control essential spheres of life that are beyond human control.[20] The causes of calamities such as illness, accidents, or droughts lie in the nonhuman realm and are attributed to angry spirits or offended deities. To avert dangers and ensure the community's well-being, it is necessary to establish contact with these nonhuman powers, to appease them, or to direct them toward human interests. Only certain gifted people, however, are capable of mediating between the two worlds in a state of trance.[21]

Blacker describes two kinds of shamans, the called and the seekers. Some shamans are called by a divinity in dreams or in a state of possession, whereas others become shamans on the basis of their own decision.[22] In both cases, the method of acquiring superhuman powers is the same: ascetic discipline (gyo), that is, the transformation of the bodily, social, and spiritual self. The ascetic practices can be divided roughly into fasting and being showered with cold water. The dietary regulations relate to the avoidance of meat, salt, cooked food, and, as in Daoism, the "five grains," namely, rice, wheat, barley, oats, and beans. Further practices include the reciting of powerful words whose power develops only in combination with ascetic practices, and travel, perhaps in the form of nomadic wandering or pilgrimages to holy places.

A practice that has now died out is self-mummification as Buddha (sokushimbutsu). Ascetics take a vow to systematically starve themselves to death over a period of one, two, three, or even four thousand days. At first, their diet consists of nuts, berries, bark, or pine needles (mokujiki), whose quantities are systematically reduced until total fasting is reached.[23] The ideal is to die sitting in the lotus position on the last day of the fast. The body, which by that time consists of skin and bones, is laid for three years in a sarcophagus, in which mummification takes place. The mummies are then given caps and prayer beads like those of Buddhist abbots and laid out in the temple at the place where the image of Buddha is normally found.

Another form of asceticism consists in exposing oneself for extended periods, in the depths of winter, to ice-cold water. Waterfalls are ideal; ascetics prefer to stand under them between two and three o'clock in the morning. Pails of water are often used as substitutes, the shamans showering themselves with as many as a thousand pails of ice-cold water per day. It goes without saying that all these practices transform not only the bodily but also the social self. For one thing, they generally preclude normal social relations, at least for the time being. The ascetic has to withdraw from his family, wear strange clothing and hairstyles, eat different foods, and behave in unusual ways.

Thus the person adopts a new social role as an ascetic and outsider, to which the local people react in different ways. Some revere ascetics or shamans as holy, while others fear them, and still others don't take them seriously. In any case, the bodily transformation entails a rupture, usually a radical one, in the shaman's social self. At the same time, the shaman communicates with superhuman powers, which partially substitute for social relations.

In Japanese shamanism as well, ascetic practices result in an empowerment that takes different forms depending on the type of shaman.[24] Some have the gift of exorcism, of "opening" holy places, of communicating with animals, of serving as mediums, or of receiving oracles. Other shamans demonstrate their power by walking on glowing coals, immersing themselves in boiling water, or climbing a ladder made of swords.[25]

Christians

Early Christianity is certainly characterized by ascetic virtuosity. Not only were certain Christians ready to suffer and die as witnesses to their faith, but many were willing to accept great privation.[26] St. Antony, as described in Athanasius's biography, corresponds to the type of the ascetic virtuoso whose life is at the same time related as a model for others.[27] Antony voluntarily accepted suffering connected with poverty, loneliness, torture, strict bodily discipline, and the repression of bodily needs such as food, sleep, sexuality, and cleanliness. Thus Athanasius reports that after the death of his parents, Antony sold his inheritance and gave the money to the poor. He associated with older ascetics and learned strict bodily discipline from them. He slept on the ground and fasted. He tried to intensify his asceticism, to live on water, salt, and bread, and refused to care for his body.[28]

One day, Antony left his village community and shut himself up in a tomb where he was tortured by demons: he was beaten, tormented with loud noise, and frightened by the appearances of dangerous animals. Finally he took up his abode in an abandoned castle in the desert and forbade occasional visitors to enter it.[29] There he lived for twenty years. Later on, Antony pushed his asceticism still further, wore rough garments, and no longer washed himself at all.[30] In his *Vita* we find the three elements of the transformation of the bodily, social, and spiritual selves through ascetic discipline, social isolation, and interaction with superhuman powers.

What is the result of this voluntary asceticism and of deprivation both physical and mental? Athanasius reports that during the twenty years Antony spent in seclusion he seemed not to have aged at all. Furthermore, he had acquired superhuman powers. When he and his entourage wanted to cross the Arsinoe canal, which was swarming with crocodiles, his prayer sufficed for them to cross safely.[31] Furthermore, Antony's asceticism put him in a state in which he could recognize demons and drive them away with a word. He healed many people of bodily ills and freed others from demons. He had visions and experienced other gifts of grace. For instance, he saw the monk Amun's soul fly up to heaven. Not fearing death, he was prepared to die as a martyr.[32]

Christian religious virtuosity in the Middle Ages followed the same basic model of self-transformation. This model is exemplified by the life of St. Francis of Assisi, in the legendary form in which it was handed down by St. Bonaventure.[33] Bonaventure reports that Francis's self-transformation began when he was suffering from an extended illness.[34] His conversion was given visible form when he began to chastise his body. He practiced sexual abstinence, wore a rough undergarment, lived in poverty, and exposed himself to disease, dirt, and cold. He sought martyrdom in the land of the Saracens. Often he ate only uncooked foods, such as vegetables and fruits. For many years he touched neither bread nor wine (Bonaventure, 39). When he ate cooked food, he mixed it with ashes or water to rid it of taste. At other times he lived simply on bread and water. His discipline was so strict that he ate barely enough to keep his body alive (44). He called his body "Brother Ass," because he thought it should work hard, be frequently whipped, and be fed the simplest foods (49).

He slept on the bare ground, often sitting up or with a piece of wood or a stone as a pillow. Even when it was very cold, he wore only a light cape. Shortly before his death, in order to increase his merit he inflicted still greater suffering on himself; he was so plagued by various diseases that scarcely any part of his body was free of intense pain (152).

When overcome by sensual lust, he scourged himself. He advised his fellow friars to avoid looking at women or conversing with them (48). In caring for lepers, he went so far as to kiss their wounds. As Bonaventure writes, he had been entirely transformed into the image of the crucified Christ (141). Nails grew out of his own skin on his hands and feet, and Christ's wounds appeared, the stigmata completing the process of his bodily self-transformation (138–50).

Francis's social and spiritual self-transformation took place on the same model. He separated himself from the family of his father, a merchant, gave away his wealth, and lived among the poor and the sick (19). He withdrew into solitude, where he battled with demons that tried to prevent him from praying (106). Sometimes he lived with his fellow friars, and sometimes with animals. When contemplating heavenly splendor, he was so absentminded that he was unaware of the time, the place, or the people he encountered (106). Thus a complete restructuring of social relations took place.

But such acts enabled him to carry out miracle cures (19). He had visions and received messages from the Holy Ghost that allowed him to discover hidden relics (62). He brought peace to the city of Arezzo by driving out its demons. His virtues of humility and obedience gave him great power over rebellious spirits and enabled him to keep their unruly audacity and violence in check (64).

Bonaventure reports countless other miracles performed by the saint. For example, Francis spoke with animals and taught a sheep to go to church. The sheep knelt on entering the church and bleated before the altar to the Virgin Mary (86). Francis had prophetic gifts and predicted the outcome of battles (115–18). He looked into people's hearts and knew their innermost secrets (119). Even his handwriting performed miracles later on (120). He knew about events that were taking place at a great distance. Francis's miracles, to which Bonaventure devotes a whole chapter (125–37), became still more frequent after he received the stigmata. Thus his bathwater healed diseased animals, and a hailstorm was ended by vision that he had.

Francis's redefinition of salvation is found in his allegory "of true and perfect joy." He explains to his clerk, Brother Leo, that true joy does not consist in bishops, kings, and all the professors in Paris joining the order, or in converting all unbelievers, or in being able to perform miracles. True joy consists in humility and self-denial:

What is true joy? I return from Perugia, and arrive here in the dead of
the night, and it is wintertime, muddy, and so cold that water freezes
on the hem of my habit, forming chunks of ice that constantly strike
against my legs, breaking the skin, so that blood flows from the wounds.
I stand in front of the gate, dirty and freezing, and after I've knocked and
called out for a long time, a friar comes and asks: "Who is it?" And I
answer: "Brother Francis." And he answers: "Get lost. This is no time to
wander around. You will not get in here." And as I insist, he adds: "Hit
the road! You are a simpleton and idiot. From now on, you will not get
back in here. We are so numerous and so good that we no longer need
you." And I stand again at the door and say: "For the love of God, take
me in for at least this night!" And he answers: "No! Go to where the
cross-bearers are, and ask for admission there!" I tell you, if, then, I am
patient and do not get upset, that is what true joy and true virtue and the
soul's salvation consists in![35]

The idea of self-empowerment is very strongly developed in Francis of Assisi.
He frequently presents himself as a new version of Christ. I have mentioned, for instance, his "reception" of the stigmata.[36] He even staged the
last hours of his life on the model of Christ. To that end, he had himself
carried, mortally ill, from the palace of the bishop of Assisi to the little
chapel of Portiuncula, where the passage in St. John's gospel about the Last
Supper was read to him. Finally, he was given bread, which he blessed and
then tried to break and distribute. At the same time, he maintained it was
Thursday, though it was not. In all reports regarding his death, there is no
indication that he received the last sacraments of the Church,[37] which also
indicates that he was no ordinary mortal. The people of Assisi were pleased
that the saint was dying, because his body would provide them with an exceptionally potent and lucrative source of relics.[38] His later veneration and
the miracles ascribed to him are further results of his virtuosity.

The life of St. Catherine of Siena, too, which was composed shortly after her death by her father confessor, Raimondo da Capua (apparently with
the intention not only to present her life as a model for others to follow but
also to recommend her for sanctification), follows the basic pattern of self-
transformation.[39] The redefinition of suffering as producing salvation and
the empowerment that it entails become clear in one of Catherine's visions,
in which Christ suggests that she imitate him in suffering. The more she
follows him in suffering, the more she will resemble him in the state of
grace. Hence, for his sake she should consider sweet as bitter and bitter as
sweet (Raymond of Capua, 90).

Catherine's transformation into a virtuosa begins with self-contempt (154). In consequence of her will to transform herself, she was led into all kinds of temptations, often sexual in nature, which she countered with various forms of ascetic discipline. She flogged her body with an iron chain until it bled, and prolonged her night vigils until she was able to get by almost without sleep (53ff.).

Among other practices that were supposed to help her more closely approach her "heavenly spouse" was caring for the poor and the sick. She engaged in these activities as ascetic exercises in self-discipline and self-denial that pushed her body to the limits of its endurance. In caring for the sick, for instance, she exposed herself to leprosy and was infected. She also cared for a woman with advanced breast cancer. One day, when the smell of the open wound was so unbearable that it nauseated Catherine, she put her mouth and nose directly on the wound and left them there "until the Spirit had conquered the rebellious feeling of nausea and tamed the flesh that was trying to oppose the spirit" (141). On another occasion, when changing the wound's dressing, she had to vomit. In order to force her body to submit, she poured the pus that had flowed from the wound into the water she had used to wash it and drank from the bowl (147). As a reward, she had a vision in which Jesus invited her to drink from the wound in his side (148). Afterward, she went to communion daily, if she could, and fasted when she could not. However, this allegedly made her stronger, not weaker.

The ever more frequent states of holiness paralleled Catherine's physical transformation (152).[40] Her rigorous fasting altered her "lifeblood" and thus the course of physiological processes (152). Catherine now ate only sacred foods, living on communion wafers, drinking from Christ's wounds (148, 170, 173), and was breast-fed by Mary in person (179). Her bodily appearance also increasingly resembled Christ's. He not only personally lent her his stigmata but also gave her, as his "dearest daughter," his heart, after he had taken hers a few days before (174–76, 165).

Next, Catherine's practices were concentrated entirely on subjugating her body through self-flagellation, sleep deprivation, extreme fasting, exertion to the point of exhaustion, and nausea-producing acts. These practices produced ecstasies and visions in which her body was further transformed by eating divine food. As an expression of this bodily transformation, we can also cite a report that on one occasion, in the presence of witnesses, Catherine floated for a while above her bed after taking communion (173).

As for the transformation of Catherine's social self, it was manifested in her relations with her fellow citizens. Although these included supporters and followers, Raymondo's biography makes it quite clear that many people considered Catherine sick, eccentric, overly devout, or hypocritical (150–63). Evidently there was a great deal of gossip, which Raymondo repeatedly tries to refute. Thus he mentions that on her deathbed, Catherine condemned self-glorification and extolled the veneration of God (334). From his point of view, this statement shows that Catherine's opponents who considered her vain were doing her an injustice. Many of them thought that so young a woman would do better to marry and have children than to starve herself to death and be constantly fainting. But her frequent ecstasies also altered her subjectively perceived interaction and communication, her spiritual self. Raymondo tells how her soul sank ever more into contemplation. She hardly prayed anymore, and went into ecstasy before she could finish her paternoster (97).

Her social self was thus increasingly shaped by her communication with Christ, Mary, and the saints. She married Christ when he rewarded her for her strict fasting by appearing to her one day in the company of his mother, John the evangelist, the apostle Paul, the founder of the Dominican order, and the prophet David. While David played his harp, Mary took Catherine's hand and gave him her son as her husband. Christ accepted her, putting a ring with pearls and diamonds on her ring finger. After the vision, she was able to see the ring her whole life long, though it remained invisible to others (99–101).

Raymondo's biography recounts meetings and personal conversations with Mary Magdalene, with whom Catherine identified. Although she also continued to participate in the social world, traveling and advising the pope, she had replaced her profane self with a holy one. This becomes clear in her encounter with the body of St. Agnes, which lies in the town of Montepulciano. When Catherine bent down to kiss her feet, Agnes raised one foot. When, on a second visit, she approached Agnes's head and bowed down to it, manna rained down from the sky (294–95). All this shows that Catherine had already been included in the heavenly company. Her increasingly frequent states of ecstasy represented anticipations of eternal felicity. Raymondo describes Catherine as totally absorbed in thoughts and feelings about paradise (185).

The transformation of the bodily, social, and spiritual selves eventuates in the empowerment of the holy self. Put another way, Catherine can perform miracles. Her biographer and confessor distinguishes between spiritual and bodily miracles, the spiritual miracles being based simply on Catherine's own reports. Raymondo constantly seeks to convey the theologically correct view of miracles, according to which Catherine did not herself possess this power, but God worked through her. The repeated insistence on this point of view suggests that the laity saw Catherine herself as the bearer of charismatic power. After her death, her relics were regarded as capable of producing salvation and performing miracles.

For the most part, Catherine's spiritual miracles are associated with the conversion of people who were considered particularly obstinate (197–218). Catherine often engaged in lengthy negotiations with God in order to have these miracles performed, always prevailing, it appears, through her patience and persistence.

Her bodily miracles consisted in resuscitation of the dead, cures from disease, and the alleviation of pain by touching or the laying on of hands, often in connection with the plague outbreak in Siena in 1374. For example, Catherine healed a pious woman of her pains by touching her. And Raymondo reports that everyone was overwhelmed by the power that the Creator had given Catherine (228). Her ability to perform miracles was not limited to her time Siena but continued during her travels.

Miracles of another kind concern exorcisms and prophecies. Catherine possessed the gift of driving out demons and evil spirits (241–49). She could read people's innermost thoughts and knew their past sins, even though they themselves might have forgotten them; she could also predict future events, such as the Great Schism (250–67). She had the power to multiply loaves of bread so as to feed a mass of people. As a rule, virtuosos do not die a normal death, and their power continues even after death. Catherine was no exception. Raymondo leaves no doubt as to her direct ascension to heaven. At the hour of her death, her confessor, who was in Genoa at the time, heard her voice, promising him protection and support (337). And a pious woman in Rome had a vision that is obviously supposed to represent Catherine's reception into heaven, where she was personally greeted and welcomed by God and Mary (339–42). When her body lay in state, it had to be protected from the crowds that tried to grab bits of her clothing and even of her body (344). The dead Catherine performed a multitude of miracles; indeed, her power seemed to grow rather than to diminish (346–55).

Jews

Robert Cohn is probably correct in arguing that Jewish virtuosity is a rather peripheral phenomenon. Charismatic forms of Judaism develop especially where the rabbinical tradition of textual exegesis is less established as an institution or cannot adequately meet the community's religious needs, as in North Africa and Eastern Europe.[41] Nonetheless, Judaism has undeniably produced ascetic forms. But Jewish virtuosity seems more strongly community oriented than is Christian virtuosity, and it is less fixated on extreme bodily suffering than the virtuosity of other traditions.[42]

Rabbi Nahman of Bratislava is said to have engaged in severe asceticism when he was young. In winter he rolled in the snow, and in summer he allowed insects to bite and sting him.[43] Above all, he tried to keep his sex drive under control, for this seemed to him the most important aspect of ascetic self-discipline.[44] It was also this overcoming of his older self that made Rabbi Nahman a zaddik, a mediator between God and his community. Samuel Dresdner describes the zaddik as a living saint, who is not only a technical mediator between heaven and earth but also stands between them. He is bound to humans, but his fate is not; his primary attention is given to the heavenly sphere.[45] But he is prepared to suffer for the sake of humans.[46] There are many collections of stories about miracles performed by zaddiks.

Nathan of Gaza's description of his prophetic awakening is an interesting document:

> Whosoever knoweth me can truthfully testify that from my childhood unto this day not the slightest fault [of sin] could be found with me. I observed the Law in poverty, and meditated on it day and night. I never followed after the lusts of the flesh, but always added new mortifications and forms of penance with all my strength, nor did I ever derive any worldly benefit from my message. [. . .] I was undergoing a prolonged fast in the week before the feast of Purim. Having locked myself in a separate room in holiness and purity, and reciting the penitential prayers of the morning service with many tears, the spirit came over me, my hair stood on end and my knees shook and I beheld the *merkabah*, and I saw visions of God all day long and all night, and I was vouchsafed true prophecy like any other prophet.[47]

Gershom Scholem has rightly called Nathan an ascetic rabbi. The passage just quoted confirms my impression that Jewish virtuosity also follows my model of self-transformation. But since this subject matter seems quite controversial in the literature and there are few studies on it, a nonspecialist should not be drawing his own conclusions. I will therefore go no further into virtuosity in Judaism.

Muslims

As in the case of Judaism, the literature on Islam often leaves the impression that there was hardly any radical Islamic virtuosity. The new *Ency-*

clopedia of Islam contains no article on the concept of *zuhd* (asceticism).
Although at certain times and among certain groups strict asceticism and
sexual abstinence were stigmatized as heterodox and culturally disapproved
of, asceticism plays an important role in Sufism and not always a heterodox
one.[48] Richard Gramlich cites many different forms of ascetic renunciation.
Poverty, humility, sleep deprivation, strict diets, and sexual abstinence
count as typical ascetic virtues. Vincent Cornell mentions similar but more
moderate forms in Morocco.[49] Here I will limit myself to describing the life
of Rabi'a, an eighth-century female mystic.[50]

Among the ascetic practices of Rabi'a were a celibate life, fasts, and living in the desert and in a cell (Smith, *Rabi'a the Mystic,* 7). It is reported
that she once spent seven days and nights without food or sleep, praying
all night long (21). She willingly endured illness and suffering and ignored
bleeding wounds (22–23). Like other ascetics, she did without any comforts
when sleeping. She used a brick as a pillow (25). After a vision in which she
was rebuked for sleeping instead of praying, she gave up sleeping for the rest
of her life (27).

Rabi'a went through phases of loneliness interspersed with companion-
ship. Her social life changed fundamentally. Social contacts were reduced
to a religious entourage, to other mystics, to pupils that followed her, and to
those seeking advice (13). Her true contacts were increasingly spiritualized
and occurred in prayers and visions. She claimed to have turned her back
on human beings since she had known God (24). Her spiritual contact with
God is described as an intimate relationship. She called God her joy, her
desire, her refuge, her friend, her provider of nourishment, her goal, and her
confidant. Longing for him, she said, kept her alive (28). Emphasizing the
non-instrumental nature of her relationship to God, she does not seek him
out of fear of hell or hope of paradise; the encounter with God is an end in
itself and an anticipation of the paradisiacal condition (29–30, 88–110).

The motif of the virtuoso's increase in power is also found in Islamic
mysticism. For example, Ibn Arabi claims that he is "the seal of Muhammadan holiness"; in a dream, he saw that two bricks were missing in the
Kaaba, one gold and one silver, and he took their place and thus completed
the Kaaba's holiness.[51] The outstanding ascetic and martyr al-Hallaj is supposed to have said: "I am the Absolute Truth."[52] In addition, he could perform miracles by pointing with his finger; in one instance, he brought a
dead parrot back to life.[53] Rabi'a too is said to have performed miracles. A
thief who trying to steal from her could not find his way out of her cell. She
could read thoughts and predict the future. When she prayed, a dead camel
came back to life and locusts were driven out of a field.[54] She could fly on

her prayer carpet and use her finger as a lamp.[55] On her pilgrimage to Mecca, the Kaaba came to meet her.[56] As in other religions, the saints' legends are endless in number. Islamic saints are also venerated both during their lives and after their deaths. People pray directly to them, and many believers go to the saints' tombs in search of blessings.[57] Cornell reports that in Moroccan Islam the status of a saint is made manifest by miracles, including reading thoughts and demonstrations of power, such as healing, flying, or walking on water. Depending on the group in question, the emphasis may fall on miracles involving knowledge or miracles involving power.[58]

Buddhists

In its early form, Buddhism was probably a movement of itinerant ascetic-contemplative virtuosos on an all-out quest for salvation, which Buddha, in one of his lessons, calls the attainment of the "highest peace." He explains that the goal of salvation cannot lie in things, which are themselves—like humans—susceptible to aging, illness, death, and dirt. The goal of salvation lies in a state that is free of these four conditions.

> There are four noble goals, monks. Which four? Someone looks at the misery of growing old who is himself going to grow old, and he seeks after the highest peace, which never grows old, Nirvana. Susceptible to illness himself, he looks at the misery of illness and seeks after the highest peace, which is without illness, Nirvana. Susceptible to death himself, he looks at the misery of death and seeks after the immortal highest peace, Nirvana. Susceptible to dirt himself, he looks at the misery of dirt and seeks after the unsoiled highest peace, Nirvana. There are these four noble goals, monks.[59]

The crises of aging, illness, dying, and impurity that Buddhism strives to surmount are fully in accord with the basic assumptions of my theory of religion. However, at least in ancient Buddhism, this goal of salvation can be attained only by the virtuoso monk. For the laity, there is relative salvation but no liberation from the misery of rebirth. To that extent it is not surprising that Theravada Buddhism in particular has codified the path to enlightenment and salvation as a monastic discipline, guided by Gautama.[60] The *Visuddhi-Magga* of the fifth-century Buddhaghosa systematizes the practices of Buddhist virtuosos. It distinguishes several levels on the path to enlightenment or purity.[61] For the first level of self-discipline it lists thirteen purification exercises, through which the ascetic can acquire certain virtues such as frugality, strict renunciation, or effort of will.[62] The ascetic vows to carry out these exercises. There are exercises for various kinds of ascetic practice: wearing a robe made of rags, wearing only three garments, eating a strictly limited amount of food, eating only what one receives by going "house to house," eating only once a day, eating from the cooking pot, "rejecting later meals," dwelling in the forest, dwelling under a tree, dwelling outside, dwelling in a cemetery, sleeping wherever one happens to be, and sleeping sitting up. The exercises thus concentrate on restrictions regarding clothing (no. 2), nutrition (no. 5), and social contacts and sleeping comfort (no. 6). In a few cases they also concern overcoming fear. Thus, for example, the cemetery ascetic is forbidden to throw things at demons roaming about in the night and howling (Buddhaghosa, 77).

The next level of ascetic practices is called "collection," and might also be described as concentration, meditation, or contemplation. A teacher prescribes for the ascetic a certain object for spiritual exercises that serve to promote specific virtues. There are forty such objects of meditation, which are described in detail. They are divided into ten visible objects, or *kasina*, ten objects of repulsion, ten recollections, four stations of Brahma, four formless states, one perception of repulsive food, and one analysis of the four elements. Then there are various exercises, each adapted to specific characteristics, which promote virtues that the ascetic in question lacks. "A suitable lodging for one of greedy temperament," for example, "has an unwashed sill and stands level with the ground [. . .] full of bats [. . .] in bleak surroundings, threatened [by lions, tigers, etc.] with a muddy, uneven path, where even the bed and chair are full of bugs. And it should be ugly and unsightly, exciting loathing as soon as it is looked at" (109).

As objects of meditation, the *kasina* exercises prescribe earth, water, air, and fire; the colors blue, yellow, red, and white; bright light; and enclosed space. The goal is equanimity, an emotionally neutral condition, an ideal balance between positive and negative emotions in which the ecstatic conditions of bliss that have appeared in the meantime are neutralized. The *kasina* exercises can be characterized as a moderate ascetic discipline that entails, for example, "being pained by an uneven seat" or "being pestered by mosquitoes" (172).

The demands made by virtuoso practices increase significantly when we turn to objects of disgust. Here we are not only confronted with death but must also remain indifferent on viewing repulsive human bodies. Corpses are meditated upon: bloated corpses, blue corpses, festering corpses, split-open corpses, corpses that dogs and jackals have fed upon, scattered body parts, bodies hacked to pieces, blood-smeared corpses, corpses full of worms, and skeletons (185–203). Here, too there are detailed instructions. Thus, for example, it is advised not to approach the corpse from headwind, because one might then have to vomit (189). Men should not meditate on the corpses of women, since even in their bloated condition they might captivate a man's heart (191). And one should not visit corpses at the wrong time of day, when it might look as though they could rise up and pursue one (193). Not least, the contemplation of disgusting objects serves to suppress sexual desire (201–2).

"For a living body is just as foul as a dead one, only the characteristic of foulness is not evident in a living body. [. . .] So men delight in women and women in men without perceiving the true nature of its characteristic foulness. [. . .] But in the ultimate sense there is no place here even the size of an atom fit to lust after" (201–2). To attain equanimity when looking upon disgusting objects, the ascetic should recall that this contemplation exercise brings him closer to the liberation "from aging and death" (188).

The next exercises consist of six contemplations: on the Enlightened One (Buddha), the law (*dharma*), the community (*sangha*), morality, generosity, and heavenly virtue; these are followed by contemplations on death, the body, breathing, and peace. Here, too, the goal is "the destruction of illusion." In reference to a classical sutra we read: "Bhikkhus, I shall teach you the unformed—the truth—the other shore—the hard to see—the undecaying—the lasting—the undiversified—the deathless—the auspicious—the safe—the marvelous—the shelter" (320).

The following exercises are connected with the four "divine abidings": Loving-kindness, compassion, gladness, and equanimity, and then with the "boundless space," the "boundless consciousness," "nothingness," and "neither perception nor non-perception" (321–71). The explanations regarding "collection" close with observations on the repulsive nature of food and the human body.

Because the *Visuddhi-Magga* is addressed to monks, social transformation is already presupposed in the form of separation from family and homeland and the acceptance of discipline either alone or in a monastic community. What does the ascetic who has completed all these exercises achieve? The *Visuddhi-Magga* holds out the prospect of attaining "five kinds of direct knowledge": magical powers, the knowledge of the Divine Ear, the knowledge of Penetration of Minds, the knowledge of Recollection of Past Life, and the knowledge of the Passing Away and Reappearance of Beings (409).

Magical powers include the ability to make oneself visible or invisible. The virtuoso can pass through walls, barriers, and mountains; he can walk on water, fly through the air sitting cross-legged, and even reach the sun and the moon. Buddhist legends about virtuosos report that a monk who was the eldest of his order was thought to have died and was laid on a funeral pyre. But not a single thread of his clothing caught fire. According to another legend, a courtesan poured hot oil over the head of a lay sister, but it simply rolled off her (419–20).

In addition to magical powers, the virtuoso acquires the ability to perceive sounds coming from the world of Brahma, to know the states of consciousness of other people, to recall the forms of existence in earlier ages of the world, and even to recognize people's status as reborn. If he looks toward hell, for instance, he sees "the beings in hell undergoing great suffering" (466). But he can also know what deeds led to these punishments in hell.

Although in the literature dealing with virtuosos these magical abilities are treated as rather embarrassing, their detailed presentation demonstrates their central importance for the relations between virtuosos and the laity. In his excellent study on the forest ascetics in Thailand,[63] Stanley Tambiah tells of Acharn Mun, a master of meditation and a saint, who goes through the phases I have identified. He too subjects himself to strict ascetic practices such as sleep deprivation, fasting, and overcoming fear. He and his relics perform miracles that are especially important for the pious laity. Forest monks also make objects sacred by transferring to them spiritual virtues and energies they have acquired through their practices.[64]

Japanese Virtuosos

Shugendo is an ascetic religious movement in Japan that is associated with mountains as the dwelling place of superhuman powers. Originally, Shugendo was a loose movement of itinerant ascetics who later settled in certain mountainous areas and performed rituals for the religious laity. Its practitioners are divided into three categories: the laity, monks or priests, and itinerant ascetics. Depending on their status, they perform different practices and pursue different salvation goals. Here we are interested chiefly in the practices of the ascetics (yamabushi).[65]

The transformation of the profane self into a holy self takes place through a series of practices. Hartmut Rotermund mentions meditation, fasting, mountain exercises, and pilgrimages. Making pilgrimages seems to have two possible meanings: homelessness, and traveling to holy places that transfer their power to the pilgrim. It is said that when going on pilgrimages, the yamabushi often used paths known only to them.[66] Pilgrimages were accompanied by fasting, but this was not always strictly observed.

Miyake defines ascetic practices in a way that is entirely compatible with my theory, as symbolic transformations of a profane person into a holy one by means of mystical training at a holy place.[67] Ascetics retire to the mountains and spend the whole winter there, living in caves. In earlier times, the dead were placed in these caves, since they were seen as entrances to the underworld. Asceticism involves not only dwelling in borderline areas but also engaging in practices such as standing under an ice-cold waterfall and extreme fasting.[68] One of the earliest reports on these practices, in the form of an explanation of their meaning by a *sendatsu* (a high-ranking *yamabushi*), comes from the Kokonchomonju, a collection of stories from the year 1215:

> When the *sendatsu* orders you [. . .] to perform arduous tasks such as cutting wood and drawing water, confessing your sins and being beaten with a stick, this means that you are redeeming the pains of Hell. When he allows you so little to eat that you are nearly dying of starvation, you shall thereby redeem the miseries of the Hungry Ghosts. When you carry heavy burdens over steep mountains and valleys, you are thereby expiating the pains of the Beasts.[69]

The variant more strongly marked by esoteric Buddhism sees ascetic practices as a path toward the achievement of one's own Buddha nature. For this purpose, the novice must move through ten stages: hell (*jigoku*), hungry spirit (*gaki*), animals (*chikusho*), devil (*shura*), human being (*ningen*), heaven (*ten*), apprentice (*shomon*), self-enlightened person (*enkaku*), enlightened being (*bosatsu*), and Buddha (*butsu*). Each of these stages has its own practices.[70] Hitoshi Miyake summarizes this process of transformation as follows:

> At first the initiate convinces himself of his ability to be a Buddha in his very body. Then his sins are weighed by the leader and he confesses his sins. Thus he can cancel his sins. After these preparations the austerities begin. The initiates recognize the importance of water by abstaining from water. They use water in order to become reborn as a Buddha. Sumo and dancing are carried out as a celebration for this rebirth. Once more the initiate burns off his sinful desires in the fire ritual. He changes his body physiologically by abstaining from grains for seven days. And at last he receives a *mudra* of the cosmos itself and/or its incarnation [. . .] from the main leader. Thus he accomplishes becoming a Buddha in this body.[71]

The transformation of the bodily self is accompanied by a reshaping of the social self. For one thing, clothing and hairstyle symbolize the fact of belonging to another category of people.[72] Furthermore, ascetics isolate themselves from their fellow human beings, at least while they are in seclusion in the mountains. Both as wandering, homeless ascetics and as monks who live permanently in the mountains, they have withdrawn from traditional social roles and created new social relations.

What do these ascetic practices and the ascetics' self-transformation achieve? The answer varies, depending on whether the interpretation is more strongly marked by indigenous tradition or by esoteric Buddhism. In exercising their strict discipline, ascetics are reported to have visions of superhuman beings, and to see this as proof that they themselves have been granted superhuman powers by divinities. As H. Byron Earhart confirms, the goal of these ascetic exercises is primarily to renew or acquire superhuman powers that can then be put in the service of others.[73] In the spring, decked with green branches, ascetics return from the mountains to the villages, where they are greeted as virtuosos who have gained the power of the mountain god.[74] Earhart reports that for some Shugendo priests who never left the mountains, "the goal of life consisted in attaining ritual purity, whereas itinerant *yamabushi* strove to periodically revive and renew their power. However, ordinary members of the movement strove to acquire transcendent religious power in order to cope with the crises of everyday life—birth, illness, death."[75]

Carmen Blacker reports in still greater detail on the kind of superhuman powers gained through asceticism. It was believed that after climbing several holy mountains, standing under waterfalls and fasting, *yamabushi* would have the ability to control demons and drive out the evil spirits that cause disease and madness. With the gift of second sight, they could see the causes of illnesses and understand the language of animals and natural sounds. And with special concentration, they could make the fire spirit obey.[76]

The hardest ascetic practices, Rotermund explains, were required of those who strove to acquire superhuman powers.[77] The relation of these *yamabushis* to the laity consisted in healing them by exorcism.[78] Miyake mentions that Shugendo ascetics and priests sometimes acted as soothsayers and exorcists, using magical formulas and amulets. Some demonstrated their magico-religious powers in ways less useful to the laity, such as flying through the air, walking on sword blades or fire, or immersing themselves in boiling water.[79] All these practices, however, show that the principal effect of self-transformation consists in an empowerment of the holy self. This effect is not accidental but willed.

Daoists

As an illustration of Daoist virtuosity, I have selected the Chinese tale of the Seven Daoist Masters, an introduction to Daoist doctrine and practices that presumably goes back to oral traditions and was intended for the religious laity and novices.[80] The story describes the transformation of Wang Ch'ung-yang, one of the most important patriarchs of the school of "complete perfection," and that of his seven pupils—Ma Tan-yang, Sun Pu-erh, Ch'iu Ch'ang-ch'un, Liu Ch'ang-sheng, T'an Ch'ang-chen, Hao T'ai-ku, and Wang Yü-yang—into "immortals." This tale offers eight case studies through which we can typify transformation in virtuosos.

When Wang, a prosperous man, decided to seek enlightenment, he conceived a plan that would allow him to free himself of earthly concerns. He pretended to have had a stroke, and acted so strangely that soon all his friends, relatives, and servants kept away from him. His wife took over his business, and a servant simply brought food to his room three times a day. This solitude lasted for twelve years, during which Wang sought enlightenment and finally found it. Afterward, he followed the instructions Daoist immortals had given him, and set off on a quest for seven future pupils. He lived as a hermit, then as a beggar, and finally as a Daoist teacher.

His first pupils, a couple named Ma Tan-yang and Sun Pu-erh, also created a new social identity for themselves. First, they handed over all their property to Wang, so that he could use it to construct a meditation center. The estate, which had earlier been very busy, now became a rather unsociable place. After their initiation, the couple lived abstinently and considered each other "brother and sister in Dao."[81] Sun Pu-erh decided to seek enlightenment in Loyang, a place filled with power. When Wang tried to stop her, pointing out the dangers to which a beautiful woman traveling alone was exposed, she disfigured her face, blackened it, slipped out of the house, and lived from then on as a beggar.

Further examples of the complete transformation of social identity could be given. In addition to solitary life as a beggar, there are other amusing varieties and new forms of association. For example, during their training the seven pupils constituted a close community and later on repeatedly met each other as "immortals." Liu Ch'ang-sheng lived for over a year in a brothel in the company of attractive women in order to get his sex drive under control. When he had succeeded, he withdrew again to the loneliness of the mountains, achieved immortality after three years of meditation, and joined the heavenly community.

During his twelve years of isolation, Wang did not grow older; instead, he looked younger and healthier afterward than he had before.[82] We are reminded of the *Life of St. Antony*. The transformation of the bodily self is carried out through certain kinds of abstinence and control over the body. Alcohol, sexual longing, the desire for wealth, and yielding to anger must be avoided. The bases for surmounting these dependencies are meditation and "inner alchemy." Novices are to meditate for eight hours a day, but they are not bound to endure other ascetic discomforts. Other schools of Daoism prescribe a far more rigorous regimen.

The effects of self-transformation into an "immortal" are impressive. The two immortals that Master Wang has initiated disappear, changing themselves into a ray of light. Master Wang's spirit rises up to heaven, where he bows down before the Lord of the T'ai-pa star. The latter's scribe reads him a scroll that declares him to have been granted the title of an Enlightened Master who opens the way. The miraculous feats of "immortals" are awe-inspiring too. Daoist masters can develop such intense inner heat that they melt the snow around them and do not grow cold in winter even when spending the night in the open. They can predict the future and make rain, as did Ch'iu Ch'ang-ch'un. When on another occasion an attempt was to be made to poison Ch'iu, he foresaw the plot and took precautions that allowed him to survive. At the emperor's request, Ch'iu prayed for rain for three days under a blazing sun, until finally a cloud appeared and rain saved the harvest, thus preventing a famine. One "immortal" put out a great fire in the city of Han-yang by spitting a mouthful of wine onto the fire. Talismans of the "immortals" protect villages from the plague and bring them prosperity. These stories go on and on.[83] Through their ascetic discipline the "immortals" have acquired superhuman powers and are therefore in a position to avert calamity and suffering for ordinary mortals.

On the Logic of Virtuoso Practices

The examples presented above show that virtuoso practices—regardless of cultural differences, differing salvation goals and the paths to them, and processes of historical change—follow a logic that transcends time and place. For one thing, virtuosos pass through three phases of self-transformation. They work on their bodies, which they reshape by means of various exercises and deprivations so that they express a certain ethos and symbolize a new social status. They restructure their social relations by giving up their traditional bonds to family, relatives, neighbors, and friends, and joining groups of like-minded people or living among strangers or in solitude. Other social contacts focus on pupils, those seeking help, or laypersons from whom they receive support. In addition, there is a "spiritual" transformation. Social contacts become less important than communication with superhuman powers or concentration on the "sacred" that slumbers within, which has to be developed and activated. The result is always the achievement of superhuman power. Yet this power tends to be seen not as the goal of the exercise but as a gift of grace, an unintentional side effect, or a subordinate goal. Nonetheless, the very quantity of traditional legends reporting miracles shows that these play a major role in confirming the special status of virtuosos.

Virtuosos accept suffering in order to achieve first a temporary and then an eternal state of salvation. They have the strength to defy misfortune and suffering, which, on the one hand, brings them nearer to salvation and, on the other, provides the foundation for their special religious status, distinct from that of the laity and religious officials. The end result is that they transform themselves, with or without the help of higher forces, into superhuman powers that can avert misfortune, overcome crises, and produce or mediate salvation. In other words, virtuosos provide one model of the genesis of charisma.[84] What makes powers superhuman is primarily their ability to dispense blessings and salvation. As a rule, human beings can attain this status only by willingness to accept suffering and by mastering it. This constitutes the virtuosos' central achievement, which at the same time reveals the logic of religion. The promise to avert misfortune, to overcome crises, and to provide salvation presupposes powers that can keep this promise. Virtuosos show us how these powers originate and how the promise is made credible.

CHAPTER SEVEN

Turning toward Salvation:
Religious Propaganda

This study has sought to arrive at a theory of religion by systematizing the self-representations of various religions. Up to this point, I have used as my sources for analysis religious practices by laypersons and by virtuosos, and I have examined the premises and expectations that are implied in these practices. I have shown how communication with superhuman powers is central to their meaning. In this chapter, I will turn to religious propaganda, that is, efforts to move people to a religious change of direction or, to use the term broadly, a "conversion." These texts too are religious self-representations. If my interpretation of religious practices is based on more than a secondary aspect of religion, it must also be supported by religious propaganda. To that extent, this chapter puts the preceding chapters to the test. Here are the central questions: What reason is given for religious reorientation? What achievements do religions claim for themselves in conversion discourses? And what promises do religions make to those who convert?

Calls for conversion or evidence of an altered way of life may be addressed to members of one's own religious group in order to urge them to adhere more strictly to their religious duties. They may also be addressed to nonmembers so as to persuade them to join the group. Or they may take the form of mass appeals to whole population groups in the hope of moving them to a religious and moral revival, as we see in the case of prophetic movements. In what follows, I shall examine stories of conversion, reports of enlightenment, and prophetic appeals.

Conversion and Propaganda

In scholarly literature, conversion is commonly seen as an individual act of rethinking and reorienting the way one leads one's life, achieved through a sudden experience, a painful inner transformation, or a process of education. This emphasis on the individual, however, seems to represent a specifically Christian and thus historically contingent restriction of the concept of conversion. The way this concept is understood has repeatedly changed in the course of history. In early Christianity it was connected chiefly with ascetic trends that called for sexual abstinence in marriage or for withdrawal into the solitude of the desert.[1] Today, conversion is more often seen as a move from one religious group or denomination to another. On this view, conversions take place when Christians become Muslims, Hindus become Christians, or Jews become Buddhists, or even when Protestants become Catholics. On the other hand, moving from one Protestant denomination to another is seldom described as "conversion." Historically, mass conversions have not been uncommon. The Christianization of central and northern Europe and the spread of Buddhism in China, Japan, and Tibet were largely collective processes.[2]

In a classic study, Arthur Nock sought to define the concept of conversion more precisely, in order to distinguish between conversion and adherence.[3] To that end he emphasized differences between the various religions of late Roman antiquity. Whereas early Christianity made strong demands regarding one's way of life and membership in the community, the mystery religions required less strictness and exclusivity on the part of their adherents. Nock's definition, modeled on early Christianity, locates the concept of conversion very close to those of devotion or commitment. It indicates a radical rethinking of the individual's self-perception and lifestyle. The convert reorganizes his or her life on the basis of specifically religious principles.[4] Conversion presupposes a society with relatively strong social differentiation. For this reason alone, conversion does not occur in all religions, especially not in those where religious and political affiliations are inseparable.

Even in the fields of sociology and religious studies, conversion is not defined in a unified way; there are various methods of understanding and describing it.[5] One can choose, for example, a "culturally immanent" approach such as that of Lewis Rambo, who argues that "conversion is what a group or a person calls conversion."[6] This option may at first seem plausible. It solves the problem of the absence of conversion in a few traditions and takes into account the changeability of the concept, but it makes the concept of conversion analytically unusable. Which concepts in foreign languages are to be considered equivalents of the concept of conversion, and which not? What do we do with religious groups that have no concept of conversion but do recognize comparable processes, such as the quest for enlightenment? How do we deal with contradictions between the definitions offered by religious officials, local communities, and a convert's self-conception? Analytical concepts that are forced to get involved in theological debates do not lend themselves to systematic theory building.

Sociological literature on conversion concentrates almost exclusively on contemporary phenomena in industrialized countries.[7] Two perspectives are dominant. One of these defines conversion in purely operational terms as a change from one religious group to another. Based on the sociology of organizations and studies on social movements, this perspective equates conversion with success by religious organizations or movements in recruiting new members. Some authors highlight the attraction exercised by social groups and networks.[8] The convert is seen as a relatively passive part of his own process of conversion, a kind of tabula rasa that can be written upon at will. It is assumed that any special rethinking or commitment on the part of the individual concerned is either irrelevant or learned after the event. The content of religious ideas and practices, as well as the value judgments expressed in the way groups and organizations are structured, are thus regarded as relatively arbitrary and less important than measurable market factors. There is little investigation into who actually influences whom within social networks, and why the influence doesn't work in the opposite direction.

Authors taking this approach pursue a kind of religious market research based on the psychology of advertising. They are primarily concerned with the growth or contraction of religious groups, not with meaningful action. As in advertising, it is assumed that any product can be sold to anyone if only it is marketed correctly. But unlike the psychology of advertising, this approach fails to investigate even the affinity between religious taste and socioeconomic or demographic characteristics such as class, level of education, gender, age, regional origin, and cultural shaping.

The fact that this way of proceeding was developed chiefly in the United States, from the 1960s on, makes its perspective easier to understand. The existence of a religious marketplace is assumed, a marketplace that targets especially white, middle-class young people who are experimenting with religion. But this assumption underestimates the human capacity for action and the convert's active participation in his or her own conversion. Historically, its usefulness is limited, because it is based on cases in which the costs of apostasy are small. Moreover, it is relatively unspecific analytically. The grounds and mechanisms it uses to explain religious conversion are applicable to nearly all recruiting processes, whether these involve religious communities, gangs, political parties, or rabbit-breeding associations.

This approach does, however, attribute great importance to the convert's role learning and thus points to an important analytical level.

In contrast to supply-oriented approaches, those based on action theory seek to reconstruct, understand, and explain the process of conversion from the convert's point of view.[9] Many of these studies have contributed valuable insights into the dynamics of such transformations. Earlier investigations repeatedly showed that conversions were reactions to crises and thus, in my terminology, to experiences of misfortune and suffering. William James coined the term "the sick soul" in describing the reintegration of the self as the central meaning of conversion.[10] Sociological theories or models of conversion have, of course, also been based on the close connection between crisis and conversion. Thus John Lofland and Rodney Stark, in their classic essay, spoke of the "tensions" or "problems" that make people into religious seekers.[11] In his survey of the literature on conversion, Lewis Rambo expressly takes experiences of crisis as his starting point. These crises may be religious, political, psychological, or cultural in kind.[12]

In order to lend more precision to the debate, David Snow and Richard Machalek, using a study of conversions in the United States in the 1970s, proposed a series of indicators. They pointed out that converts, perceiving themselves as new persons, reinterpret their biography, adopt a new, comprehensive explanatory schema, abandon analogical thinking, and learn to play the convert's role.[13] A before-and-after temporal dimension acquires central importance.[14] As a rule, the period before is described as crisis ridden, independently of whether an awareness of crisis existed beforehand. This dimension becomes empirically accessible through autobiographical accounts of conversion. Moreover, this new definition of the self implies a modification of behavior with regard to other people and groups. Conversion entails a reevaluation of social relations as well as new connections and social distancing from old ones.

I could make things easier for myself by referring to reported experiences of crises and seeing my theory as confirmed by them. Conversions would then be seen as reactions to experiences of calamity and suffering, and the turn toward religion would represent a confirmation of the belief that conversions can avert misfortune, overcome crises, and provide salvation. But such a solution is unacceptable both empirically and methodologically. First, the concept of crisis is somewhat vague. After the fact, one can find a "crisis" in the life of every convert. Second, before their conversions, converts are not always conscious of being in crisis, and for that reason some writers deny that crisis experiences cause conversions. According to these writers, a sense of crisis can also be the result of conversion, as converts reevaluate their lives retrospectively and perceive their earlier life as characterized by crisis.[15]

It is conceivable that a true sense of crisis is not formed even after the fact, and that what actually happens is that converts adopt a conversion story standardized by the religious community, through which they confirm for themselves and others their membership in the new group. In suggesting this, I am not claiming that conversions are never connected with subjective experiences of crisis. But it is equally possible that the rhetoric of crisis derives from conversion scripts. It is also conceivable that subjective experience intersects here with the interpretations objectively available. Converts feels that they are understood because they find their experience of crisis in the conversion script.

One can no more infer a factual crisis from the rhetoric of crisis than one can infer a factual absence of crisis from a lack of consciousness of crisis, since consciousness of something can be repressed. Consider, for instance, alcoholics who think their dependency is not a problem. No matter how it is used, the explanation of conversion based on the theory of crisis often lacks convincing proof and leads to insoluble problems of interpretation. Crises, especially "unconscious" ones, can be found in every person if we dig deep enough. Most people, however, do not react to crises by converting. So my theory would not be very convincing if I were to base it on the crisis rhetoric used by converts.

Such explanations fail to support my theory on methodological grounds as well. In my analysis of the meaning of religious practices, I have already rejected subjective interpretations and referred instead to the objective level of "liturgies." Here I will proceed in a similar manner, interpreting conversion narratives not as subjective explanations but as religious propaganda, in the sense of religions' self-representation. The meaning of religion develops most reliably, from a methodological point of view, in institutionalized meanings. However, these too include conversion narratives or experiences of enlightenment.

As I have repeatedly stressed, my theory of religion offers not a functional but rather an interpretive explanation of religion. Averting misfortune, overcoming crises, and providing salvation are not latent functions of religion but represent the claims of religion. They are therefore expressed in the respective institutionalized structures of meaning. So I am concerned here not with "objective" crises, however these might be defined, or with the factual overcoming of crises and the production of a psychic or social equilibrium, but rather with the "promises" of a religion as these are expressed in its propaganda. Clearly something "happens" to individuals who "convert," no matter whether this process is defined as a change of association, a change of faith, or religious commitment. At least in their own self-conceptions, converts often become different persons, reorder their lives, associate with different people, and communicate with different superhuman powers or with the same powers in a different way. But sociology's methods are inadequate to achieve access to this inner process of transformation or even to grasp it theoretically. As a rule, we study not conversions but converts, whom we use to reconstruct the process of conversion. To be sure, one can undertake an ethnographic study of conversion and try to follow or reconstruct the process in detail.[16] But since the investigator usually becomes acquainted with converts only after their conversion, and since conversion consists in being socialized into a religious community and learning its religious practices and ideas, conversion narratives are always reconstructions that are guided by a pre-set script. How closely the convert adheres to a script may vary a great deal. But in general we can say that a "conversion" that contradicts the group's script will not be recognized as a conversion. Hence, all conversion narratives must be conventionalized to a certain degree. Many Christian conversion stories refer, for example, to St. Paul or St. Augustine, and many Buddhist accounts of enlightenment refer to Gautama. It would be a misunderstanding of the genre of such conventionalized narratives to read them as empirically verifiable reports of an experience.

Codified and conventionalized conversion stories thus represent models for successful and correct conversions, which are recommended for imitation by others. To that extent they obviously serve the needs of propaganda. A model is propagated that demonstrates how religion keeps its promise. In this respect, reports of enlightenment in the Buddhist or Daoist traditions resemble conversion narratives in the Abrahamic religions.

Nearly all religions have propaganda that is addressed inwardly, to their own members. In nineteenth-century Protestantism, the concept of an "inner mission" was widely used for this. In Judaism, the *haredim* recruit among Jews who, from the *haredim*'s point of view, have fallen away from right belief. Most fundamentalist movements recruit new members within their own religions. Some religious traditions, such as Buddhism and Christianity, also recruit among members of other religions.

In all these recruitment efforts, stories of religious reorientation play a major role, whether they are reports of conversions or legends about saints, the enlightened, immortals, the founders of religions, or prophets. So narratives of all these types can be compared as forms of propaganda. Narratives are produced that provide grounds for the new commitment and religious rethinking. My own interpretation focuses on the structure of meaning in such narratives: on the one hand, the occasion for religious conversion, and, on the other, the promise made in the event of conversion. From the point of view of my theory of religion, religious propaganda must consist primarily in stimulating the demand that a religion be able to avert misfortune, overcome crises, and dispense salvation. I expect all three elements in such narratives, but not necessarily in the following order: an actual experience of calamity or the recognition of a menacing or harmful condition, the "experience" of an external or internal superhuman power, and finally the promise of salvation, which is connected with activating this power or with devotion to it.

Conversion Narratives

The prototype of Christian conversion narratives is the transformation of Saul into Paul, as he himself reports it.[17] Saul is represented as a persecutor of the followers of Jesus, whom he considers members of a heterodox Jewish sect. As he heads for Damascus, where he is to arrest Christians, a light from heaven suddenly flashes about him. He falls to the ground and hears a voice saying to him: "Saul, Saul, why do you persecute me?" The voice identifies itself as Jesus. When Saul asks what he should do, the voice tells him to go to Damascus, where he will receive further instructions. The men accompanying Saul can see the light, but they do not hear the voice.[18] Saul, who is dazzled and cannot see, is led to Damascus and there he meets Ananias, who says to him: "The God of our fathers appointed you to know his will, to see the Just One and to hear a voice from his mouth; for you will be a witness for him to all men of what you have seen and heard. And now why do you wait? Rise and be baptized, and wash away your sins, calling on his name."[19]

The narrative next makes a threefold reference to misfortune and suffering. First, Saul seeks to bring misfortune on Christians. But Jesus demonstrates his power to protect them in this case. Second, Saul remains blind for three days. And third, he understands that he has to suffer in order to make his transition. Furthermore, the narrative makes the experience of superhuman power central. Saul experiences a direct revelation in which he communicates with the resurrected Jesus. After returning to Jerusalem, Paul prays in the temple, enters into a state of ecstasy, and sees Jesus.[20] Here he already anticipates the eternal state of salvation that was promised him through baptism and the forgiveness of his sins.

A more recent example from colonial India confirms the influence of the Pauline model. Sundar Singh grew up in late nineteenth-century India as a member of the Sikh community, but he was educated primarily in the

Hindu scriptures. He corresponds to the type of the religious seeker looking for answers to existential questions. Despite his initial, profound rejection of the missionary school, which he left after a short time, Singh ultimately converted to Christianity and became a Christian sadhu. He describes his conversion, which estranged him from his family, as follows: Full of doubts, he prays for a revelation. If there is a God, he should show himself to him, otherwise he intends to commit suicide. Expecting Buddha, Krishna, or another Hindu divinity to be revealed to him, he suddenly sees a light in the room. In this light, Jesus appears to Singh and asks him why he is persecuting him.[21]

Another model of the Christian conversion narrative comes from the writings of Eusebius. This theologian reports that Constantine, in his efforts to overthrow his rival Maxentius, had only a small, inferior army at his disposal.[22] Since Maxentius had made use of magical powers to achieve his ends, Constantine also sought the help of a god. Various gods were eliminated because they proved themselves incapable of warding off misfortune. But Constantine's father believed in a god who had always proved powerful. Constantine now prayed to this god, who answered in the form of two visions. First, Constantine saw, over the noonday sun, a trophy in the shape of a cross, with the inscription "In hoc signo vinces." On the following night, Christ appeared to him and advised him to reproduce the sign and use it as protection against his enemy. All this was done. He was victorious. And the god who had revealed himself as the Christian god was from then on befittingly revered by Constantine.

It is not hard to identify the three elements here, though they refer to an entirely different context, and they function "magically." Misfortune in the form of a military defeat is averted. The experience of a divine reality is described in two visions in which the Christian god reacts to Constantine's attempt to communicate. And this god proves his superior power by protecting Constantine against his enemy's stronger forces and enabling him to win a victory. In the rest of the text it becomes clear that superhuman powers are measured by their ability to ward off dangers and to provide power and success.

St. Augustine's *Confessions* can be interpreted as a long conversion narrative describing, in a dialogue with God, his transformation from a sinner on his way to damnation into a saved Christian.[23] In this autobiographical narrative, a professional rhetorician puts to work all the stylistic tools at his disposal in order to propagate his religion in its battle against "paganism." As such, it is a particularly interesting case for our purposes, and because of its complexity it must be examined in greater detail.

Although Augustine's conversion is often reduced to the command *Tolle, lege* ("take up [the book] and read") in book 8, there can be no doubt that he describes his conversion not as a spontaneous "experience" but rather as a gradual process. In doing so, he draws on earlier models, but he also wants to offer himself as a paradigm of successful conversion. So I will assemble all the descriptions of conversion in the *Confessions* and analyze them as Augustine presents them.

The first report of a conversion occurs in book 4. Augustine writes about a student friend who had been baptized while he was sick and near death. Augustine assumed that after his friend recovered, he would not take the baptism seriously. But to his surprise, the friend was upset by his mockery. Before they were able to work out their differences, the friend had a relapse and died (Augustine, 57ff.). This story shows the act of baptism being performed in a crisis situation, evidently on the assumption that it is the last opportunity to ensure eternal salvation for a man who is deathly ill. However, when a short time later Augustine himself fell ill and was near death, he did not ask to be baptized (86–88). This could be seen as a cleverly chosen counterexample intended to demonstrate his stubbornness. But conversion is usually represented less as an act carried out by human beings than as an act of divine grace. In any case, the friend does not serve as a model for Augustine's own conversion.

Throughout the *Confessions*, Augustine reports on his intellectual transition from Manichaeism to Neoplatonism and finally to Pauline Christianity. And it is certainly no accident that his turn toward Paul takes place at the end of book 7, that is, immediately before the description of Augustine's own conversion. Before we get to that point, however, Augustine narrates other conversions.

Unable to make up his mind, Augustine seeks out his friend Simplicianus, a leading Neoplatonist who later succeeded his pupil Ambrose as bishop of Milan. Simplicianus tells him the story of the rhetorician Victorinus's conversion. One day, Victorinus confessed that he was a Christian. As a rhetorician, he had publicly defended the pagan gods and taken part in pagan rites; but in his old age he had read the Bible and Christian authors. Simplicianus was still not sure how serious the conversion was, since Victorinus did not want to make it public. Consequently, Victorinus changed his behavior, fearing that Christ would reject him at the Last Judgment. He had himself officially baptized and publicly confessed his belief, as was usual in his time, before a large audience (147ff.). He then had to give up his position as a rhetorician, because Christians were not allowed to hold such a position under Emperor Julian. Augustine sees very clearly that Simplicianus has told him this story in order to get him to convert. He confirms the propaganda goal of the conversion narrative when he writes: "But when that man of Thine, Simplicianus, related to me this of Victorinus, I was on fire to imitate him; for this very end had he related it" (152).

Still other conversion models are inserted before we arrive at Augustine's own. First, a certain Ponticianus comes to visit Augustine and finds him reading the Apostle Paul. Their conversation moves from Paul to Antony to the desert fathers. Finally, Ponticianus reports on his own conversion, which took place when he was still an imperial official. During a walk with a colleague, he stopped at a cottage where he found Athanasius's "Life of St. Antony." Reading it suddenly opened his eyes and those of his friend, so that they decided to give up their posts and convert to Christianity. Both of them were engaged to be married, but their brides, on hearing of the men's decision, spontaneously "dedicated their virginity unto God" (157).

It is the example set by these men and women that eventually leads Augustine to examine his own life, putting him into a state of despair that he describes as an illness. In his extremity he seeks refuge in a garden, where, as he sits weeping, he hears a child's voice uttering the famous words "Take up and read!" He interprets this as a command from God instructing him to open the Bible and read the first passage on which his eye falls. That was also how Antony's conversion took place (167). The passage in Romans 13:13–14 ("not in reveling and drunkenness, not in debauchery and licentiousness, not in quarreling and jealousy. But put on the Lord Jesus Christ and make no provision for the flesh, to gratify its desires"), which seems to refer directly to his sensual life, dissipates his last doubts and resistance. Augustine converts.

Following Victorinus's example, Augustine resigned his office as a rhetorician. But he had an explanation ready that was far more profane than that of Victorinus and that did not bring him into conflict with others: he claimed to be sick. "In this very summer my lungs began to give way, amid too great literary labour, and to breathe deeply with difficulty, and by the pain in my chest to show that they were injured, and to refuse any full or lengthened speaking; this had troubled me, for it almost constrained me of necessity to lay down that burden of teaching, or, if I could be cured and recover, at least to intermit it" (171).

Augustine's baptism took place in a rather unspectacular fashion. The crisis had been surmounted, the patient healed. The conversion narrative includes threats of misfortune in the event that conversion does not take place, as well as characterizations of God as a conqueror of crises and a rescuer.[24] It also throws light on conversion as propaganda, from Paul to Antony and on to Victorinus and Ponticianus.

Ignatius of Loyola's decision to lead his life in accord with religious principles, as he describes it in his autobiography, largely corresponds to our model.[25] A soldier and a playboy, Ignatius is so severely wounded in battle that he almost dies. After receiving the last rites, he is miraculously healed. In order to pass the time, he asks for books, but his host's library contains none of his favorite chivalric novels. He finds only a book about the life of Christ and one about the saints. He is fascinated by St. Francis of Assisi and the Dominicans, and makes up his mind to follow their example. He undergoes an increasingly intense inner conflict, which he interprets as a battle between worldly, demonic powers and God. One night he has a vision. He sees Mary with the child Jesus in her arms. From that moment on, he gives up worldly life and turns to his religious mission. Here again we find the central themes. The experience of serious injury, healing through the power of God in the form of the last rites, and, in his vision of Mary, a further experience of the reality of a superhuman power.

Conversions to Islam have produced narratives that in some ways differ totally from those produced by Christianity. Over and over, they occur in unspectacular ways and without the subjective inner struggles that are described in Christian accounts of conversion. Historically, many conversions were connected with Islam's political expansion and the power of attraction exercised by a new civilization on conquered peoples.[26] Conversion also offered tax reductions, career opportunities, and social advancement, as well as access to social support networks. But this picture is one-sided. Many reports of conversion, especially those provided by intellectuals, emphasize that Islam's persuasive force lies in its rationality when compared with polytheism, Judaism, or Christianity; hence, such reports are often used for propaganda and polemics.[27] In addition to intellectual grounds, dreams and visions frequently play an important role, as for instance in the case of Said ben Hasan, an educated Jew. During a serious illness he has a vision in which he hears a voice telling him he will survive if he reads the Al-Hamd sura.[28] He does as he is told, survives, and converts to the Muslim faith.

Active missionary work is also performed in Islam; one example is the Sufi mission in the Ottoman Empire in the sixteenth century.[29] In these narratives, conversions to Islam take place chiefly as reactions to miraculous events. An unbeliever is converted by the miracle-working powers of a Sufi holy man, and Christian knights convert because they attribute Muslim knights' superior strength to Islam.[30] These proofs of power in battle, or in the ability to heal or to perform miracles, are often cited as the grounds for conversion. The theme of contests in which Allah manifests his superior power is also found in Otemish Hajji's report on the conversion of Uzbek Khan (1313–1341). The impetus for conversion came from Allah himself, who inspired four (Sufi) saints to go to the ruler's residence and challenge the "infidel magicians" gathered there to a religious duel.[31] One of the saints and an infidel magician climb into a hot oven. While the magician burns up, the Muslim emerges unharmed. Seeing this demonstration of power, the khan and his people immediately convert to Islam.[32] Allah alone has proved that he can effectively protect his followers against harm.

As a rule, Judaism does not proselytize among non-Jews, and for that reason conversions to Judaism have produced fewer paradigmatic conversion narratives. Nonetheless, particularly in the Middle Ages, conversion narratives played a certain role as means of propaganda and polemics. Documents indicate that during the Middle Ages even Christian officials and scholars sometimes went over to Judaism. These include, in the ninth century, a certain Bodo, who worked at the court of Louis the Pious and later called himself Eleazar, and, in the eleventh century, Andreas, archbishop of Bari.[33] On the other hand, some conversions to Judaism were kept secret for obvious reasons or did not produce any typical propaganda reports.[34]

Conversion can also be connected with fears that the old gods will take revenge and cause calamities for human beings. A few examples are associated with the spread of Buddhism in Asia. As we saw in chapter 2, Buddhism's first attempt to gain a foothold in Japan failed because an epidemic broke out.[35] In Tibet, an outbreak of plague and other diseases caused Buddhist monks to be expelled, even though monastic communities and laymen had already been living there in accord with Buddhist precepts for twelve years.[36] *The Testament of Ba* mentions that the conversion of the Tibetan ruler Trhi Desongtsen to Buddhism met with a variety of objections. Buddhism, it was said, was not the traditional religion. People distrusted it because it did not provide for the pacification and veneration of the tutelary gods. It was feared that it would harm the ruler, threaten the government's ability to carry out its tasks, and cause epidemics among humans and animals. When a famine broke out, it was attributed to the ruler's conversion to Buddhism.[37] All these fears confirm the basic assumptions of my theory of religion.

Reports of Enlightenment

In Buddhism, the quest for enlightenment is clearly connected with the experience of human liability to calamity and crisis. According to legend, it was encounters with age, illness, and death that allowed the bodhisattva Vipassi and then Gautama to follow the path to renunciation of the world.[38] For Gautama, the search for enlightenment led to a series of erroneous paths until finally the "middle" way was found to be the right one. Enlightenment produces an inner distancing from the world and its apparent good or ill fortune and ends in a condition of absorption into the eternal, the timeless, and the immutable. In the Buddhist tradition, Gautama's narrative of enlightenment underwent many rewritings that then served as models for later stories.[39] A good example is provided by Tambiah's classic study *The Buddhist Saints of the Forest and the Cult of Amulets*, which begins with an analysis of the hagiography of Phra Acharn Mun.[40]

The Singhalese monk Asmandale Ratanapala's self-reformation, described by Michael Carrithers, is an attempt to escape from a disastrous condition of impurity—presumably involving sexual transgressions with other monks—and to achieve the holy condition of purity. In following this path, Ratanapala is excluded from the monastery and plagued by sickness, which he interprets as punishment for his offenses. But his quest for purity and enlightenment finally succeeds when, after overcoming many obstacles, he manages to gather a small group of monks around him and retires with them into the forests.[41]

The basic interpretive model is also seen in less spectacular cases, such as the reports of two Japanese women who visited a Zen meditation center in search of enlightenment.[42] Nakayam Momoyo was a pious woman. She was married to a Buddhist missionary who spent most of his time in faraway Hawaii. She herself ran a kindergarten. But she derived all her joy in life from her son, whom she raised mainly on her own. When her son was killed in the last months of the Second World War, she lost all will to live and all pleasure in life; but the voice of her son urged her to go on living. She sought out a Zen center and wrote about her struggle with meditation. In the end, she did achieve enlightenment and experienced life with her dead son as full of joy. She thanked Buddha and the Patriarchs for making her life worth living again.[43]

An entirely different kind of experience of misfortune is reported by Nachii Keido. When still young, she left her parents' home "to escape from this burning house of the triple world." She immediately joined a convent and devoted her religious life to Kannon, the goddess of compassion. Nachii Keido was a simple woman who had had little education. She wanted to understand the nature of Kannon but doubted her ability to do so. She finally found the solution to this painful problem in Zen meditation. Her early uncertainty left her, and she became one with Kannon.[44]

A report on the conversion of a German to Tibetan Buddhism may seem more banal, but it also revolves around the motif of overcoming fear and suffering.[45] The convert, "Holger M.," writes:

> In my room, I had all kinds of Buddhas, which I had brought back from my travels, both thangkas and statues, and I counted them: there were twenty-seven, altogether . . . and for some reason I bought a little thangka at the Swayambunath temple . . . showing the bodhisattva Avalokitesvara, as Chenresig, four-armed . . . as I sat there with my negative thoughts, prey to my fears, it was as if someone were knocking, knocking so softly on the top of my head . . . I felt it quite bodily, felt that someone was knocking . . . and then I stopped for a moment and looked up . . . and saw this Avalokitesvara sitting directly opposite me, yes, . . . on this thangka, and it had four hands and four arms, and it said to me, yes, you need not fear . . . well, I thought . . . take refuge in Buddha, take refuge, nothing can happen to you, and afterward I thought, okay, it's interesting that refuge comes to you in this way.[46]

Prophetic Promises

Under the rubric of prophetic propaganda I am subsuming the ideologies of messianic, millenarian, apocalyptic, or fundamentalist movements that promulgate a religious message of salvation in which conversion or radical change is called for.[47] As a rule, the fate of political or religious communities is at stake. What these ideologies have in common is a view of the present as a time of calamity and corruption, as well as the proclamation of a future state of salvation either for a people or for the elect. Salvation is often produced by a savior or a messiah, usually after a period of destruction.

The prophets of the Sun Dance movement, for example, have a paradigmatic character among Indian tribes threatened with annihilation, and express the whole tragedy and the hope for divine intervention. All Indians had to dance constantly, without interruption, and then the Great Spirit would come in the following spring and bring much game with him. All Indians who had died would be resurrected and be young and strong. Even the blind would see again. When the Old Man returned, then the Indians would return to the mountains, far away from the whites, who would no longer be able to harm them. Then a great flood would come, and drown all the whites. After the water subsided, only Indians would live on the land, and there would be a great abundance of all kinds of game.[48]

In the case of messianic expectations, the appearance of the savior is often connected with special rituals—in this case, dancing—or with an inner conversion that is expressed outwardly in the way life is led, as in fundamentalist movements. Prophetic appeals emphasize the necessity of turning toward right action or right belief, and threaten disaster and punishment in the event that this turnaround does not take place. Salvation can also be produced, via the logic of salvation history, as a consequence of divine dispensation.[49] Internally, such movements and ideas may be diverse, salvation often being conceived as a reformist or revolutionary return to an authentic order. But even rulers have claimed messianic legitimation for themselves, as did Shah Ismail, the founder of the Safavid dynasty, or the Ottoman sultan Suleiman.[50] In the context of my theory of religion, such details play only a subordinate role.

Abrahamic Traditions

Prophecy and messianism are central components of the Jewish tradition that have been nourished by experiences of being exiled, conquered, repressed, expelled, and persecuted.[51] The prophet Isaiah represents a classic formulation of pre-exilic messianic expectations. A ruler is announced under whose dominion peace and justice will be established. Even nature will be peaceful and well disposed toward humans. "The wolf shall dwell with the lamb, the leopard lie down with the kid; the calf, the beast of prey, and the fatling together, with a little boy to herd them. [. . .] So rain will be provided for the seed with which you sow the ground, and the bread that the ground brings forth shall be rich and fat."[52]

The post-exilic text concerning the prophet Haggai describes the return of the Jewish people out of the Babylonian captivity. Haggai's prophecies depict a condition of calamity and suffering that is traced back to the fact that the temple in Jerusalem was not rebuilt. "That is why the skies above you have withheld [their] moisture and the earth has withheld its yield, and I have summoned fierce heat upon the land—upon the hills, upon the new grain and wine and oil, upon all that the ground produces, upon man and beast and upon all the fruits of labor."[53]

The way out of calamity leads through the reconstruction of the temple. God will make the temple splendid by filling it with the treasures of all peoples, with silver and gold, and it will be a place of peace. The building of the temple will bring about the destruction of other kingdoms and make Jerusalem powerful, prosperous, and peaceful. "And I will overturn the thrones of kingdoms and destroy the might of the kingdoms of the nations."[54] On the day of salvation, Zerubbabel, the Lord's chosen, will become king.

The sermons delivered by Savonarola in 1494 focus on the prophet Haggai (or Aggeus), drawing a parallel between Jerusalem and the situation in Florence. The Medici had just fled the city, and a new order had to be established. "I tell you, do first those two things I told you another time, that is, that everyone go to confession and be purified of sins, and let everyone attend to the common good of the city; and if you will do this, your city will be glorious. [. . .] But if you will not do what I tell you, God will elect those who [. . .] want to see you divided, and this will be your final destruction."[55]

Savonarola repeatedly warned the citizens of Florence to turn their lives around. They had to do penance and adopt a Christian way of life; otherwise they were in danger of being punished in hell. But he also wanted a kind of mass conversion. His message was political as well as individual, and related to the condition of the community as a whole. In another sermon full of apocalyptic expectations, Savonarola spoke of the conversion of pagan nations. But this could happen only if the citizens of Florence and the church had already renewed themselves.[56] In his sermon of December 10, 1494, he spoke particularly clearly about his anticipation of a new age. He described Florence as a patient full of wounds. Florence needed a physician who could slowly heal it, wound by wound. That physician was Christ. The cure consisted in two steps. First, everyone had to be spiritually renewed and go to confession and communion during the approaching Christmas season. Second, all citizens had to become politically active and establish a Christian republic. In this way Florence would become God's agent. Savonarola intended this promise to be taken not only in a spiritual sense but also in a very concrete political and economic sense. It had been revealed to him, so he claimed, that Florence was to become a model for all Italy. As a new center of power, it would increase its political influence and its wealth. The pious city, like the Jerusalem of the Second Temple in Haggai's prophecy, is a powerful and rich city:[57]

> This Florence is the navel of Italy, and your counsels will reshape everything through the light and grace that you will be given by God. [. . .] Florence will have countless riches, and God will increase all you have. [. . .] You will extend your dominion and in this way possess temporal and spiritual power, and you will have such an abundant blessing that you will say: "We don't want any more!"[58]

The path laid out by Savonarola thus leads from sickness to grace. He confirms this prophecy once more in his report on the revelations he has had and his embassy to Paradise. There he received the following message: "Florence, dear to our God and the Lord Jesus Christ, my Son, and also to me, hold fast to the faith, be constant in prayer, and firm in patience. Through these means you will gain glory with men and eternal salvation with God."[59]

Savonarola's apocalyptic expectations run along the same lines. Florence, Rome, and Italy find themselves at the end of an age, the fourth age. The first age was that of the Apostles, the second that of the martyrs, the third that of heretics, and the fourth that of the indifferent.[60] But now a new age is dawning: "It is necessary that this fourth age come to an end, that the church renew itself, that the fifth age begin, the conversion of unbelievers take place, and the Christians stand where they have to fight against the Antichrist."[61]

The model for the new age is provided by primitive Christianity, a society with a pious way of life that is pleasing to God.[62] Savonarola also frequently refers to seven ages, which end with the Last Judgment. His apocalyptic speculations, which were influenced by Joachimite millenarianism, are somewhat inconsistent systematically but very effective rhetorically.

In Islam, the idea of a messiah is expressed in the expectation of a Mahdi, a "guided one" who establishes a kingdom of justice.[63] Following the Hadith literature, which is also discussed in detail by Ibn Khaldun, this idea of a righteous leader developed in early Islam, often connected with longing for the Prophet Muhammad's original community.[64] As Mercedes Garcia-Arenal notes, Islamic messianism embodies the longing for the original order, in which the community was divinely guided. At the same time, it seeks to realize this idea of an eternal righteous order for the whole of humanity.[65] In Islam, the messianic idea is politically ambivalent, for it can be used both to criticize and to legitimate the ruling power, as it was under the Ummayads, Abbasids, and Fatimids, and in the Ottoman Empire.[66]

Messianic ideas also vary between the Sunni and Shiite traditions.[67] In Shiite Islam, the Mahdi is considered to be immanent. He lives hidden among us, and precisely when he will reveal himself and act is uncertain. When he shows himself, however, he will do away with the calamities of this world and create a kingdom of righteousness and peace.[68] The Mahdi's function is to produce righteousness, release the whole world from repression, suffering, and war, and introduce an age of spiritual and physical bliss.[69] The whole world will then turn to Islam.[70] Similarly, a late twentieth-century Shiite treatise declares that the Qur'anic prophecy of the inevitable victory of Islam after the return of the Mahdi will be realized. He will battle evil, heal the world's illnesses, and establish a world order based on the Islamic doctrine of righteousness, fairness, and virtue. From then on there will be only one religion and one government in the world.[71]

The prophetic and millenarian ideas of the Abrahamic traditions clearly confirm the central meaning of religion's promise to avert disaster, overcome crises, and provide salvation. Salvation is primarily related not to a vague beyond but to the here and now, the social and political order of the present or the future.

East Asian Traditions

Prophetic propaganda is not limited to Abrahamic religions; it is also found in Buddhism and Daoism. Daoist messianism probably first developed with the collapse of the Han dynasty (206 BCE–220 CE).[72] It incorporates the idea of a royal savior, which is already found in Confucius's *Analects*, and thus remained associated with the notion of an ideal ruler. The Chinese ruler needed the mandate of heaven; but heaven could withdraw its mandate from an unworthy or incompetent ruler. Bad harvests, catastrophic floods, earthquakes, epidemics, and social unrest were interpreted as signs that the ruler had lost his mandate. Daoist messianism picks up this idea and drafts harmonious utopias. Thus, for example, the past age of great peace (T'ai-ping) is described as a time when nature itself was not threatening but constantly productive and moderate. There were no bad harvests or premature deaths, and the climate was friendly to humans.[73]

As in Islam, the idea of a royal savior is ambivalent in Daoism, for it can be interpreted in a revolutionary or a restorative way. Rulers can appropriate it in order to legitimate themselves, but the idea can also develop a revolutionary process directed against corrupt rulers or a whole dynasty. For instance, Lao-tzu, having become a god, proclaimed: "Men are in despair; everywhere epidemics and famines rage. In order to change your fate, I will make the Han government totter. [. . .] I have revealed myself many times in order to save humanity. [. . .] Few understand me, many do not believe in me."[74]

A strong apocalyptic tone is found in the work *Spirit Spells of the Abyss*, in which a great flood is predicted that will destroy half of humanity. Wind and rain do not come at the desired time of year, and the harvest no longer ripens. Humans become evil and are wiped out by epidemics. Only the Daoists will be saved, and then a new redeemer will appear, an emissary sent by the god Lao to help them establish the kingdom of peace.[75]

Erik Zürcher has developed a model of Daoist messianism that contains six elements: the crisis, the savior, his helpers, the apocalyptic battle, the separation of those destined for salvation from those doomed to death, and the creation of an ideal order.[76] This Daoist messianism influenced Buddhist messianism in China. The crisis is not only a cosmological turning point but also a punishment inflicted by heaven for humans' moral depravity. The savior has superhuman powers and is either a high-ranking immortal or a god, and his helpers are saints with superhuman powers. In an apocalyptic battle, evil people are destroyed and only pious Daoists survive. They live in a paradisiacal condition for thousands of years. It is not hard to see that Daoism's prophetic propaganda claims that it can protect people from disaster and bring them into a lasting state of salvation.

We find the same paradigm in South Asia. The *Kalachakra Tantra*, written during a period when Indian Buddhism was threatened by the expansion of Islam, contains a prophecy: in the present age of degeneration, the Muslim barbarians will take control of South Asia and eliminate the true religion from their empire. At the end of this period, however, a Buddhist warrior-king will emerge in the inner-Asian kingdom of Sambhala, and with the help of the Brahmin gods he will defeat the barbarians' armies in a decisive battle. The king will reestablish Buddhist dharma, and a realm of happiness, prosperity, and uprightness will be established.[77]

The writings of Nichiren (1222–1282), founder of a branch of Japanese Buddhism named after him, bear the clear imprint of a catastrophic situation in Japan.[78] In his letters and other writings, Nichiren describes an apocalyptic scenario. Famine and epidemics rage. The death toll of humans and animals is massive and seemingly endless. People, horses, and cattle lie dead in the street. Bridges, lookout points, and trade routes are littered with the bones of the dead. Beggars are seen everywhere. Half of the households have disappeared. Parents have lost their children, children their parents. People are so desperate that they eat the flesh of the dead.[79]

Nichiren blames this catastrophic situation on other schools of Buddhism—such as Jodo (Pure Land) Buddhism, Shingon Buddhism, and Zen Buddhism—which are spreading false doctrines and practices and denying the supreme authority of the Lotus Sutra. But everyone can be saved, even those who have committed the worst sins. The only ones who cannot be forgiven are those who spread disbelief and false doctrines, who slander the law (dharma) or merely pretend that they are realizing Buddhist principles and put themselves above others.[80] So long as false doctrines are being spread, beneficent gods and the heavenly ruler will leave the country,[81] and evil demons will take their place.[82] Only when the authority of the Lotus Sutra alone is considered valid will peace be restored, and people be able to live in contentment and tranquillity, copying sutras and meditating.[83] As in Islamic messianism, disaster can be overcome only if the right religion prevails everywhere. In some religious movements and ideologies, this salvation-producing unity is achieved through conversion, and in others through the destruction of unbelievers. But salvation is always connected with the establishment of the right religion, with right practice, and with right belief.

Even in modern Japan we find millenarian and apocalyptic movements. Omotokyo, a religious group founded in 1892, acquired great influence between 1910 and 1935.[84] In its various manifestos, millenarian and apocalyptic elements appear in diverse forms. The first divine message of 1917 announces that Japan needs Shinto and its tutelary gods. Foreign lands live in the age of wild animals; they are evil. Japan also lives in barbarism, but the *kami* will transform the country, and their commands will then be strictly followed.[85] In the 1980s and 1990s, apocalyptic expectations were prominently represented by Aum Shinrikyao, with deadly results for many.[86]

In general, these texts confirm the meaning of the practices analyzed earlier. Whether in the form of conversion narratives, reports of enlightenment, or prophetic promises, religions represent themselves as means of averting misfortune, overcoming crises, and providing salvation.

CHAPTER EIGHT

The Future of Religion

What is the future of religion? For a long time, this question seemed already to have been answered: the future of religion would be played out under the sign of "secularization." Whether this is understood as social differentiation, disenchantment, privatization, or deinstitutionalization, almost everyone seems to agree that religion nowadays has to accept a serious loss of importance and influence. A few people have tried to console themselves by describing secularity as religion's self-transformation in the modern world. But that is about as encouraging as describing the decay of the body after death as the realization of human life. What distinguishes Western modernity from other social formations so dramatically that it is said to spell the end of the universality of religion? This question has to be answered, particularly if we want to resolve the problem of secularization.

From the outset, debate about religion in the modern age has suffered from not being conducted on the basis of a unified concept of religion, not to mention a unified theory of religion. Discussion of secularization often focuses less on trends in religious development than on various understandings of religion, on anthropological assumptions, and especially on ways of imagining "modernity." What in Max Weber still consisted in an empirically grounded, institution-related analysis of trends toward rationalization in Western modernity was soon reduced to a teleological theory of modernization no longer capable of distinguishing between an analysis of the actually existing conditions and the anticipation of a normative ideal based on the philosophy of history.

In order to engage in a meaningful debate on secularization, we need a clear concept of religion and a theory of religion in which an answer to the question of secularization is not already implicit. I have defined religion as a system of practices with relation to superhuman powers. This definition has the advantage of leaving open the questions of the universality of religion and secularization as ones that should in principle be answered empirically. It does not declare religion to be either an anthropological or a social necessity; nor does it imply its inevitable disappearance in modernity. Empirically, it is probably safe to say that there is no society in which religion as I have defined it is lacking. Even critics of religion like Marx and Freud presuppose the universality of religion at least in premodern times, but they then assume that humanity can and should free itself of such ideas. In most premodern societies there is an institutionally anchored belief in the existence of invisible superhuman powers; and practices of making contact, interacting, and communicating with those powers pervade everyday life. This belief is presumably shared by the vast majority of human beings. Whether or on what grounds that has changed in the modern age is debatable. Are religion and modernity incompatible, as is so often said? Have the banning of religion from politics, the economy, and culture and the adoption of a scientific mode of thinking made religion largely obsolete and reduced it to the level of a hobby? Or is religion a firmly established component of human culture, the social order, and individual self-interpretation that can be repressed but not abolished? What answer emerges from my theory of religion?

I want to develop my answer in two stages. First, the (premodern) universality of religion has to be explained. Why are there religions in all societies known to us? How did religion originate, and how does it reproduce itself? To answer these questions I turn to both phylogenetic and ontogenetic explanations that are compatible with my theory of religion. But I do not rely on them for the correctness and fruitfulness of my theory. I am responsible only for my own theory, not for those additional explanations, although I find them plausible.

Second, I will analyze the arguments involved in the secularization debate with regard to their logical consistency and their empirical validity. I myself maintain that although religion is not a necessary component of human culture and existence, its disappearance is extremely unlikely.

On the Universality of Religion

Thomas Hobbes expressed his conviction that only the human species had religion. Since the effects of religion are felt only in our species, we must suppose that the seeds of religion slumber only in humans.[1] Given humanity's apparent monopoly on the religious and the universality of religion, at least in premodern societies, how can we explain the genesis and reproduction of religion? With regard to its phylogenetic origins, two theoretical traditions, which in my view complement each other, have offered the most convincing answers: (1) the Durkheimian theory, and (2) philosophical anthropology in the tradition of Arnold Gehlen. Both offer theories less of religion than of culture, especially of institutionalization.[2] With regard to ontogenesis, I still find a modified psychoanalytic approach the most convincing. I find this combination of phylogenetic and ontogenetic explanations superior to cognitive-evolutionary approaches.[3]

Phylogenetic theories emphasize the replacement of instinctual regulation by cultural regulation in the evolution of the human species. The development of religion is thus part of a complex process in which the human brain grows and assumes new functions. Instincts gradually give way to differentiated forms of communication, reflection, the regulation of social relations, and the interpretation of the social and natural environment. In other words, culture becomes a biological necessity for human beings.

Durkheim argues entirely along these lines when he attributes to religion the social function of coordination. Human societies need a basic set of unified concepts, rules of behavior, and norms, rituals, and ideals. Coordination is achieved by means of sacralization, which makes the central demands of society appear naturally given and enforced through superhuman sanctions. Durkheim's interpretation of the sacred as a projection of the social offers only a partial explanation of important aspects of this process. For one thing, his reduction of the religious to the social is hard to maintain. Durkheim succeeds in doing so in his study only because he declares totemism, that is, a social classification system, to be the most elementary form of religion. But this argument leads to an inconsistent distinction between the sacred and the profane, since he regards magic as asocial and therefore excludes it. Magic represents the limit of his theory of projection, insofar as the superhuman powers contacted in "asocial" magical practices cannot embody the projection of the social.

I therefore suggest that the distinction between religion and magic be abandoned in favor of a distinction between actions that are related to superhuman powers and those that are not. From this follows a distinction between religious and nonreligious cultures. It makes sense to assume that in the course of human evolution there has been no purely religious stage, in which all actions were related to superhuman powers. As Durkheim persuasively showed in his distinction between the sacred and the profane, all categories of thought are based on a perception of difference.

In principle, the reduction of instinct forced the human race to regulate and institutionalize to a significant degree its internal and external relations. This necessity becomes acute when people are confronted by their own powerlessness, as in the case of their bodily mortality, their lack of control over the natural environment, or the instability of social relations.[4] For that reason, illness and death, droughts and floods, domination and war represent threats that are universally made the object of religious interpretation and religious action.

On this view, the achievement of religious institutions is based on the fact that they uphold the ability to act in situations where people feel powerless and incapable of action. In bringing threats into significant relation to superhuman powers, people can attempt, by communicating with these powers, to actively manage such situations rather than panicking or despairing. As I have shown, after calamities such as earthquakes or serious epidemics, the participants in religious rituals increase in number and evince greater emotional intensity. In this existential sense, religion is a way of coping with contingency.[5] My theory of religion is thus fully compatible with a phylogenetic explanation of religion that underlies central sociological traditions.

This phylogenetic theory of the genesis of religion can be complemented by an ontogenetic theory of the reproduction of religion, which explains how ideas about the existence of superhuman powers develop and are reproduced in individual human beings. Ontogenetic theories cannot explain the genesis of religion as a social institution, but they can help us understand why belief in the existence of superhuman powers is both plausible and universal. The most convincing ontogenetic explanations go back to Freud, considerably modifying some essential theses of his psychoanalytic theory.[6] For Freud, religious ideas are based on the father figure and the Oedipal phase of child development. At the same time, Freud assumed that such religious ideas could be overcome both ontogenetically and phylogenetically. For him, religious ideas were illusions needed neither by the healthy ego nor by enlightened (mature) society.[7]

This view of Freud's was altered in various respects. For one thing, the connection between the idea of God and the Oedipal phase was abandoned, while possible object relationships were broadened and earlier phases of development were taken more fully into account. All this has been competently summarized and further developed, though given a somewhat religious coloring, by Ana-Maria Rizzuto.[8] Here I am concerned primarily with her position, since her work is constantly cited as fundamental.[9]

In contradistinction to Freud, Rizzuto replaces the father with the mother as most important object relation in early child development, but without neglecting other persons and objects. Moreover, she assumes that the idea of God is a necessary part of the construction of the ego and, contrary to Freud, that it is not something to be overcome. According to Rizzuto, religion is an integral component of true humanness that allows humans to create invisible but meaningful realities and thus to give expression to the imagination's power to transcend the boundaries of the empirical world.[10]

Rizzuto assumes that every person develops an idea of God. This idea is not identical with theologians' rationalistic concept of God but represents a highly personal and idiosyncratic imagination that adapts to changing circumstances and needs. Narcissistic vulnerabilities and fears lead young children to construct fantasies and images of threatening or rescuing powers in the form of monsters, heroes, or other superhuman beings over which they usually exercise magical control. According to Rizzuto, this is also the starting point for the idea of God. Along with this colorful collection of characters surrounded by intense fantasies, wishes, and fears emerges an idea of God. At first, this god may emerge as one among many, but he soon takes on a special, superordinate status on the basis of diverse sociocultural, religious, familial, and epigenetic influences.[11]

For Rizzuto, the difference between the fiction of God and other fictions lies chiefly in the sociocultural domain, namely, in the reaction of adults. Whereas adults laugh at witches, fairies, monsters, and Santa Claus as childish fictions, they reinforce the belief in the idea of God. Although God is as invisible as other fictions, he becomes a reality; he has the power to see everything and sometimes punishes. Otherwise, Rizzuto follows the Freudian approach, interpreting the idea of God essentially as an intensification of the image of the parents.

If we now combine the phylogenetic and ontogenetic explanations with my theory of religion, we find that they confirm my thesis that religion is a system of practices especially concerned with warding off and overcoming crisis situations. Religion not only makes it possible for the inexplicable to be explained; it also maintains people's ability to act in situations in which they run up against their own limits.

From this phylogenetic and ontogenetic explanation of the universality of religion, however, we should not infer a cheap justification of religion, for the result is certainly ambivalent. On the one hand, religion allows humans to continue to act even when overtaxed. Religious practices offer humans a structure in situations in which they might otherwise oscillate between panic and despair. On the other hand, the institutionalization and internalization of religious ideas can also prevent people from rationally coping with their fate themselves when they are capable of doing so. I do not intend to make a value judgment about such possible outcomes. But this explanation of the universality of religion does have implications for the prognosis of religion.

Secularization, Disenchantment, and Deinstitutionalization

Before discussing how my theory of religion throws light on the problem of secularization, I should first explain what is at stake. Although I could draw on a whole series of intelligent attempts at clarification,[12] I will define the concept of secularization more narrowly, since applying it to a multiplicity of heterogeneous phenomena has partially deprived those attempted clarifications of their productivity. It would be better not to lump together social differentiation, religious institutions' loss of power, the disenchantment of thinking, and deinstitutionalization in the form of a dramatic decline in membership of religious associations, as if they were all expressions of the same process or mutually conditioned each other.

Further confusion has been introduced into the secularization debate by describing it as a conflict between European "representatives" and American "opponents" of secularization.[13] Trivializing and provincializing the debate in this way has concealed the real reasons for the dissension, which lie in the confrontation between two incompatible theoretical approaches, different historical experiences, and different attitudes toward religion. From my point of view, both theoretical approaches—the market theory and the modernization theory—are inadequate; both historical experiences are contingent, and neither is universalizable; and the two attitudes are equally irrelevant for sociological explanations.

American religious experience has been shaped by voluntary associations, while European religious experience has been shaped by ecclesiastical structures. Many American sociologists of religion are closely connected with religious groups and would therefore like to treat secularization as an illusion, whereas their European colleagues enjoy empty churches. One side adopts a simplistic religious market theory, the other an outmoded theory of modernization. Theorists of the religious market are fixated on the behavior of individual religious consumers. They ignore the connection between religion and the changing structures of modern societies, consider everything merely a function of market conditions, and in essence conduct religious market research.[14] In this way, they avoid or flatten out the issues involved in the debate about secularization. Theorists of modernization, on the contrary, overload the concept of secularization with assumptions and arguments that are not necessarily connected with each other logically or empirically. Ultimately, they present secularization as a metaphysical concept whose "essence" is revealed in a variety of processes such as institutional differentiation, disenchantment, deinstitutionalization, privatization, and depoliticization. But in doing so, they are conflating the meaningful concept of secularization in the sense of institutional differentiation with assumptions regarding the latter's supposed consequences. In order to disentangle these elements, I will introduce conceptual distinctions between secularization, disenchantment, and deinstitutionalization.[15]

The concept of secularization refers to a transformation of social orders, namely, to the process of freeing social institutions from religious control. This process results in the emergence of relatively autonomous spheres with their own standards and rules: on the one hand, secular institutional complexes such as the economy, politics, and culture; on the other, a rather clearly delimited religious sphere.

The concept of disenchantment refers to a transformation of structures of consciousness in terms of their rationalization. Empirically, this rationalization can best be connected with two processes, the adoption of a scientific mode of thought in which religious categories and interpretations are replaced by scientific ones, and an ethicization of religious ideas in the form of an internal rationalization of religious thinking and an internalization and deritualization of religious practice.

The concept of deinstitutionalization refers to the transformation of religious institutions, and especially to the shrinking membership in religious groups and declining participation in religious practices. Some theorists see a trend toward privatization as a consequence of this deinstitutionalization.

By the concept of secularization, therefore, I refer solely to the process of institutional differentiation through which secular spheres—that is, social spheres free of religious premises and norms—emerge.[16] In contrast, the so-called secularization debate is often unconcerned with secularization in this sense at all, but instead deals with religion's actual or supposed loss of importance in the modern age, which can be situated on three different levels: the structure of social institutions, individual consciousness, and religious organizations. On each of these levels, however, that loss of importance has a different meaning and requires different kinds of empirical testing and theoretical explanation. Thus, in examining each level separately, I shall ask: Have secularization, disenchantment, and deinstitutionalization actually taken place, and if so, to what extent? Do they necessarily imply that religion has lost importance? And are they causally connected with each other?

Secularization has clearly taken place in the West, at least partially, as well as in countries that are guided by the West or that have been forced to adopt its model; but it has occurred in different degrees, in different forms, at different points in time, and with different consequences. Even in Western countries, the separation of institutions, especially between church and state, has been carried out with variable consistency. Theorists of discourse, somewhat inaccurately, tend to date the development of a liberal model to the eighteenth century. Only in the United States were religions disestablished at that time, and even then only at the federal level; in the individual states, disestablishment was not completed until the second half of the nineteenth century. In many countries, such as Prussia, religion was less differentiated as an autonomous sphere than it was nationalized and domesticated. As king of Prussia, Frederick William III (1770–1840) was at the same time head of the Lutheran Church, which he forcibly united with the Reformed Church to form the Evangelical Church in Prussia. For this new foundation he even drafted liturgies; so he can hardly be regarded as fostering secularization in the sense of institutional differentiation.

The democratic-liberal and authoritarian traditions have left enduring traces behind them. Whereas in the United States there are still no governmental religious statistics, Germany even supports churches by collecting tax for them. In Scandinavian countries, the Lutheran Church still enjoys a privileged status, though in Sweden its privilege has recently been abolished. At the same time, different ideas regarding the role of the secular exist in the West, ideas largely determined by whether religion is organized as a church or as a voluntary association. Whereas the American model is based on secularity—that is, on the theoretical neutrality of the state with regard to religious groups—the French model aspires to secularism in the sense of a postreligious state ideology and church. Germany clings desperately to the churches' privileges and tries to ignore the political and legal problems that flow from these privileges.

In the West, there are also tendencies to relax institutional boundaries. In the United States, governmental funds are increasingly allocated to religious organizations that are active in social work and recruit members in this way. In Europe, some people are rediscovering their Christianity and, out of fear of Muslims, want to strengthen the "dominant Christian culture." If this "dominant culture" then wanted to tell them how they should spend their Sundays or how they should behave in the bedroom, these people would quickly lose their enthusiasm. The idea arose only as a means of disciplining "the other." In the West, only very marginal groups support broad dedifferentiation or even theocratization. In other words, secularization in the sense of social differentiation has taken place to a certain degree, and in the West it seems to be widely accepted.[17] However, the sociological model of secularization suggests a uniformity that largely ignores the complexity of historical reality, as David Martin showed a long time ago.[18]

Does secularization necessarily lead to religion's losing its influence? At first glance, we find examples both for and against this view. The secularization of the educational system or the introduction of civil marriage ceremonies obviously reduces the social control that religious institutions can exercise over people. On the other hand, the influence of religious institutions in the United States coincides with a much stricter separation between church and state than is known in Germany. And the differentiation between politics and religion was what made it possible for the Catholic Church to present itself as the opposition in communist Poland.

Institutional differentiation implies the achievement of a relative autonomy for all areas of society, and thus also for religion. Not only politics and economics are being released from religious control; religion also is being freed from political tutelage and other compromises that it would otherwise have to accept because of the way it was intertwined with other areas of society. For that reason, it is quite conceivable that religious institutions will gain more independence and importance as a result of secularization. They can create their own public sphere and thus exert influence on the common discourse. Whereas religions that are barely separated from other institutions are also under their control, those that are relatively autonomous can criticize from an independent standpoint the ethics and practices of other spheres of society. Religion is no longer omnipresent as it was in premodern Europe, for example, but as a result it has acquired greater autonomy.

Nevertheless, religion and its importance have undeniably changed, in Europe at least. Anyone who strives to pursue a consistently religious way of life, in which all social spheres are imbued with religious norms, is bound to be hampered by differentiation. If one can successfully litigate against the sound of church bells but cannot put an end to the persistent nuisance of telemarketing, something must have changed in the structures of power. The "dominant culture" is no longer Christian but capitalist.

Let us now turn to the second question, whether disenchantment in the sense of the adoption of a scientific mode of thought and an ethicization of religions has taken place. Has religious thinking been replaced by secular thinking? Have religious categories been replaced by secular ones? Has the focus of religious practice shifted from ritual to ethics? And can these processes be seen as resulting from secularization? Here, too, contradictory examples come to mind.

It is certain that scientific thinking has gained hugely in authority. It is the mode of thought we learn in schools and universities, and it is the norm in almost all our central institutions. In determining where to locate a business, we resort not to geomancy but to market research. We send medical samples for testing to laboratories, not to spiritual mediums. Even religious groups that oppose the theory of evolution express their religious belief in the Creation in a pseudo-scientific language by calling it "scientific creationism" or "intelligent design." But scientific thinking has in no way displaced religion. To convince ourselves of this, we have only to go into a bookstore in Germany or the United States and look at the sections on religion, spirituality, esotericism, or self-help. These sections are a catchall for do-it-yourself religions, and they make money by offering re-enchantment. Over recent decades, the market for such books has grown enormously.

Thus we can note trends toward both disenchantment and (re)enchantment of the world. Disenchantment and re-enchantment are obviously not alternatives but, rather, simultaneous, even mutually determining processes. For many people, scientific thinking and religious thinking operate on different levels, which are not essentially in competition with each other. Many believe in the evolution of humankind and also in a creator-God. They trust their physician, but take additional precautions by praying or lighting a candle. They may believe that human existence is meaningless, but when they suffer misfortune, they are raising the problem of theodicy.

If we turn to a second dimension of disenchantment, that of deritualization and ethicization, we encounter another contradictory picture. On the one hand, since the late eighteenth century, liturgical reforms reflecting this trend have been made in many denominations: consider, for example, Franz Joseph's reforms in the Habsburg Empire, the development of Reform Judaism, or the Second Vatican Council. In the public sphere, religion is often associated with "good works." Religious institutions are legitimated not only by carrying our rituals such as baptism, weddings, and, especially, funerals; with regard to their public role, they are assessed largely in terms of their social commitment and their competence in ethical matters. Churches are involved in caring for the sick and the weak, the persecuted and the deprived. They run hospitals, retirement homes, and kindergartens. They collect "bread for the world" and demand a voice in matters such as genetic research, climate change, pornography, and abortion.

On the other hand, religious movements have developed that are centered on charismatic practices. One of the fastest-growing is Pentecostalism, which has prominent affective-ecstatic and "magical" characteristics.[19] When groups of this kind seek to reform the world, they usually try to do so by means of conversion. They may represent strict personal ethics, but they also speak in tongues and believe in miracle cures and the power of the devil.[20]

Moreover, both the adoption of scientific thinking and the ethicization of religions precede secularization in the sense of institutional differentiation. Both are, at least partially, intrareligious developments.[21] For example, the ethicization of the Christian religion was already occurring in sixteenth-century ascetic Protestantism as well as in seventeenth-century Catholic Jansenism.[22] These two examples alone make it difficult to explain the process as a function of secularization. Instead, it could be argued that the adoption of scientific thinking and ethicization created the presuppositions for secularization.

As to the question of deinstitutionalization, we can safely say, with respect to Europe, that churches have lost a great many members and that few people attend services. This is less true of the United States, though there, too, fewer than 30 percent of church members attend services. Furthermore, religiousness is seen as a value in the United States. That is one reason why people tend to exaggerate when surveyed regarding their participation in institutionalized religious life.[23] The decrease in church membership is partially compensated by new religious groups or movements within the main denominations. It is worth noting the success of American mega-churches resulting from the refashioning of their liturgies on the model of the staging of mass-media performances. Deinstitutionalization may have less to do with secularization than with liturgies that no longer correspond to people's religious ideas or lifestyles. Outside the industrialized countries of the West, however, this is not generally the case, as the worldwide growth of charismatic Christianity and Islam clearly show.

It has often been suggested that deinstitutionalization is causally connected with the privatization of religion. In the 1960s, Thomas Luckmann argued that religion had lost its public role and had become subjective and private.[24] At the same time, he preferred to consider this not as a sign of the disappearance of religion but as a function of secularization. Accordingly, he described religion more broadly as "self-transcendence," thus making religion an indispensable ground for the construction of the person. This view was further developed into the thesis of a religious supermarket, in which religious consumers fill their own baskets.

In my opinion, this is a crass exaggeration of the situation in contemporary Western societies. The mainline churches still have more members than the religious "shopping malls" have customers. Even if there is an unmistakable trend toward religious voluntarism and subjectivism, especially among younger members of the middle class in Western countries, it seems to me highly problematic to simply project them linearly. "Spirituality" and "Sheilaism"[25] may prove in the long run to be transitional phenomena. We certainly cannot exclude the possibility that future generations will turn to more stable religious institutions.

The assumption implicit in the privatization thesis, that religion is being increasingly depoliticized, has turned out to be untenable too. Its falsity not only was demonstrated long ago by José Casanova but can easily be confirmed by anyone who carefully follows the news. All over the world, both traditional churches and new religious movements have acquired influence over politics, a trend that has been under way for decades, and perhaps never really ceased.[26] Even if privatization of religion is occurring, it does not necessarily follow from secularization.

The concept of secularization has also been used to describe processes of change within religious institutions. Some see secularization in the way religious ideologies and morals have been adapted to dominant modes of life, such as capitalism and democracy. Steve Bruce, for example, argues that evangelical and charismatic groups in Great Britain and the United States now hardly ever make ascetic demands on their members.[27] Even if this is correct, it does not mean that religion has lost importance, but at most that it has adapted to worldly needs. Why must religion be ascetic and reject the dominant culture? In contrast, Mark Chaves emphasizes the internal professionalization of religious institutions and the consequent loss of authority on the part of religious actors. In this he sees a form of secularization, but he does not quite convince me. Thus Talcott Parsons, for instance, characterized "secularization" as a religious success and claimed that modern industrial societies are imbued with a religious ethics.[28]

In sum, neither disenchantment nor deinstitutionalization is a trend that necessarily follows from secularization. Both claims involve a simplistic exaggeration of complex and contradictory processes. On the one hand, we cannot neglect the fact that secularization has altered the status of religion in modern societies. On the other hand, we must beware of overemphasizing the differences between earlier and present-day forms of religion. All too many perceptions of difference are based on stereotypical images of the religions of earlier periods and other cultures, which are then compared with exaggerated images of our own religious present.

The central difference consists primarily in the liberation of social institutional structures from religious control. The circumstances under which religion is politicized or depoliticized, religious thinking is repressed by scientific thinking or coexists with it, and religious groups gain or lose members cannot be simply deduced from the process of secularization.

Hence, certain guidelines suggest themselves for future research. First, undifferentiated chatter about secularization must be abandoned. Secularization as institutional differentiation must be clearly distinguished from processes of disenchantment and deinstitutionalization. Whether and how these processes are interconnected cannot be answered by means of philosophical deduction but requires concrete case studies. Secularization is not a metaphysically given historical process; as a rule, it is produced by governmental policies. In view of numerous starting points, interests, and power relations, secularization can take place historically in extremely different ways. For that reason one must determine as precisely as possible how the relations between the state and religious associations are formed in any given case.

The Return and the Future of Religion

How can we explain the "return of religion" in recent decades from the point of view of my theory of religion? How can we interpret the apparently contradictory tendencies toward secularization and dedifferentiation, toward disenchantment and re-enchantment, toward deinstitutionalization and the emergence of new religious movements, toward the spiritualization and the politicization of religion? First, we should bid farewell to imaginations of "modernity" based on the philosophy of history and accept existing modernity in all its diversity of forms and contradictoriness. Instead of seeing modernity as a linear, teleological process and treating contrary processes as curious deviations, we should investigate the internal relation of these apparent contradictions. Secularization, disenchantment, and deinstitutionalization are not natural events; in them, needs and interests are articulated and pursued in the framework of structural possibilities and ideological orientations. Since these presuppositions vary, the results also vary.

Moreover, we must correctly assess the significance of religion. Theories that conceive religion primarily as ethics, as a worldview, or even as aesthetics are not capable of explaining the dynamics of religious developments. My theory may offer a more fruitful avenue. I have identified the averting of misfortune, the overcoming of crises, and the provision of salvation as the central promise made by religions. Drawing on Freud, I have distinguished three domains that are addressed by religions: the mortality of the human body, humans' lack of control over their natural environment, and the fragility of human relations based on differences in power. The more humans are exposed to such crises, the more they will resort to religious means to cope with these threats. Moreover, these crises do not disappear but shift to new locations, triggering further religious responses.

For a long time, Western modernism could propagate quite persuasively a belief in its constantly growing ability to control nature, the human body, and social orders. Progress in the natural sciences and technology is certainly impressive. Science and technology, capitalism and democracy have reduced people's liability to crises. Scientific research has made huge progress, especially in the realm of medicine. Diseases that invariably killed people a century ago are now prevented by vaccines or can be easily cured. The average lifespan has risen enormously. Not only infant mortality but also—far more importantly and dramatically—the percentage of women who die in childbirth has greatly decreased. Pregnancy and birth now pose only a relatively small risk. People survive even the most serious accidents. In addition, the democratic-capitalist welfare state has succeeded in organizing a relatively high level of social stability. Yet these scientific, technological, and political means of coping with misfortune benefit chiefly those who live in industrialized countries.

Nonetheless, crises have hardly diminished, even in the West. Indeed, many new threats have emerged, including the unintended consequences of scientific and technological innovations. New epidemics have broken out, such as AIDS and avian flu. People die from the achievements of our technological civilization. Modern biological, chemical, and atomic weapons have the potential to annihilate people on a massive scale. Industrial production endangers the health of many who work in factories, coal mines, and elsewhere. The consequences of climate change are still impossible to assess.

In the course of its development, capitalism has produced economic prosperity for large sections of society. But it is a revolutionary force that constantly overturns social relations in accord with market conditions and technological innovations. It creates new selves, alters people's traditionally predetermined opportunities, the structure of their needs, and their relations to others. It offers opportunities for advancement, but also undermines traditional power relations and patriarchal authority, destroys family ties, makes work and income the central criteria for evaluating people, imposes social and geographical mobility, and subjects people to the unpredictability of the market and changing labor conditions. One person's social advancement often means a decline in social status or even impoverishment for someone else. Many of these insecurities emerged in the West during the nineteenth and twentieth centuries.

Neoliberal globalization is repeating some of these developments. In the West, the dismantling of the welfare state and the outsourcing of jobs lead to existential anxieties. In Asia and Latin America, on the other hand, a capitalistic revolution in social relations is taking place. Countries that are not participating in globalization appear to have poor prospects and little hope. No matter whether one is directly affected by globalization or excluded from it, its transformative social and economic effects are accompanied by deep insecurities. Capitalism itself often seems to be an irrational, magical force that one can deal with only by using magical means.[29] In addition, the importance of the nation-state is decreasing. Globalized society increasingly resembles the great empires of the past. As a result, group identities and expectations of solidarity are frequently shifted from the nation to other levels of social aggregation, especially ethnic and religious ones.

Finally, a loss of legitimacy in political regimes contributes to the growth and politicization of religions. Political failure has always been interpreted as a withdrawal of religious legitimation. The greater the failure and the greater the share of the population that is prevented from defending its own interests, the more likely are people to turn to religious means of salvation, whether in politicized or depoliticized forms. These developments provide a seedbed for religious groups ranging from fundamentalists to Pentecostalists. What is striking about these movements is the dominant role played by the religious laity, who find in religious associations not only a new identity and solidarity but also direct access to superhuman powers, which promise them protection and blessings.[30] In other words, the crises that people cope with through religious practices have not disappeared; they have simply shifted.

Human beings' inadequacy in the face of all the problems that confront them is a permanent feature of their condition. We cannot surmount the vulnerability and mortality of our bodies; nor will we be able, at any time in the foreseeable future, to exert full control over our natural environment; nor will we succeed in erasing the fact and problematic consequences of differences in power, privileges, and unjust domination. But these are exactly the problems that religions promise to overcome either concretely in this world or abstractly in a future state of salvation. Although not everyone relies on this promise or even believes in the existence of superhuman powers, given the insurmountable threats to humanity it would be unrealistic to expect religion to disappear.

At the same time, my theory of religion suggests that not all religions will be able to maintain or increase their importance in the future. If the center of religion is the promise of salvation, religions that are conceived essentially as ethics or aesthetics will have a hard time sustaining themselves. In the West, at least since Kant, we know that morality does not require religion. And although aestheticizing the religious may be useful for "furnishing the soul," it cannot help overcome crises.[31] The future belongs, rather, to religions that take their promise seriously and represent it credibly. The theory of religion I have developed here should not be interpreted as defining an "essence" of religion. My theory does not seek to prove that all religions are "ultimately" alike, but it does aim to make them comparable by reference to a general structure of meaning underlying them. Naturally, religions differ with regard to the ways they conceive superhuman powers, how they interpret misfortune and crises, and what paths they take toward salvation. These differences arise not only from social and cultural factors but also, and especially, from each specific religious tradition. At the same time, these various religious conceptions and motives for action have their own effects on social and cultural developments as Max Weber has brilliantly demonstrated. But I chose a different topic.

Instead, given widespread confusion regarding the concept of religion and the dominance of functionalist explanations, I have proposed a content-based definition and an interpretation that justifies the use of "religion" as an analytical concept and makes comparative studies of religions possible. This generalization is a necessary presupposition for a more precise definition of the cultural and structural properties of concrete religions and religious traditions. In this way, particularization receives a point of reference, and the peculiarities of religions can be illuminated from a clear point of view. Without such a reference point, invoking the uniqueness of religious and cultural phenomena remains an empty exercise. In addition, the theory of religion set forth here allows us to reinterpret the dynamics of different religious developments and the present-day return of religions.

Theoretical schemata based on evolutionism and modernization, which apply the standard of rationalization, have classified religions in accord with value hierarchies and models of progress that range from magical religion to religions of salvation, from polytheism to monotheism, from ethnic religion to world religion, from ritualism to ethical religion. These classifications ultimately serve to evaluate religions theologically, and they are usually constructed in such a way that Protestantism is postulated as the highest form of religion and the one best suited to modernity.

In contrast, my approach conceives religions as complexes of religious practices that reflect communities' and individuals' typical experiences of contingency and hopes for salvation. It proposes to study religions in their social and cultural contexts and to use the latter as the standard for classifying them. It therefore pays attention to practices that are reserved for specific social groups and individuals—practices that vary in accord with the gender, age, rank, income, status, or ethnicity of those who perform them. Since all these practices express fears of misfortune, experiences of crisis, and hopes for salvation, my theory provides insight into the state of societies, groups, and movements that go unnoticed by conventional religious theories or by political, sociological, and economic analyses. It takes religion seriously and helps us explain its enduring power in the age of globalization.

NOTES

For bibliographical details of works cited in the notes, see the bibliography.

CHAPTER ONE
Religion as Discourse

1. Lawrence, *Shahrastani on Indian Religions.*

2. Haußig, *Der Religionsbegriff in den Religionen.*

3. Asad, *Formations of the Secular.*

4. Almost a century ago James Leuba cited more than fifty such definitions in *A Psychological Study of Religion, Its Origin, Function, and Future.* See also Smith, "Religion, Religions, Religious."

5. Pertinent remarks may be found in Balagangadhara, *"The Heathen in his Blindness . . ."*

6. Kippenberg, *Discovering Religious History in the Modern Age;* Bellah, *Beyond Belief.*

7. Pollack,"Vom Tischerücken zur Psychodynamik"; Luckmann, *The Invisible Religion.*

8. Gay, *The Enlightenment;* Locke, *The Reasonableness of Christianity.*

9. Gay, *Deism.*

10. Wuthnow, "Spirituality and Spiritual Practice."

11. Lincoln, *Discourse and the Construction of Society.*

12. Asad, *Genealogies of Religion;* Dubuisson, *The Western Construction of Religion.*

13. Chidester, *Savage Systems;* Jensen, *Manufacturing Confucianism;* King, *Orientalism and Religion;* Sugirtharajah, *Imagining Hinduism.*

14. Balagangadhara, *"The Heathen in His Blindness . . . ,"* 1ff.

15. Dubuisson, *The Western Construction of Religion,* 17ff.

16. The enormous number of quotation marks in Max Weber's texts seeks to lend expression to precisely this problem.

17. Asad, *Genealogies of Religion,* 27–54.

18. See also McCutcheon, *Manufacturing Religion.*

19. See Feil, *Religio*, vols. 1–3.

20. Smith, *The Meaning and End of Religion*.

21. Martin, *A General Theory of Secularization*.

22. Casanova, *Public Religions in the Modern World*.

23. Hugh-Jones and Laidlaw, eds., *The Essential Edmund Leach*, 1:323.

24. Weber, *Economy and Society*, 1:468–517.

25. See King, *Orientalism and Religion*, 60.

26. See the above-cited works by Jensen, King, Sugirtharajah, and Chidester.

27. Acosta, *Natural and Moral History of the Indies*, 300.

28. Paper, *The Spirits Are Drunk*.

29. Ibid., 3.

30. Claerhout and De Roover, "The Question of Conversion in India."

31. Ibid.

32. Quoted in Magenschab, *Andreas Hofer*, 57.

33. Ch'en, *The Chinese Transformation of Buddhism*.

34. See Gombrich and Obeyesekere, *Buddhism Transformed*.

35. Marshall D. Sahlins has argued brilliantly in many of his pieces against these tendencies. See, for example, *How "Natives" Think*.

36. Chakrabarty, *Rethinking Working-Class History*.

37. Polanyi, *Primitive, Archaic, and Modern Economies*.

38. Dubuisson, *The Western Construction of Religion*, 189.

39. Malinowski, *Primitive, Archaic, and Modern Economies, and Other Essays*, 30–31.

40. See Malinowski, Introduction to Fortune's book *Sorcerers of Dobu*, xix–xxxii.

CHAPTER TWO
Religion as Social Reference

1. Cancik, "Apologetik/Polemik." There is no need for me to demonstrate the obvious fact that all societies recognize religious specialists, which preconceives the distinction between religious and nonreligious practices.

2. Weber, *Economy and Society*, 468ff.

3. Acosta, *Natural and Moral History of the Indies*, 300.

4. Malinowski, Introduction to Fortune, *Sorcerers of Dobu*, xx.

5. Simmel, *Soziologie*, 247–336.

6. Fletcher, *The Barbarian Conversion*, 64.

7. Ch'en, *The Chinese Transformation of Buddhism*; Kapstein, *The Tibetan Assimilation of Buddhism*.

8. Goldenberg, *The Nations That Know Thee Not*.

9. Exod. 20:2–3, 5. All Hebrew Bible quotations are drawn from *Tanakh: The Holy Scriptures*.

10. Exod. 20:23–24.

11. See Matt. 12:1–8; Mark 2:18–28; Luke 6:1–11; 11:37–54. All New Testament quotations are drawn from the Revised Standard Version.

12. Matt. 23:13, 23, 25, 27, 29.

13. Matt. 24:23–24; Acts 13:6.

14. Acts 14, 17:16–34, 19:21–40; Rom. 2.

15. 1 Cor. 8, 10:14–22; Gal. 4:8–20; see also Harnack, *Die Mission und Ausbreitung des Christentums in den ersten drei Jahrhunderten.*

16. 1 Cor. 10:14.

17. 1 Cor. 10:20–22.

18. Lauchert, *Die Kanones der wichtigsten altkirchlichen Concilien, nebst den Apostolischen Kanones*; Reichert, "Elvira, Synode von."

19. For an overview, see Waardenburg, ed., *Muslim Perceptions of Other Religions.*

20. See Gimaret, "Shirk."

21. All sura translations are drawn from *The Qur'an*, trans. M.A.S. Abdel Haleem.

22. Sura 4:48.

23. Sura 4:171–72.

24. Sura 98:6.

25. Tabari, *The Book of Religion and Empire*, 165–66.

26. Ibid., 167.

27. See Lawrence, *Shahrastani on Indian Religions*, Introduction.

28. Lawrence, *Shahrastani*; see also Waardenburg, ed., *Muslim Perceptions of Other Religions*, 29–30.

29. Lawrence, *Shahrastani*, 16–17.

30. Steinschneider, *Polemische und apologetische Literatur in arabischer Sprache . . .*

31. Harvey, *An Introduction to Buddhism*, 9–31.

32. Horner, ed., *The Book of Discipline (Vinaya-Pitaka)*, vol. 4 (Mahavagga), 15.

33. Ibid., 32–45; Müller, ed., *Sacred Books of the Buddhists.*

34. Ibid., 16–19; Walshe, ed., *The Long Discourses of the Buddha*, 67–71. Here and on the following pages I do not standardize the writing of the Buddhist terms but write them as they are written in the respective sources (Pali *Sutta*, *Dhamma*; Sanskrit *Sutra*, *Dharma*), or else I use the words in their modern, Westernized form.

35. Müller, ed., *Sacred Books of the Buddhists*, 26–55; Walshe, ed., *Long Discourses of the Buddha*, 71–90.

36. Walshe ed., *Long Discourses of the Buddha*, 133–41.

37. Another example can be found in the Samannaphala Sutta "The Fruit of Contemplative Life Discourse," in *Long Discourses of the Buddha*, 91–109.

38. Ch'en, *The Chinese Transformation of Buddhism*, 14–64.

39. Zürcher, *The Buddhist Conquest of China*; Schmidt-Glintzer, *Das Hung-ming chi und die Aufnahme des Buddhismus in China.*

40. Ch'en, *The Chinese Transformation of Buddhism*, 16.

41. Ibid., 42–50.

42. Ibid., 18–41.

43. Zürcher, *The Buddhist Conquest of China*, 290ff.

44. Kohn, *God of the Dao*, 115–18.

45. Kohn, ed., *Laughing at the Tao*, esp. 102–5.

46. Jones, *Ages Ago*, 35–38.

47. Endres, ed., *Die Sieben Meister des wunderbaren Tao*; Wong, trans., *Seven Taoist Masters.*

48. Wong, trans., *Seven Taoist Masters*, 153–72.

49. Kasahara, ed., *A History of Japanese Religion*, 50ff.

50. Aston, trans., *Nihongi*, 66.

51. See Kapstein, *The Tibetan Assimilation of Buddhism*, 54–65.

52. In Tibet, many warned of epidemics and famines; see ibid., 53.

53. Aston, trans., *Nihongi*, 67.

54. Ibid.; De Bary, ed., *Sources of Japanese Tradition*, 1:100–101; Kasahara, *A History of Japanese Religion*, 54.

55. Sansom, *A History of Japan to 1334*, 77.

56. According to McMullin, "Historical and Historiographic Issues in the Study of Pre-modern Japanese Religions," we can speak of the structured and self-confident tradition functioning independently from Buddhism only since the ending of the Japanese Middle Ages, around 1600.

57. Reader, *The Simple Guide to Shinto*, 33–34.

58. Ibid., 56.

59. Boot, "Shunmu-ki and Denchu Mondo, 47.

60. See Ketelaar, *Of Heretics and Martyrs in Meiji Japan*, 14.

61. For polemic, see Newman, "Islam in the Kalacakra Tantra."

62. Sastri, *A History of South India from Prehistoric Times to the Fall of Vijayanagar*, 425.

63. Baldon, "Christmas," in *Encyclopedia of Religion*, 3:460.

64. Gombrich, *Precept and Practice*; Gombrich and Obeyesekere, *Buddhism Transformed*.

65. Ch'en, *Buddhism in China*; Ch'en, *The Chinese Transformation of Buddhism*; Kohn, *Laughing at the Tao*; Zürcher, *The Buddhist Conquest of China*.

66. Ch'en, *Buddhism in China*, 48–50.

67. Ibid., 50.

68. Ibid., 473ff.

69. De Bary and Bloom, eds., *Sources of Chinese Tradition*, 793.

70. Wong, trans., *Seven Taoist Masters*, 44–45, 74–75.

71. Cavin, *Der Konfuzianismus*, image opposite p. 160.

72. Dean, *Taoist Ritual and Popular Cults of Southeast China*.

73. Kitagawa, *Religion in Japanese History*, 38.

74. Ibid., 43; Earhart, *Religions of Japan*, 32.

75. Reader, *The Simple Guide to Shinto*, 55ff.

76. Kitagawa, *Religion in Japanese History*, 40.

77. See also Kasahara, *A History of Japanese Religion*, 48, 140–41. Here, however, shamanistic Buddhism is not connected with Gyogi.

78. McMullin, "Historical and Historiographic Issues in the Study of Pre-modern Japanese Religions," 5.

79. Kasahara, *A History of Japanese Religion*, 141–45.

80. Grapard, *The Protocol of the Gods*, 74ff., points out that this is a territorial association of Kami and Buddha, i.e., Bodhisattva, and not a merging of the teachings.

81. McMullin, "Historical and Historiographic Issues in the Study of Pre-modern Japanese Religions," 6.

82. Gernet, *China and the Christian Impact*, 73.

83. Ibid., 74.

84. Ibid., 26.

85. Ricci, *The True Meaning of the Lord of Heaven*.

86. Gernet, *China and the Christian Impact*, 39.

87. Mungello, *Curious Land*, 62.

88. Boxer, *The Church Militant and Iberian Expansion, 1440–1770*, 39.

89. Gernet, *China and the Christian Impact*, 77.

90. Minamiki, *The Chinese Rites Controversy from Its Beginning to Modern Times*.

91. Nizami, *Akhbar and Religion*.

92. Abu l-Fazl, *The A-in-i Akbari*, 191ff.

93. Nizami, *Akhbar and Religion*, 190–214; Abu l-Fazl, *The A-in-i Akbari*, 170–223.

94. Abu l-Fazl, *The A-in-i Akbari*, 188ff.

95. Ibid., 188.

96. Nock, *Conversion*, 68.

97. Foltz, *Religions of the Silk Road*, 84.

98. Ibid., 85–86.

99. See, for example, the excellent study by Rawski, *The Last Emperors*, 197–263.

100. Kratz, ed., *Religion und Religionskontakte im Zeitalter der Achämeniden*.

101. Quoted in Foltz, *Religions of the Silk Road*, 65.

102. Foltz, *Religions of the Silk Road*, 65.

103. Selinger, *Die Religionspolitik des Kaisers Decius*; Lactantius, *De Mortibus Persecutorum*.

104. Lactantius, *De Mortibus Persecutorum*, 71.

105. Dhammika, trans., *The Edicts of King Asoka*.

106. Pattanayak, *Religious Policy of the Imperial Gangas*; Sharma, *The Religious Policy of the Mughal Emperors*.

107. For the religious policy of Muslim emperors, see, for example, May, "Die Religionspolitik der ägyptischen Fatimiden," 969–1171.

108. See "Djizya," in *The Encyclopaedia of Islam*, II.

109. Sharma, *The Religious Policy of the Mughal Emperors*, 1.

110. Ibid., 1–6.

111. Ibid., 9.

112. Ibid., 15–69.

113. Schimmel, *The Empire of the Great Mughals*.

114. Ch'en, *Buddhism in China*, 191.

115. Foltz, *Religions of the Silk Road*, 73.

116. Reischauer, *Ennin's Travels in T'ang China*, 228.

117. Ibid., 226.

118. Ibid., 227.

119. Ibid., 232; see also Lieu, *Manichaeism in Central Asia and China*, 128–31.

120. Rawski, *The Last Emperors*, 197–294.

121. See Harrison, *Divinity and History*.

122. Herodotus, *The Histories*, 187 [Bk. 2, 146].

123. Ibid., 149 [Bk. 2, 49].

124. Ibid., 86, 87 [Bk. 1, 179–85].

125. Ibid., 96 [Bk. 1, 130].

126. Parker, *Athenian Religion*.

127. Biruni, *Alberuni's India*. Subsequent references to this work appear in parentheses in the text.

CHAPTER THREE

Scholarly Imaginations of Religion

1. See, for example, Capps, *Religious Studies*; Kippenberg, *Discovering Religious History in the Modern Age*.

2. Waardenburg, "The Problem of Representing Religions and Religion," 31–56.

3. Troeltsch, "Der Deismus"; see also Cassirer, *The Philosophy of the Enlightenment*.

4. Gay, *Deism*.

5. The continuity of these approaches is also expressed in Allen, "Phenomenology of Religion."

6. Schleiermacher, *On Religion*, 147.

7. Otto, *The Idea of the Holy*, 22.

8. Schleiermacher, *On Religion*, 134.

9. Ibid., 135.

10. Ibid., 189ff.

11. Ibid., 115.

12. Ibid., 108; De Wette, *Über die Religion, ihr Wesen, ihre Erscheinungsformen und ihren Einfluss auf das Leben*, 2.

13. Schleiermacher, *On Religion*, 147.

14. Otto published a new edition of Schleiermacher's speeches in 1899. Yet he became a follower of Fries in the circle of the historico-religious school in Göttingen; see Otto, *Kantisch-Fries'sche Religionsphilosophie und ihre Anwendung auf die Theologie*.

15. Van der Leeuw, *Religion in Essence and Manifestation*; Van der Leeuw, *Der Mensch und die Religion*; Kippenberg and Luchesi, eds., *Religionswissenschaft und Kulturkritik*.

16. Van der Leeuw, *Religion in Essence and Manifestation*, 680.

17. Ibid., 679.

18. Eliade, *Die Religionen und das Heilige*, 48ff.

19. Eliade, *The Sacred and the Profane*, 11ff.

20. Van der Leeuw, *Phänomenologie der Religion*, 671ff.; see also Eliade, "Methodological Remarks on the Study of Religious Symbolism."

21. Eliade, *The Sacred and the Profane*, 11; Eliade, "Methodological Remarks on the Study of Religious Symbolism," 88.

22. Van der Leeuw, *Religion in Essence and Manifestation*, 680.

23. Eliade, *The Myth of the Eternal Return*.

24. See, for example, McCutcheon, *Manufacturing Religion*.

25. For the concept of revelation as basic for understanding religion, see Gräb, "Von der Religionskritik zur Religionshermeneutik."

26. Freud, *The Future of an Illusion*; Freud, *Civilization and Its Discontents*.

27. Marx and Engels, *The German Ideology*; Marx, "Critique of Hegel's Philosophy of the State." For a good overview, see also McLellan, *Marxism and Religion*.

28. Feuerbach, *The Essence of Christianity*.

29. Comaroff and Comaroff, *Ethnography and the Historical Imagination*; Comaroff and Comaroff, *Of Revelation and Revolution*; Comaroff and Comaroff, eds., *Millennial Capitalism and the Culture of Neoliberalism*; Taussig, *The Devil and Commodity Fetishism in South America*; Meyer, *Translating the Devil*.

30. Tylor, *Religion in Primitive Culture*; Frazer, *The Golden Bough*.

31. Horton, "African Traditional Thought and Western Science."

32. Boyer, *Religion Explained*; Boyer, "Religious Thought and Behaviour as By-products of Brain Function."

33. Boyer, "Religious Thought and Behaviour as By-products of Brain Function," 119.

34. Boyer, *Religion Explained*, 4.

35. Hume, *Writings on Religion*, 114.

36. Marett, *Anthropology*, 235ff.

37. Ibid., 210–11.

38. McDougall, *An Introduction to Social Psychology*.

39. Newberg, D'Aquili, and Rause, *Why God Won't Go Away*, 129.

40. Ibid., 135–36.

41. Ibid., 140.

42. Ibid., 35–53, 86.

43. Ibid., 134.

44. Ibid., 8–9.

45. Ramachandran and Blakeslee, *Phantoms in the Brain*.

46. Ibid., 177–78.

47. Ibid., 179.

48. Durkheim, *The Elementary Forms of Religious Life*, 425.

49. Hobbes, *Leviathan*.

50. Leach,. *Political Systems of Highland Burma*.

51. Bellah, *Beyond Belief*.

52. Luckmann, *The Invisible Religion*; Simmel, "Religion."

53. Luhmann, "Die Ausdifferenzierung der Religion"; Luhmann, *Die Religion der Gesellschaft*.

54. Pollack, *Säkularisierung—ein moderner Mythos?* Beyer, *Religions in Global Society*.

55. Durkheim, *The Elementary Forms of Religious Life*, 44.

56. Weber, *Economy and Society*, 399ff.

57. For an interesting reinterpretation of the Weberian approach, see Sharot, *A Comparative Sociology of World Religions*.

58. Bourdieu, "Genesis and Structure of the Religious Field."

59. Stark and Bainbridge, *A Theory of Religion*.

60. Finke and Stark, *The Churching of America, 1776–1990*; Stark, *The Rise of Christianity*.

61. For a critique, see Sharot, "Beyond Christianity"; Bruce, *Choice and Religion*; Chaves, "On the Rational Choice Approach to Religion."

62. Stark, *The Rise of Christianity*, 163–89.

63. Weber, *Economy and Society*, 56.

CHAPTER FOUR

Religious Practice and the Promise of Salvation

1. I agree for the most part with Melford Spiro, "Religion."

2. I am using the term "system" not in the sense of system theory but in a general sense.

3. I am aware that I am using the term "liturgy" more broadly than is commonly done. Bernhard Lang has described this liturgic perspective in his important book *Sacred Games*.

4. To simplify language issues, I am subsuming the term "manipulation" under the term "communication."

5. Berger, *The Sacred Canopy*; Luckmann, *The Invisible Religion*; Berger and Luckmann. *The Social Construction of Reality*. See also Dobbelaere and Lauwers, "Definition of Religion."

6. Merton, *Social Theory and Social Structure*, 73–138.

7. When Luhmann speaks of dealing with contingencies as a function, he is using "contingency" in a rather empty manner. See Luhmann, "Die Ausdifferenzierung der Religion"; Luhmann, *Die Religion der Gesellschaft*. For a good critique of Luhmann's view, see Pollack, *Säkularisierung—ein moderner Mythos?*

8. Merton, *Social Theory and Social Structure*, 82ff.

9. Durkheim, *The Elementary Forms of Religious Life*.

10. Spiro, "Religion," 85ff.

11. James, *The Varieties of Religious Experience*, 72. Spiro, "Religion," 96, defines religion as an institution "consisting of culturally patterned interaction with culturally postulated super-human beings"; see also Bruce, *God Is Dead*, 2.

12. On the following pages I consistently use the term "superhuman power" and avoid the term "supernatural power," since the concept of nature, as Durkheim has already pointed out, is a specifically modern one, which presupposes a law like the order of nature.

13. Augustine, *Confessions*, 10. The religious meaning of images is covered in my definition. See also Hans Belting's excellent book *Likeness and Presence*.

14. Lang, "Kult."

15. Spiro has already discussed this; see "Religion," 85ff.

16. Berger, *The Sacred Canopy*.

17. Berger, *The Heretical Imperative*.

18. G. Lienhardt, *The Shilluk of the Upper Nile*, 162, quoted in Sperber, "Apparently Irrational Beliefs."

19. Griaule, *Conversations with Ogotemmeli*, 2–3.

20. Bellah et al., *Habits of the Heart*, 221.

21. Turner, *The Social Theory of Practices*.

22. Geertz, *The Interpretation of Cultures*, 109.

23. Freud, *The Future of an Illusion*, 30–31.

24. Oldenburg, *The Religion of The Veda*, 181.

CHAPTER FIVE
Averting Misfortune

1. This formula is spoken at the Japanese Setsubun festival at the beginning of spring.

2. See, for example, Dean, *Taoist Ritual and Popular Cults of Southeast China*, 116, illustration.

3. See also the discussion in Staal, "The Meaninglessness of Ritual."

4. Leach, *Political Systems of Highland Burma*.

5. Griaule, *Conversations with Ogotemmeli*.

6. Freud, *The Future of an Illusion*; Freud, *Civilization and Its Discontents*.

7. Le Goff, *The Birth of Purgatory*; Lopez, *Buddhist Scriptures*.

8. Lang, "Kult."

9. Kitagawa, *On Understanding Japanese Religion*, 139.

10. Earhart, *Religions of Japan*.

11. See also Schipper, *The Taoist Body*, 8.

12. Rawski, *The Last Emperors*, 197–294.

13. Saso, *Blue Dragon, White Tiger*, 161–92.

14. Dean, *Taoist Ritual*, 100.

15. Eberhard, *Chinese Festivals*.

16. Saso, *Taoism and the Rite of Cosmic Renewal*, 8.

17. Saso, *Blue Dragon, White Tiger*, 93.

18. Eberhard, *Chinese Festivals*, 7–8.

19. Teiser, *The Ghost Festival in Medieval China*, 41–42.

20. *Evangelisches Gesangbuch*, 1115.

21. Ibid, 1150–51.

22. Ibid., 1154–55.

23. "Freitag," In *Lexikon der islamischen Welt*, 183.

24. Chaudhri, *Muslim Festivals and Ceremonies*, 15.

25. Bieritz, *Das Kirchenjahr*.

26. Chaudhri, *Muslim Festivals and Ceremonies*; Grunebaum, *Muhammadan Festivals*.

27. Saso, *Taoism and the Rite of Cosmic Renewal*, 15–41.

28. Harrell, "Domestic Observances."

29. Bodde, *Festivals in Classical China*, 388–89.

30. Poo, *In Search of Personal Welfare*.

31. Cohen, "Chinese Religion"; Eberhard, *Chinese Festivals*; Stepanchuk and Wong, *Mooncakes and Hungry Ghosts*.

32. Bodde, *Festivals in Classical China*, 388–90.

33. Lagerwey, *Taoist Ritual in Chinese Society and History*.

34. Cohen, "Chinese Religion," 290.

35. Feuchtwang, *Popular Religion in China*; Modder, *Chinese Temple Festivals*, 12ff.

36. Saso, *Blue Dragon, White Tiger*, 169.

37. Stepanchuk and Wong, *Mooncakes*, 1–26.

38. Aijmer, *The Dragon Boat Festival on the Hupeh-Hunan Plain, Central China*.

39. Stepanchuk and Wong, *Mooncakes*, 46.

40. Eberhard, *Chinese Festivals*, 113–27.

41. Stepanchuk and Wong, *Mooncakes*, 61.

42. Teiser, *Ghost Festival*, 8.

43. Stepanchuk and Wong, *Mooncakes and Hungry Ghosts*, 72.

44. Hardacre, "Ancestor Worship," 266.

45. Seidel, Anna. "Yü-huang."

46. Saso, *Taoism and the Rite of Cosmic Renewal*, 18.

47. Kohn, *God of the Dao.*

48. Saso, *Taoism and the Rite of Cosmic Renewal*, 21.

49. Shimazono, "Traditional Japanese Religious Society."

50. Bock, ed., *Engi-Shiki.*

51. Philippi, *Norito.*

52. Bock, ed., *Engi-Shiki*; Nelson, *Enduring Identities*; Nelson, *A Year in the Life of a Shinto Shrine*; Picken, *Essentials of Shinto*, 171ff.

53. Bock, ed., *Engi-Shiki*, 2:66.

54. See also Horne, ed., *The Sacred Books and Early Literature of the East.*

55. Philippi, *Norito*, 45–49.

56. Therefore there were links for using Shinto as a nationalist cult. See, for example, Hardacre, *Shinto and the State, 1868–1988.*

57. Philippi, *Norito*, 50. For a more thorough explanation of the ritual see p. 8 of the same work.

58. Reader, *The Simple Guide to Shinto*; Nelson, *A Year in the Life of a Shinto Shrine.*

59. Kitagawa, *On Understanding Japanese Religion*; Nelson, *A Year in the Life of a Shinto Shrine*, 40.

60. Shimazono, "Traditional Japanese Religious Society," 134–38.

61. Bellenir, *Religious Holidays and Calendars*, 170ff., 194ff.

62. Ibid., 171.

63. Deut. 6:4, in *Tanakh.*

64. See also, for example, the handbook *In Sure and Certain Hope*, 79.

65. Al-Nawawi, *Al-Maqasid.*

66. Harrell, "Domestic Observances."

67. Stepanchuk and Wong, *Mooncakes and Hungry Ghosts*, 65.

68. Levering, Miriam. "Ta-hui and Lay Buddhists."

69. Ibid., 191; Harrell, "Domestic Observances."

70. Earhart, *Religion in the Japanese Experience*; Ebersole, *Ritual Poetry and the Politics of Death in Early Japan*, 123ff., 171ff., 265ff.

71. A thorough presentation can be found in Smith, *Ancestor Worship in Contemporary Japan*, 69ff.

72. For a summary, see http://tanutech.com/japan/jfunerals.html. For a comprehensible presentation, see Juzo Itami's excellent film *The Funeral* (1987).

73. For Christianity, see, for example, Post, *Disaster Ritual.*

74. For Jewish prayer in general, see Hammer, *Entering Jewish Prayer.*

75. Stein, ed., *Seder ha-avodah.*

76. Ibid., 245–376.

77. Ibid., 261.

78. Ibid., 323.

79. Birnbaum, trans., *Daily Prayer Book.*

80. Stark, *Tägliches Handbuch, in guten und bösen Tagen.*

81. *Alles mit Gott.*

82. Lee, *Family Prayers, with Forms for Occasional and Private Use.*

83. Padwick, *Muslim Devotions.*

84. Uddin and Yusuf, *Reflections of Pearls.*

85. http://www.inid.de/wissenswertes/61-bittgebet-im-islam/134-das-bittgebet-im-islam.

86. Al-Nawawi, *Al-Maqasid.*

87. Patai, *On Jewish Folklore;* Patai, "Folk Judaism."

88. Gaster, "Amulets and Talismans."

89. Sharot, *Messianism, Mysticism, and Magic,* 42–43; Gaster, "Amulets and Talismans," 243–46.

90. http://judaism.about.com/librar y/3_blessingsprayers/bl_mezuza.htm.

91. An article about folk Christianity is missing in the *Encyclopedia of Religion.* The article "Popular Christianity" attributes all these practices to cultural contact with other religions.

92. An acquaintance of mine who was on the mailing list of the evangelical preacher Oral Roberts handed me a pamphlet containing content of this kind in 1982.

93. This is repeatedly mentioned by Pat Robertson in his 700 Club, a TV show I watched regularly from October 1981 until May 1982.

94. Padwick, *Muslim Devotions,* 235ff.

95. *Prophetic Medical Sciences,* part 2, p. 1, and part 5, p. 34.

96. Padwick, *Muslim Devotions,* 94ff.

97. Patai, "Folk Islam."

98. Quoted from the Revised Standard Version.

99. See, for example, Kushner, *When Bad Things Happen to Good People.*

100. Jakubowski-Tiessen and Lehmann, eds., *Um Himmels Willen;* Hanska, *Strategies of Sanity and Survival.*

101. Bergdolt, *Der Schwarze Tod;* Nohl, *Der schwarze Tod.*

102. Burmeister, *Der Schwarze Tod.*

103. Breidert, ed., *Die Erschütterung der vollkommenen Welt,* 7–8.

104. Quoted in Zeilinga de Boer and Sanders, *Earthquakes in Human History,* 99.

105. Breidert, ed., *Die Erschütterung der vollkommenen Welt,* 53–73.

106. Winchester, *A Crack in the Edge of the World.*

107. Bartleman, *Azusa Street,* 47.

108. http://www.globalsecurity.org/org/news/2005/050110-god-tsunami.htm. For further discussion, see http://www.channel4.com/culture/microsites/C/can_you_believe_it / debates/tsunami. html.

109. http://www.beliefnet.com/story/174/story_17443_1.html.

110. http://mediamatters.org/items/200601050004.

111. Despeux, "Talismans and Sacred Diagrams"; Sakade, "Divination as Daoist Practice."

112. Eno, "Deities and Ancestors in Early Oracle Inscriptions."
113. Sakade, "Divination as Daoist Practice," 541–42.
114. Teiser, "Introduction," especially p. 22.
115. Harrell, "Domestic Observances."
116. Ibid.
117. Kohn, ed., *The Taoist Experience*, 106–15.
118. Piyadassi, *The Book of Protection*.
119. Perera, *Buddhist Paritta Chanting Ritual*, 35ff.
120. Ibid., 41–42.
121. Ibid., 40.
122. Lagerwey, *Taoist Ritual in Chinese Society and History*; Thompson, "Chiao."
123. Lagerwey, *Taoist Ritual in Chinese Society and History*, 51ff.
124. Thompson, "Chiao."
125. Schipper, *The Taoist Body*, 81.
126. Saso, *Taoism and the Rite of Cosmic Renewal*, 32ff.
127. Thompson, "Chiao," 239; Schipper, *Taoist Body*, 81
128. Schipper, *Taoist Body*, 81.
129. Ibid.
130. Lagerwey, *Taoist Ritual in Chinese Society and History*, 61–62.
131. Feuchtwang, *Popular Religion in China*, 179ff.
132. Ibid., 179–81; Lagerwey, *Taoist Ritual in Chinese Society and History*, 52.
133. Shimazono, "Traditional Japanese Religious Society," 137–38.
134. Takei and Keane, *Sakuteiki, Visions of the Japanese Garden*, 188.
135. Yampolsky, ed., *Selected Writings of Nichiren*, 14.
136. Zeilinga de Boer and Sanders, *Earthquakes in Human History*, 170ff.
137. Smith, *Ancestor Worship in Contemporary Japan*, 44.

CHAPTER SIX
The Radical Quest for Salvation

1. Athanasius, *The Life of Antony and the Letter to Marcellinus*, 43–44.
2. Durkheim, *The Elementary Forms of Religious Life*; Freud, *Civilization and Its Discontents*.
3. Brown, *The Body and Society*.
4. Marcus, *Piety and Society*; Kaelber, *Schools of Asceticism*.
5. McGinn, *The Foundations of Mysticism*, xvi.
6. Ibid., 16.
7. Frank, *Geschichte des christlichen Mönchtums*.
8. Buddhaghosa, *The Path to Purification*, 72–74.
9. Ibid., 64ff.
10. Kieschnick, *The Eminent Monk*.
11. Weber, "The Social Psychology of the World Religions," 287.
12. Bourdieu, "Genesis and Structure of the Religious Field."
13. Francis, *Subversive Virtue*.
14. Cohn, "Sainthood on the Periphery."

15. Otto, *Mysticism East and West*, 16–37, provides a good discussion of this topic.

16. For the positive evaluation of suffering, see Weber's discussion of Nietzsche in "The Social Psychology of the World Religions," 270ff.

17. Woodward, *The Book of Miracles*.

18. Eliade, *Shamanism*, 33–34. Subsequent references to this work appear in parentheses in the text.

19. Eliade, "Shamanism."

20. Blacker, *The Catalpa Bow*, 21.

21. Ibid., 21–22.

22. Ibid., 85.

23. Ibid., 87ff.

24. Jones, trans., *Ages Ago*.

25. Blacker, *Catalpa Bow*, 235–320.

26. Musurillo, ed. and trans., *The Acts of the Christian Martyrs*; Chadwick, *Western Asceticism*; Russell, *The Lives of the Desert Fathers*; Doran, ed., *The Lives of Simeon Stylites*.

27. The narrative also serves theological goals, particularly anti-Arian polemics. Athanasius, *The Life of Antony and the Letter to Marcellinus*, 82, 91–97; Brakke, *Athanasius and Asceticism*.

28. Athanasius, *The Life of Antony and the Letter to Marcellinus*, 31–40.

29. Ibid., 41ff.

30. Ibid., 66–67.

31. Ibid., 43.

32. Ibid., 47ff., 75–79, 96–99. Athanasius reports theologically correctly that Antony does perform miracles himself but that they are done by "the Lord bringing his benevolence to effect through Antony and curing those who were afflicted" (p. 92). Yet this does not change anything for those who witness his deeds, since it is the presence of Antony and his words that make the effects happen.

33. Bonaventure, *The Life of St. Francis*.

34. Bonaventure, *The Life of St. Francis*, 9. Subsequent references to this work appear in parentheses in the text.

35. Quoted in Feld, *Franziskus von Assisi und seine Bewegung*, 207–8.

36. Feld, *Franziskus von Assisi*, 68.

37. Feld, *Franziskus von Assisi*; Feld, *Franziskus von Assisi und seine Bewegung*, 314–18.

38. Feld, *Franziskus von Assisi*, 94.

39. Raymond of Capua, *The Life of St. Catherine of Siena*. The advantage of this source is that it expresses the piety of Catherine's times. Subsequent references to this work appear in parentheses in the text.

40. Raymond talks about the destruction of the corporeal nature (ibid., 147).

41. Cohn, "Sainthood on the Periphery"; Diamond, *Holy Men and Hunger Artists*.

42. Dresner, *The Zaddik*; Marcus, *Piety and Society*.

43. Green, *Tormented Master*; Marcus, *Piety and Society*.

44. Green, *Tormented Master*, 37ff., 167ff.

45. Dresner, *The Zaddik*, 124ff.

46. Ibid., 157ff.

47. Scholem, *Sabbatai Sevi*, 204.

48. Gramlich, Richard. *Weltverzicht*; Cornell, *Realm of the Saint*.

49. Cornell, *Realm of the Saint*, 109ff.

50. Attar, *Muslim Saints and Mystics*; Schimmel, *Mystical Dimensions of Islam*; Smith, *Rabi'a the Mystic and Her Fellow-Saints in Islam*. Subsequent references to the last work appear in parentheses in the text.

51. Schimmel, *Sufismus*.

52. Ibid.

53. Gramlich, *Die Wunder der Freunde Gottes*, 394.

54. Ibid., 320–21.

55. Smith, *Rabi'a the Mystic and Her Fellow-Saints in Islam*, 32–36.

56. Gramlich, *Die Wunder der Freunde Gottes*, 240.

57. Smith, *Rabi'a the Mystic and Her Fellow-Saints in Islam*, 176.

58. Cornell, *Realm of the Saint*, 112–20.

59. Nyanaponika, ed., *Die Lehrreden des Buddha aus der Angereihten Sammlung*, 197.

60. Bigandet, *The Life, or Legend, of Gaudama, the Buddha of the Burmese*, vol. 2; Tambiah, *The Buddhist Saints of the Forest and the Cult of Amulets*.

61. Buddhaghosa, *The Path to Purification*; see also Tambiah, "The Buddhist Arahant."

62. Buddhaghosa, *The Path to Purification*, 59ff. Subsequent references to this work appear in parentheses in the text.

63. Tambiah, *The Buddhist Saints of the Forest and the Cult of Amulets*.

64. Ibid., 243.

65. Miyake, *Shugendo*; Rotermund, *Die Yamabushi*; Kasahara, ed., *A History of Japanese Religion*.

66. Rotermund, *Die Yamabushi*, 94.

67. Miyake, *Shugendo*, 78.

68. Earhart, *A Religious Study of the Mount Haguro Sect of Shugendo*, 19.

69. Blacker, *Collected Writings of Carmen Blacker*, 190.

70. Miyake, *Shugendo*, 88; Blacker, *Collected Writings of Carmen Blacker*, 190–93.

71. Miyake, *Shugendo*, 92–93.

72. Rotermund, *Die Yamabushi*, 127–41.

73. Earhart, *A Religious Study of the Mount Haguro Sect of Shugendo*, 3.

74. Miyake, *Shugendo*, 88.

75. Earhart, *A Religious Study of the Mount Haguro Sect of Shugendo*, 3; see also Averbuch, *The Gods Come Dancing*.

76. Blacker, *Collected Writings of Carmen Blacker*, 186.

77. Rotermund, *Die Yamabushi*, 142.

78. Ibid., 119–27.

79. Miyake, *Shugendo*, 60–71, 127–29.

80. Wong, trans., *Seven Taoist Masters*.

81. Ibid., 40 (where the older spelling "Tao" is used).

82. Ibid., 17.

83. Ibid., 120–72.

84. Not the only model, of course. See also Tambiah, *The Buddhist Saints of the Forest and the Cult of Amulets*, 321ff.

CHAPTER SEVEN

Turning toward Salvation

1. Brown, *The Body and Society*.

2. Fletcher, *The Barbarian Conversion*; Kapstein, *The Tibetan Assimilation of Buddhism*.

3. Nock, *Conversion*.

4. James, *The Varieties of Religious Experience*; Simmel, "Religion."

5. See Wiesberger, *Bausteine zu einer soziologischen Theorie der Konversion*; Wohlrab-Sahr, *Konversion zum Islam in Deutschland und den USA*; Knoblauch, Krech, and Wohlrab-Sahr, eds., *Religiöse Konversion*.

6. Rambo, *Understanding Religious Conversion*, xiv.

7. The decisive theoretical impetus was made by Lofland and Stark, "Becoming a World-Saver."

8. Snow and Philipps, "The Lofland-Stark Conversion Model"; Snow and Machalek, "The Convert as a Social Type"; Snow and Machalek, "The Sociology of Conversion."

9. Shimazono, "Conversion Stories and Their Popularization in Japan's New Religions"; Bruce and Wallis, "Rescuing Motives."

10. James, *The Varieties of Religious Experience*, 127ff., 166ff.

11. Lofland and Stark, "Becoming a World-Saver."

12. Rambo, *Understanding Religious Conversion*, 44.

13. Snow and Machalek, "The Sociology of Conversion"; Snow and Machalek, "The Convert as a Social Type."

14. Beckford, "Accounting for Conversion."

15. For an example, see Snow and Philipps, "The Lofland-Stark Conversion Model," 43.

16. See the excellent studies by Chong, *Delivery and Submission*; and Smilde, *Reason to Believe*.

17. Acts 22. All quotations from the New Testament are drawn from the Revised Standard Version.

18. It is curious that earlier (Acts 9:7) we read: "The men who were traveling with him stood speechless, hearing the voice but seeing no one."

19. Acts 22:14–16.

20. Acts 22:17.

21. Singh, *With and Without Christ*.

22. Eusebius, *Über das Leben des Kaisers Konstantin*.

23. Augustine, *The Confessions of St. Augustine*. Subsequent references to this work appear in parentheses in the text.

24. In addition to the already quoted passage, see *The Confessions of St. Augustine*, 35, 44, 66ff., 88, 134.

25. Olin, ed., *The Autobiography of St. Ignatius Loyola*.

26. Bulliet, "Conversion to Islam and the Emergence of a Muslim Society in Iran"; Bulliet, *Conversion to Islam in the Medieval Period*.

27. García-Arenal, ed., *Conversions islamiques.*

28. García-Arenal, "Dreams and Reasons," 98.

29. Arnold, *The Preaching of Islam*; Krstic, "Narrating Conversions to Islam."

30. Krstic, "Narrating Conversions to Islam," 102.

31. De Weese, *Islamization and Native Religion in the Golden Horde*, 541–43.

32. This resembles, though in reverse, St. Francis's missionary work as described by Bonaventure.

33. Golb, *Jewish Proselytism*; Marcus, *The Jew in the Medieval World*, 353–54; Fletcher, *The Barbarian Conversion*, 289–91, 298.

34. Mulsow and Popkin, eds., *Secret Conversions to Judaism in Early Modern Europe.*

35. Aston, ed., *Nihongi*, 67.

36. Kapstein, *The Tibetan Assimilation of Buddhism*, 41–42.

37. Ibid., 53.

38. Oldenberg and Bechert, eds., *Die Reden des Buddha*, 61–67.

39. Tambiah, *The Buddhist Saints of the Forest and the Cult of Amulets*, 111–23; Tambiah, "The Buddhist Arahant"; Bigandet, *The Life, or Legend, of Gaudama, the Buddha of the Burmese*; Nyanaponika and Hecker, *Great Disciples of the Buddha.*

40. Hyanasampanno, *The Venerable Phra Acharn Mun Bhuridatta Thera, Meditation Master.*

41. Carrithers, *The Forest Monks of Sri Lanka*, 139–62.

42. King, "Awakening Stories of Zen Buddhist Women."

43. Ibid., 521.

44. Ibid., 524.

45. Bitter, *Konversion zum tibetischen Buddhismus.*

46. Ibid., 168–70.

47. See also Doren, "Wunschräume und Wunschzeiten." For further reading, see also Kippenberg's excellent article "Apokalyptik / Messianismus / Chiliasmus."

48. Mooney, *The Ghost-Dance Religion and the Sioux Outbreak of 1890*, 26.

49. Reeves, *The Influence of Prophecy in the Later Middle Ages.*

50. Arjomand, *The Shadow of God and the Hidden Imam*; Fleischer, "Seer to the Sultan."

51. For messianism in modern times, see also Scholem, *Sabbatai Sevi*; Idel, *Messianic Mystics.*

52. *Tanakh*, Isaiah 11:6 and 30:23.

53. *Tanakh*, Haggai 1:10–11.

54. *Tanakh*, Haggai 2:22–23.

55. Savonarola, *Selected Writings of Girolamo Savonarola*, 153; see also 70. For the comparison between Florence and Jerusalem, see 235; see also Savonarola, *O Florenz! O Rom! O Italien!* 116.

56. Savonarola, *Selected Writings of Girolamo Savonarola*, 153–54. Regarding penance, see Savonarola, *A Guide to Righteous Living and Other Works*, 81–97.

57. See also Savonarola, *Selected Writings of Girolamo Savonarola*, 231–37; Weinstein, *Savonarola and Florence*, 138–58.

58. Savonarola, *O Florenz! O Rom! O Italien!* 132; see also Savonarola, *Selected Writings of Girolamo Savonarola*, 73.

59. McGinn, ed. and trans., *Apocalyptic Spirituality*, 266.

60. Savonarola, *O Florenz! O Rom! O Italien!* 154.

61. Ibid., 155–56.

62. Savonarola is adhering to thought patterns typical for fundamentalists. See also Riesebrodt, *Pious Passion*.

63. Madelung, "Al-Mahdi"; see also Cook, *Studies in Muslim Apocalyptic*.

64. See Khaldun, *The Muqaddimah*, 2:156–200.

65. García-Arenal, *Messianism and Puritanical Reform*, 21.

66. Ibid.; Fleischer, "The Lawgiver as Messiah."

67. Madelung, "Al-Mahdi."

68. Arjomand, *The Shadow of God and the Hidden Imam*; Sachedina, *Islamic Messianism*; Bashir, *Messianic Hopes and Mystical Visions*.

69. Sachedina, *Islamic Messianism*, 173.

70. Ibid., 174.

71. Sadr, *The Awaited Saviour*, 11.

72. Bauer, *China und die Hoffnung auf Glück*; Seidel, "Taoist Messianism"; Ownby, "Chinese Millenarian Traditions."

73. Seidel, "Taoist Messianism," 163.

74. Ibid., 167.

75. Ibid., 169.

76. Zürcher, " 'Prince Moonlight.' "

77. Newman, "Eschatology in the Wheel of Time Tantra"; Newman, "Islam in the Kalacakra Tantra."

78. For the historical background, see introduction to Yampolsky, ed., *Selected Writings of Nichiren*; see also Matsunaga and Matsunaga, *Foundation of Japanese Buddhism*, 2:137ff.

79. Nichiren, *The Writings of Nichiren Daishonin*, 6, 891–92.

80. Ibid., 561; Yampolsky, ed., *Selected Writings of Nichiren*, 215.

81. Nichiren, *The Writings of Nichiren Daishonin*, 8; Yampolsky, ed., *Selected Writings of Nichiren*, 16.

82. Nichiren, *The Writings of Nichiren Daishonin*, 891.

83. Ibid., 126–27.

84. Yoshio, "Millenarianism in Omotokyo."

85. Ibid., 18–19.

86. Reader, *Religious Violence in Contemporary Japan*.

CHAPTER EIGHT

The Future of Religion

1. Hobbes, *Leviathan*, 168.

2. Durkheim, *The Elementary Forms of Religious Life*; Gehlen, *Man, His Nature and Place in the World*. I am aware of problems inherent in Gehlen's work and only share certain aspects of his anthropology.

3. See Boyer, *Religion Explained*.

4. Freud, *The Future of an Illusion*.

5. See Lübbe, *Religion nach der Aufklärung*; Luhmann,"Die Ausdifferenzierung der Religion"; Luhmann, *Funktion der Religion*. Luhmann's concept of contingency, by contrast, is inappropriately vague. See Pollack, *Säkularisierung—ein moderner Mythos?* Pascal Boyer has disapproved such interpretations, but his analysis of religious thoughts focuses on the abstract thought categories of subjects and not on institutionalized meanings of practices.

6. Freud, *Civilization and Its Discontents*; Spiro, *Culture and Human Nature*; Spiro, "Religion."

7. Freud, *The Future of an Illusion*.

8. Rizzuto, *The Birth of the Living God*. Rizzuto's presentation is informed by an underlying ontogenetic, prototypical monotheism. In her opinion, the lack of such belief needs to be explained (47).

9. See also Coles, *The Spiritual Life of Children*; Meissner, *Psychoanalysis and Religious Experience*.

10. Rizzuto, *The Birth of the Living God*, 47.

11. Ibid., 193–94.

12. Martin, *A General Theory of Secularization*; Dobbelaere, *Secularization*; Casanova, *Public Religions in the Modern World*; Gorski, "Historicizing the Secularization Debate"; Pollack, *Säkularisierung—ein moderner Mythos?* Graf, *Die Wiederkehr der Götter*.

13. Warner, "Work in Progress toward a New Paradigm for the Sociological Study of Religion in the United States"; Young, ed., *Rational Choice Theory and Religion*; Iannoccone, "Introduction to the Economics of Religion."

14. See also the excellent critique by Bruce, *Choice and Religion*.

15. See also Dobbelaere, *Secularization*.

16. Luhmann, "Die Ausdifferenzierung der Religion"; Luhmann, *Funktion der Religion*.

17. See also Juergensmeyer, *The New Cold War?*

18. Martin, *A General Theory of Secularization*.

19. Martin, *Tongues of Fire*.

20. Meyer, *Translating the Devil*.

21. Merton, *Science, Technology and Society in Seventeenth Century England*; Thomas, *Religion and the Decline of Magic*.

22. Weber, *The Protestant Ethic and the "Spirit" of Capitalism and Other Writings*; Honigsheim, *Die Staats- und Sozial-Lehren der französischen Jansenisten im 17. Jahrhundert*.

23. Bruce, *God Is Dead*, 204ff.

24. Luckmann, *The Invisible Religion*.

25. Bellah et al., *Habits of the Heart*; Wuthnow, "Spirituality and Spiritual Practice."

26. Riesebrodt, *Pious Passion*; Riesebrodt, *Die Rückkehr der Religionen*.

27. Bruce, *God Is Dead*, 210.

28. Parsons, "Christianity and Modern Industrial Society."

29. Comaroff and Comaroff, eds. *Millennial Capitalism and the Culture of Neoliberalism*.

30. Riesebrodt,"Was ist 'religiöser Fundamentalismus'?"

31. Weber, "Science as a Vocation."

BIBLIOGRAPHY

Abu l-Fazl, Allami. *The A-in-i Akbari.* Translated by H. Blochmann. 2nd ed. Delhi: Low Price Publications, 1965.

Acosta, José de. *Natural and Moral History of the Indies.* Translated by Frances López-Morillas. Durham, NC: Duke University Press, 2002.

Aijmer, Göran. *The Dragon Boat Festival on the Hupeh-Hunan Plain, Central China.* Stockholm: Ethnographical Museum of Sweden, 1964.

Allen, Douglas. "Phenomenology of Religion." In Eliade, *Encyclopedia of Religion* (see below), 11:272–85.

Alles mit Gott: Evangelisches Gebetbuch. 38th ed. Stuttgart: Verlag von W. Kitzinger, 1880.

Arjomand, Said Amir. *The Shadow of God and the Hidden Imam.* Chicago: University of Chicago Press, 1984.

Arnold, Thomas Walker. *The Preaching of Islam: A History of the Propagation of the Muslim Faith.* Westminster: A. Constable and Co, 1896.

Asad, Talal. *Formations of the Secular: Christianity, Islam, Modernity.* Stanford: Stanford University Press, 2003.

———. *Genealogies of Religion: Discipline and Reasons of Power in Christianity and Islam.* Baltimore: Johns Hopkins University Press, 1993.

Aston, W. G., ed. *Nihongi: Chronicles of Japan from the Earliest Times to A.D. 697.* Vol. 2. Tokyo: Charles E. Tuttle Company, 1972.

Athanasius. *The Life of Antony and the Letter to Marcellinus.* Translated by Robert C. Gregg. New York: Paulist Press, 1980.

Attar, Farid al-Din. *Muslim Saints and Mystics: Episodes from the Tadhkirat al-Auliya'* ("Memorial of the Saints"). Translated by A. J. Arberry. Chicago: University of Chicago Press, 1966.

Augustine. *The Confessions of St. Augustine.* Translated by E. B. Pusey. 1907. Reprint, New York: Everyman's Library, 1949.

Averbuch, Irit. *The Gods Come Dancing: A Study of the Japanese Ritual Dance of Yamabushi Kagura.* Cornell East Asia Series, vol. 79. Ithaca, NY: Cornell University Press, 1995.

Balagangadhara, S. N. *"The Heathen in his Blindness . . .": Asia, the West, and the Dynamic of Religion*. Leiden: E. J. Brill, 1994.

Baldon, John F. "Christmas." In Eliade, *Encyclopedia of Religion* (see below), 3:460.

Bartleman, Frank. *Azusa Street*. New Kensington, PA: Whitaker House, 1982.

Bashir, Shahzad. *Messianic Hopes and Mystical Visions: The Nurbakhshiya between Medieval and Modern Islam*. Columbia: University of South Carolina Press, 2003.

Bauer, Wolfgang. *China und die Hoffnung auf Glück: Paradiese, Utopien, Idealvorstellungen in der Geistesgeschichte Chinas*. Munich: Deutscher Taschenbuch Verlag, 1971.

Beckford, James. "Accounting for Conversion." *British Journal of Sociology* 29 (1978): 249–62.

Bellah, Robert N. *Beyond Belief: Essays on Religion in a Post-Traditional World*. New York: Harper & Row, 1970.

Bellah, Robert N., Richard Madsen, William M. Sullivan, and Ann Swidler. *Habits of the Heart: Individualism and Commitment in American Life*. Berkeley: University of California Press, 1985.

Bellenir, Karen. *Religious Holidays and Calendars: An Encyclopedic Handbook*. 2nd ed. Detroit: Omnigraphics, 1998.

Belting, Hans. *Likeness and Presence: A History of the Image before the Era of Art*. Chicago: University of Chicago Press, 1994.

Bergdolt, Klaus. *Der Schwarze Tod: Die Große Pest und das Ende des Mittelalters*. Munich: C. H. Beck, 2000.

Berger, Peter L. *The Sacred Canopy*. Garden City, NY: Doubleday, 1967.

———. *The Heretical Imperative: Contemporary Possibilities of Religious Affirmation*. Garden City, NY: Doubleday, 1979.

Berger, Peter L., and Thomas Luckmann. *The Social Construction of Reality*. Garden City, NY: Doubleday, 1966.

Beyer, Peter. *Religions in Global Society*. London: Routledge, 2006.

Bieritz, Karl-Heinrich. *Das Kirchenjahr*. 7th ed. Munich: C. H. Beck, 2005.

Bigandet, Paul Ambroise. *The Life, or Legend, of Gaudama, the Buddha of the Burmese*. 2 vols. 4th ed. London: K. Paul, Trench, Trübner, 1911.

Birnbaum, Philip, trans. and ed. *Daily Prayer Book*. New York: Hebrew Publishing Company, 1949.

Biruni, Muhammad Ibn Ahmad, al-. *Alberuni's India: An Accurate Description of All Categories of Hindu Thought*. New York: Norton, 1971.

Bitter, Klaus. *Konversion zum tibetischen Buddhismus: Eine Analyse religiöser Biographien*. Göttingen: E. Oberdieck, 1988.

Blacker, Carmen. *The Catalpa Bow: A Study of Shamanistic Practices in Japan*. London: Allen & Unwin, 1975.

———. *Collected Writings of Carmen Blacker*. Tokyo: Japan Library, 2000.

Bock, Felicia Gressitt, ed. *Engi-Shiki. Procedures of the Engi Era*. 2 vols. Tokyo: Sophia University, 1970.

Bodde, Derk. *Festivals in Classical China: New Year and Other Annual Observances during the Han Dynasty, 206 B.C.–A.D. 220*. Princeton, NJ: Princeton University Press, 1975.

Bonaventure. *The Life of St. Francis.* Translated by Ewert Cousins. San Francisco: Harper San Francisco, 2005.

Boot, Willem Jan. "Shunmu-ki and Denchu Mondo: Two Instances of Buddhist-Confucian Polemics in the Edo Period." In *Conflict and Accommodation in Early Modern East Asia: Essays in Honour of Erik Zürcher,* edited by Leonard Blussé and Harriet T. Zurndorfer, 38–53. Leiden: E. J. Brill, 1993.

Bourdieu, Pierre. "Genesis and Structure of the Religious Field." In *Comparative Social Research* 13, edited by Craig Calhoun, 1–44. Greenwich, CT: JAI Press, 1991.

Boxer, C. R. *The Church Militant and Iberian Expansion, 1440–1770.* Baltimore: Johns Hopkins University Press, 1978.

Boyer, Pascal. *Religion Explained: The Evolutionary Origins of Religious Thought.* New York: Basic Books, 2001.

———. "Religious Thought and Behaviour as By-products of Brain Function." *Trends in Cognitive Sciences* 7, no. 3 (2003): 119–24.

Brakke, David. *Athanasius and Asceticism.* Baltimore: Johns Hopkins University Press, 1995.

Breidert, Wolfgang, ed. *Die Erschütterung der vollkommenen Welt: Die Wirkung des Erdbebens von Lissabon im Spiegel europäischer Zeitgenossen.* Darmstadt: Wissenschaftliche Buchgesellschaft, 1994.

Brown, Peter. *The Body and Society: Men, Women and Sexual Renunciation in Early Christianity.* Berkeley: University of California Press, 1982.

Bruce, Steve. *Choice and Religion.* Oxford: Oxford University Press, 1999.

———. *God Is Dead: Secularization in the West.* Oxford: Blackwell, 2002.

Bruce, Steve, and Roy Wallis. "Rescuing Motives." *British Journal of Sociology* 34 (1983): 61–71.

Buddhaghosa. *The Path to Purification: Visuddhi-Magga.* Vol 1. Translated by Bhikku Nyanamoli. Berkeley: Shambhala Publications, 1976.

Bulliet, Richard W. "Conversion to Islam and the Emergence of a Muslim Society in Iran." In *Conversion to Islam,* edited by Nehemia Levtzion, 30–51. New York: Holmes & Meyer, 1979.

———. *Conversion to Islam in the Medieval Period.* Cambridge, MA: Harvard University Press, 1979.

Burmeister, Karl Heinz. *Der Schwarze Tod: Die Judenverfolgungen anläßlich der Pest von 1348/49.* Göppingen: Jüdisches Museum, 1999.

Cancik, Hubert. "Apologetik/Polemik." In *Handbuch religionswissenschaftlicher Grundbegriffe,* vol. 2, edited by Hubert Cancik, Burkhard Gladigow, and Matthias Laubscher, 29–37. Stuttgart: W. Kohlhammer Verlag, 1990.

Capps, Walter H. *Religious Studies: The Making of a Discipline.* Minneapolis: Fortress Press, 1995.

Carrithers, Michael. *The Forest Monks of Sri Lanka.* Delhi: Oxford University Press, 1983.

Casanova, José. *Public Religions in the Modern World.* Chicago: University of Chicago Press, 1994.

Cassirer, Ernst. *The Philosophy of the Enlightenment.* Translated by Fritz C. A. Koelln and James P. Pettegrove. Princeton, NJ: Princeton University Press, 1951.

Cavin, Albert. *Der Konfuzianismus.* Translated from the French by Elinor Lipper. Geneva: Edito Service, 1973.

Chadwick, Owen. *Western Asceticism: Selected Translations.* The Library of Christian Classics, vol. 12. London: SCM Press, 1958.

Chakrabarty, Dipesh. *Rethinking Working-Class History: Bengal, 1890–1940.* Princeton, NJ: Princeton University Press, 1989.

Chaudhri, Rashid Ahmed. *Muslim Festivals and Ceremonies.* London: London Mosque, 1983.

Chaves, Mark. "On the Rational Choice Approach to Religion." *Journal for the Scientific Study of Religion* 34 (1995): 98–104.

Ch'en, Kenneth. *Buddhism in China.* Princeton, NJ: Princeton University Press, 1964.

Ch'en, Kenneth. *The Chinese Transformation of Buddhism.* Princeton, NJ: Princeton University Press, 1973.

Chidester, David. *Savage Systems: Colonialism and Comparative Religion in Southern Africa.* Charlottesville: University of Virginia Press, 1996.

Chong, Kelly H. *Delivery and Submission: Evangelical Women and the Negotiation of Patriarchy in South Korea.* Cambridge, MA: Harvard University Press, 2008.

Claerhout, Sarah, and Jakob DeRoover. "The Question of Conversion in India." *Economic and Political Weekly,* July 9, 2005.

Cohen, Alvin. "Chinese Religion: Popular Religion." In Eliade, *Encyclopedia of Religion* (see below), 3:289–96.

Cohn, Robert L. "Sainthood on the Periphery: The Case of Judaism." In *Saints and Virtues,* edited by John Stratton Hawley, 87–107. Berkeley: University of California, Press, 1987.

Coles, Robert. *The Spiritual Life of Children.* Boston: Houghton Mifflin, 1990.

Comaroff, Jean, and John L. Comaroff, eds. *Millennial Capitalism and the Culture of Neoliberalism.* Durham, NC: Duke University Press, 2001.

———. *Ethnography and the Historical Imagination.* Boulder, CO: Westview Press, 1992.

———. *Of Revelation and Revolution.* Chicago: University of Chicago Press, 1991.

Cook, David. *Studies in Muslim Apocalyptic.* Princeton, NJ: Princeton University Press, 2002.

Cornell, Vincent J. *Realm of the Saint: Power and Authority in Moroccan Sufism.* Austin: University of Texas Press, 1998.

De Bary, William Theodore, ed. *Sources of Japanese Tradition.* 2nd ed. Vol. 1. New York: Columbia University Press, 2001.

De Bary, William Theodore, and Irene Bloom, eds. *Sources of Chinese Tradition.* 2nd ed. Vol. 1. New York: Columbia University Press 1999.

De Weese, Devin A. *Islamization and Native Religion in the Golden Horde.* University Park: Pennsylvania State University Press 1994.

De Wette, Wilhelm Martin Leberecht. *Ueber die Religion, ihr Wesen, ihre Erscheinungs-formen und ihren Einfluss auf das Leben.* Berlin: G. Reimer, 1827.

Dean, Kenneth. *Taoist Ritual and Popular Cults of Southeast China.* Princeton, NJ: Princeton University Press, 1993.

Despeux, Catherine. "Talismans and Sacred Diagrams." In *Daoism Handbook,* edited by Livia Kohn, 498–540. Leiden: E. J. Brill, 2004.

Dhammika, V. S., trans. *The Edicts of King Asoka.* The Wheel, Publication No. 386–87. Kandy, Sri Lanka: Buddhist Publication Society, 1993.

Diamond, Eliezer. *Holy Men and Hunger Artists: Fasting and Asceticism in Rabbinic Culture.* Oxford: Oxford University of Press, 2004.

Dobbelaere, Karel. *Secularization: An Analysis at Three Levels.* New York: Peter Lang, 2002.

Dobbelaere, Karel, and Jan Lauwers. "Definition of Religion: A Sociological Critique." *Social Compass* 20 (1974): 535–51.

Doran, Robert, ed. *The Lives of Simeon Stylites.* Kalamazoo, MI: Cistercian Publications, 1992.

Doren, Alfred. "Wunschräume und Wunschzeiten." *Vorträge der Bibliothek Warburg* 4 (1924/25): 158–205.

Dresner, Samuel H. *The Zaddik.* London: Abelard-Schuman, 1960.

Dubuisson, Daniel. *The Western Construction of Religion: Myths, Knowledge, and Ideology.* Baltimore: Johns Hopkins University Press, 2003.

Durkheim, Émile. *The Elementary Forms of Religious Life.* Translated by Karen E. Fields. New York: Free Press, 1995.

Earhart, H. Byron: *Religion in the Japanese Experience: Sources and Interpretations.* Belmont: Wadsworth Publishing Company, 1974.

———. *Religions of Japan.* San Francisco: Harper & Row, 1984.

———. *A Religious Study of the Mount Haguro Sect of Shugendo.* Tokyo: Kobundo, 1970.

Eberhard, Wolfram. *Chinese Festivals.* New York: H. Schuman, 1952.

Ebersole, Gary L. *Ritual Poetry and the Politics of Death in Early Japan.* Princeton, NJ: Princeton University Press, 1989.

Eliade, Mircea. "Methodological Remarks on the Study of Religious Symbolism." In *The History of Religions,* edited by Mircea Eliade and Joseph Kitagawa, 86–107. Chicago: Chicago University Press, 1959.

———. *The Myth of the Eternal Return; or, Cosmos and History.* Princeton, NJ: Princeton University Press, 1971.

———. *Die Religionen und das Heilige.* Darmstadt: Wissenschaftliche Buchgesellschaft, 1976.

———. *The Sacred and the Profane: The Nature of Religion.* New York: Harcourt, Brace, 1959.

———. *Shamanism.* Translated by Willard R. Trask. New York: Pantheon Books, 1964.

———. "Shamanism." In Eliade, *Encyclopedia of Religion* (see below), 13:201–7.

———, ed. *The Encyclopedia of Religion.* 16 vols. New York: Collier Macmillan, 1987.

The Encyclopaedia of Islam. Leiden: E. J. Brill, 1996.

Endres, Günter, ed. *Die Sieben Meister des wunderbaren Tao: Taoistische Geschichten aus der Schule der vollkommenen Verwirklichung.* Bern: Scherz Verlag 1991.

Eno, Robert. "Deities and Ancestors in Early Oracle Inscriptions." In *Religions of China in Practice,* edited by Donald S. Lopez, Jr., 41–51. Princeton, NJ: Princeton University Press, 1996.

Eusebius. *Über das Leben des Kaisers Konstantin.* 2nd ed. Berlin: Akademie-Verlag, 1991.

Evangelisches Gesangbuch. Ausgabe für die Evangelisch-Lutherischen Kirchen in Bayern und Thüringen. Munich: Claudius, 1994.

Feil, Ernst. *Religio.* Vol. 1: *Die Geschichte eines neuzeitlichen Grundbegriffs vom Früh-christentum bis zur Reformation.* Forschungen zur Kirchen- und Dogmengeschichte, vol 36. Göttingen: Vandenhoeck & Ruprecht, 1986.

———. *Religio.* Vol 2: *Die Geschichte eines neuzeitlichen Grundbegriffs zwischen Reformation und Rationalismus (ca. 1540–1620).* Forschungen zur Kirchen- und Dogmengeschichte, vol. 70. Göttingen, 1997.

———. *Religio.* Vol 3: *Die Geschichte eines neuzeitlichen Grundbegriffs im 17. und frühen 18. Jahrhundert.* Forschungen zur Kirchen- und Dogmengeschichte, vol. 79. Göttingen, 2001.

Feld, Helmut. *Franziskus von Assisi.* Munich: C. H. Beck, 2001.

———. *Franziskus von Assisi und seine Bewegung.* Darmstadt: Wissenschaftliche Buchgesellschaft, 1996.

Feuchtwang, Stephan. *Popular Religion in China: The Imperial Metaphor.* Richmond, UK: Curzon, 2001.

Feuerbach, Ludwig. *The Essence of Christianity.* Translated by Georg Eliot. 1893. Reprint, New York: Harper, 1957.

Finke, Roger, and Rodney Stark. *The Churching of America, 1776–1990: Winners and Losers in Our Religious Economy.* New Brunswick, NJ: Rutgers University Press, 1992.

Fleischer, Cornell. "The Lawgiver as Messiah: The Making of the Imperial Image in the Reign of Süleyman." In *Soliman le Magnifique et son temps,* edited by Gilles Veinstein, 159–77. Paris: Documentation française, 1992.

———. "Seer to the Sultan: Haydar-I Remmal and Sultan Süleyman." In *Cultural Horizons,* edited by Jayne L. Warner, 290–99. Syracuse: Syracuse University Press, 2001.

Fletcher, Richard. *The Barbarian Conversion: From Paganism to Christianity.* Berkeley: University of California Press, 1997.

Foltz, Richard C. *Religions of the Silk Road.* New York: St. Martin's Press, 1999.

Fortune, Reo. *Sorcerers of Dobu.* New York: E. P. Dutton, 1963.

Francis, James A. *Subversive Virtue: Asceticism and Authority in the Second-Century Pagan World.* University Park: Pennsylvania State University Press, 1995.

Frank, Karl Suso. *Geschichte des christlichen Mönchtums.* Darmstadt: Primus, 1993.

Frazer, James G. *The Golden Bough: A Study in Magic and Religion.* New York: Macmillan, 1900; abridged ed., 1951.

Freud, Sigmund. *Civilization and Its Discontents.* Translated by Louis Menand. New York: Norton, 2005.

———. *The Future of an Illusion.* Translated by W. D. Robson-Scott. London: Hogarth Press, 1943.

García-Arenal, Mercedes. "Dreams and Reasons: Autobiographies of Converts in Religious Polemics." In *Conversions islamiques,* edited by Mercedes García-Arenal, 89–118. Paris: Maisonneuve et Laros, 2001.

———. *Messianism and Puritanical Reform: Mahdis of the Muslim West.* Leiden: E. J. Brill 2006.

———, ed. *Conversions islamiques: Identités religieuses en Islam méditerranéen.* Paris: Maisonneuve et Laros, 2001.

Gaster, Theodor. "Amulets and Talismans." In Eliade, *Encyclopedia of Religion* (see above), 1:243–46.

Gay, Peter. *Deism: An Anthology.* Princeton, NJ: Princeton University Press, 1968.

———. *The Enlightenment: An Interpretation.* New York: Knopf, 1968.

Geertz, Clifford. *The Interpretation of Cultures: Selected Essays.* New York: Basic Books, 1973.

Gehlen, Arnold. *Man, His Nature and Place in the World.* New York: Columbia University Press, 1988.

Gernet, Jacques. *China and the Christian Impact: A Conflict of Cultures.* Translated by Janet Lloyd. Cambridge: Cambridge University Press, 1986.

Gimaret, D. "Shirk." In Eliade, *The Encyclopaedia of Islam* (see above), 484–86.

Golb, Norman. *Jewish Proselytism: A Phenomenon in the Religious History of Early Medieval Europe.* Cincinnati: University of Cincinnati, 1987.

Goldenberg, Robert. *The Nations That Know Thee Not: Ancient Jewish Attitudes toward Other Religions.* New York: New York University Press, 1998.

Gombrich, Richard. *Precept and Practice: Traditional Buddhism in the Rural Highlands of Ceylon.* Oxford: Oxford University Press, 1971.

Gombrich, Richard, and Gananath Obeyesekere. *Buddhism Transformed.* Princeton, NJ: Princeton University Press, 1988.

Gorski, Philip S. "Historicizing the Secularization Debate: Church, State, and Society in Late Medieval and Early Modern Europe, ca. 1300 to 1700." *American Sociological Review* 65 (2000): 138–67.

Gräb, Wilhelm. "Von der Religionskritik zur Religionshermeneutik." In *Religion als Thema der Theologie,* edited by Wilhelm Gräb, 118–43. Gütersloh: Gütersloher Verlagshaus, 1999.

Graf, Friedrich Wilhelm. *Die Wiederkehr der Götter.* Munich: C. H. Beck, 2005.

Gramlich, Richard. *Die Wunder der Freunde Gottes: Theologien und Erscheinungsformen des islamischen Heiligenwunders.* Freiburger Islamstudien, vol. 11. Stuttgart: Franz Steiner Verlag, 1987.

———. *Weltverzicht: Grundlagen und Weisen islamischer Askese.* Veröffentlichungen der Orientalischen Kommission, vol. 43. Wiesbaden: O. Harrassowitz, 1997.

Grapard, Allan G. *The Protocol of the Gods: A Study of the Kasuga Cult in Japanese History.* Berkeley: University of California Press, 1992.

Green, Arthur. *Tormented Master: A Life of Rabbi Nahman of Bratslav.* Tuscaloosa: University of Alabama Press, 1979.

Griaule, Marcel. *Conversations with Ogotemmeli.* New York: Oxford University Press, 1965.

Grunebaum, Gustave E. von. *Muhammadan Festivals.* New York: Schuman, 1951.

Hammer, Reuven. *Entering Jewish Prayer: A Guide to Personal Devotion and the Worship Service.* New York: Schocken Books, 1994.

Hanska, Jussi. *Strategies of Sanity and Survival: Religious Responses to Natural Disasters in the Middle Ages.* Helsinki: Finnish Literature Society, 2002.

Hardacre, Helen. "Ancestor Worship." In Eliade, *Encyclopedia of Religion* (see above), 1:263–67.

———. *Shinto and the State, 1868–1988.* Princeton NJ: Princeton University Press, 1989.

Harnack, Adolf von. *Die Mission und Ausbreitung des Christentums in den ersten drei Jahrhunderten.* Leipzig: J. C. Hinrich, 1924.

Harrell, Stevan. "Domestic Observances: Chinese Practices." In Eliade, *Encyclopedia of Religion* (see above), 4:410–14.

Harrison, Thomas. *Divinity and History: The Religion of Herodotus.* Oxford: Oxford University Press, 2000.

Harvey, Peter. *An Introduction to Buddhism.* Cambridge: Cambridge University Press, 1990.

Haußig, Hans Michael. *Der Religionsbegriff in den Religionen.* Berlin: EVA, 1999.

Herodotus, *The Histories.* Translated by Aubrey de Sélincourt. London: Penguin Books, 1954.

Hertzberg, Arthur. *Der Judaismus.* Geneva: Edito Service, 1973.

Hirsch, Leo. *Jüdische Glaubenswelt.* Gütersloh: Bertelsmann, 1966.

Hobbes, Thomas. *Leviathan.* Harmondsworth, UK: Penguin Books, 1968.

Honigsheim, Paul. *Die Staats- und Sozial-Lehren der französischen Jansenisten im 17. Jahrhundert.* Heidelberg: C. Pfeffer, 1914.

Horne, Charles F., ed. *The Sacred Books and Early Literature of the East.* Vol.12: *Japan.* New York: Parke, Austin, and Lipscomb, 1917.

Horner, I. B., ed. *The Book of Discipline (Vinaya-Pitaka).* vol. 4 (Mahavagga). Edited by H. Milford. Oxford: Oxford University Press, 1938–66.

Horton, Robin. "African Traditional Thought and Western Science." In *Rationality,* edited by Bryan R. Wilson, 121–71. Oxford: Oxford University Press, 1970.

Huang, Yongliang: *Die Sieben Meister der vollkommenen Verwirklichung: Der taoistische Lehrroman Ch'i-chen chuan in Übersetzung und im Spiegel seiner Quellen.* Würzburger Sino-Japonica, vol. 13. Frankfurt am Main: Peter Lang, 1985.

Hugh-Jones, Stephen, and James Laidlaw, eds. *The Essential Edmund Leach.* Vol. 1, New Haven, CT: Yale University Press, 2000.

Hume, David. *Writings on Religion.* Edited by Antony Flew. La Salle, IL: Open Court, 1992.

Hyanasampanno, Phra Acharn Maha Boowa. *The Venerable Phra Acharn Mun Bhuridatta Thera, Meditation Master.* Translated by Siri Buddhasukh. Bangkok: Mahamakut Rajavidyalaya Press, 1976.

Iannoccone, Lawrence. "Introduction to the Economics of Religion." *Journal of Economic Literature* 36 (1998): 1465–96.

Idel, Moshe. *Messianic Mystics.* New Haven, CT: Yale University Press, 1998.

In Sure and Certain Hope: Rites and Prayers from the Order of Christian Funerals for the Use of Lay Leaders. London: Catholic Church, International Commission on English in the Liturgy, Bishops' Conference of England and Wales. Liturgy Office, 1999.

Jakubowski-Tiessen, Manfred, and Hartmut Lehmann, eds. *Um Himmels Willen: Religion in Katastrophenzeiten.* Göttingen: Vandenhoeck & Ruprecht, 2003.

James, William. *The Varieties of Religious Experience: A Study in Human Nature.* New York: Modern Library, 1902.

Jensen, Lionel M. *Manufacturing Confucianism.* Durham, NC: Duke University Press, 1997.

Jones, Susan Wilbur, trans. *Ages Ago: Thirty-seven Tales From the Konjaku Monogatari Collection.* Cambridge, MA: Harvard University Press, 1959.

Juergensmeyer, Mark. *The New Cold War? Religious Nationalism Confronts the Secular State.* Berkeley: University of California Press, 1993.

Kaelber, Lutz. *Schools of Asceticism: Ideology and Organization in Medieval Religious Communities.* University Park: Pennsylvania State University Press, 1998.

Kapstein, Matthew. *The Tibetan Assimilation of Buddhism: Conversion, Contestation, and Memory.* New York: Oxford University Press, 2000.

Kasahara, Kazuo, ed. *A History of Japanese Religion.* Tokyo: Kosei Publications, 2001.

Ketelaar, James Edward. *Of Heretics and Martyrs in Meiji Japan: Buddhism and Its Persecution.* Princeton, NJ: Princeton University Press, 1990.

Khaldun, Ibn. *The Muqaddimah: An Introduction to History.* Translated by Franz Rosenthal. 3 vols. Princeton, NJ: Princeton University Press, 1980.

Kieschnick, John. *The Eminent Monk: Buddhist Ideals in Medieval Chinese Hagiography.* Honolulu: University of Hawai'i Press, 1997.

King, Richard. *Orientalism and Religion: Postcolonial Theory, India and "the Mystic East."* London: Routledge, 1999.

King, Sallie. "Awakening Stories of Zen Buddhist Women." In *Buddhism in Practice,* edited by Donald S. Lopez, 513–24. Princeton, NJ: Princeton University Press, 1995.

Kippenberg, Hans G. "Apokalyptik / Messianismus / Chiliasmus." In *Handbuch religionswissenschaftlicher Grundbegriffe,* vol 2, edited by Hubert Cancik, Burkhard Gladigow, and Matthias Laubscher, 9–26. Stuttgart: Kohlhammer 1990.

———. *Discovering Religious History in the Modern Age.* Translated by Barbara Harshav. Princeton, NJ: Princeton University Press, 2002.

Kippenberg, Hans G., and Brigitte Luchesi, eds. *Religionswissenschaft und Kulturkritik.* Marburg: Diagonal Verlag, 1991.

Kitagawa, Joseph M. *On Understanding Japanese Religion.* Princeton, NJ: Princeton University Press, 1987.

———. *Religion in Japanese History.* New York: Columbia University Press, 1990.

Knoblauch, Hubert, Volker Krech, and Monika Wohlrab-Sahr, eds. *Religiöse Konversion.* Konstanz: Universitätsverlag, 1998.

Kohn, Livia. *God of the Dao.* Ann Arbor: Center for the Chinese Studies, University of Michigan, 1998.

———, ed. *Laughing at the Tao: Debates among Buddhists and Taoists in Medieval China.* Princeton, NJ: Princeton University Press, 1995.

———, ed. *The Taoist Experience: An Anthology.* Albany, NY: State University of New York Press, 1993.

Kratz, Reinhard, ed. *Religion und Religionskontakte im Zeitalter der Achämeniden.* Gütersloh: Gütersloher Verlagshaus, 2002.

Kreiser, Klaus, Werner Diem, and Hans Georg Majer. *Lexikon der islamischen Welt.* 3 vols. Stuttgart: Kohlhammer, 1974.

Krstic, Tijana. "Narrating Conversions to Islam: The Dialogue of Texts and Practices in Early Modern Ottoman Balkans." Doctoral diss., University of Michigan, 2004.

Kushner, Harold S. *When Bad Things Happen to Good People.* New York: Schocken Books, 1981.

Lactantius. *De Mortibus Persecutorum.* Translated by J. L. Creed. Oxford: Oxford University Press, 1984.

Lagerwey, John. *Taoist Ritual in Chinese Society and History.* New York: Macmillan, 1987.

Lang, Bernhard. *Sacred Games: A History of Christian Worship*. New Haven, CT: Yale University Press, 1997.

———. "Kult." In *Handbuch religionswissenschaftlicher Grundbegriffe*, vol. 3, edited by. von Hubert Cancik, Burkhard Gladigow and Karl-Heinz Kohl, 474–88. Stuttgart: Kohlhammer 1993.

Lauchert, Friedrich. *Die Kanones der wichtigsten altkirchlichen Concilien, nebst den Apostolischen Kanones*. Freiburg im Breisgau: Friedrich Lauchert, 1896.

Lawrence, Bruce B. *Shahrastani on Indian Religions*. The Hague: Mouton, 1976.

Le Goff, Jacques: *The Birth of Purgatory*. Translated by Arthur Goldhammer. Chicago: University of Chicago Press, 1984.

Leach, Edmund R. *Political Systems of Highland Burma: A Study of Kachin Social Structure*. London: G. Bell, 1954.

Lee, Henry W. *Family Prayers, with Forms for Occasional and Private Use*. New York: E. P. Dutton, 1871.

Leuba, James H. *A Psychological Study of Religion, Its Origin, Function, and Future*. New York: AMS Press, 1912.

Levering, Miriam. "Ta-hui and Lay Buddhists: Ch'an Sermons of Death." In *Buddhist and Taoist Practice in Medieval Chinese Society*, edited by David W. Chappell, 181–206. Honolulu: University of Hawaii Press, 1987.

Lieu, Samuel N. C. *Manichaeism in Central Asia and China*. Leiden: E. J. Brill, 1998.

Lincoln, Bruce. *Discourse and the Construction of Society: Comparative Studies of Myth, Ritual, and Classification*. New York: Oxford University Press, 1989.

Locke, John. *The Reasonableness of Christianity: As Delivered in the Scriptures*. Edited by John C. Higgins-Biddle. Oxford: Oxford University Press, 1999.

Lofland, John, und Rodney Stark. "Becoming a World-Saver: A Theory of Conversion to a Deviant Perspective." *American Sociological Review* 30, no.6 (1965): 862–75.

Lopez, Donald S. *Buddhist Scriptures*. London: Penguin Books, 2004.

Lübbe, Hermann. *Religion nach der Aufklärung*. Graz: Styria, 1986.

Luckmann, Thomas. *The Invisible Religion: The Problem of Religion in Modern Society*. New York: Macmillan, 1967.

Luhmann, Niklas. "Die Ausdifferenzierung der Religion." In *Gesellschaftsstruktur und Semantik*, 259–357. Frankfurt am Main: Suhrkamp, 1989.

———. *Die Religion der Gesellschaft*. Frankfurt am Main: Suhrkamp, 2000.

———. *Funktion der Religion*. Frankfurt am Main: Suhrkamp, 1977.

Madelung, Wilferd. "Al-Mahdi." In *Encylopaedia of Islam*, 1230–38. Leiden: E. J. Brill, 1986.

Magenschab, Hans. *Andreas Hofer: Zwischen Napoleon und Kaiser Franz*. Graz: Amalthea, 1984.

Malinowski, Bronislaw. *Magic, Science and Religion, and Other Essays*. Boston: Beacon Press, 1948.

Marcus, Ivan G. *Piety and Society: The Jewish Pietists of Medieval Germany*. Leiden: E. J. Brill, 1981.

Marcus, Jacob Rader. *The Jew in the Medieval World: A Source Book, 315–1791*. Cincinnati: Hebrew Union College Press, 1938.

Marett, Robert R. *Anthropology*. New York: H. Holt, 1912.

Martin, David. *A General Theory of Secularization*. Oxford: Blackwell, 1978.

———. *Tongues of Fire: The Explosion of Protestantism in Latin America*. Oxford: Blackwell, 1990.

Marx, Karl, and Friedrich Engels. *The German Ideology: Including Thesis on Feuerbach and Introduction to the Critique on Political Economy*. Amherst, NY: Prometheus Books, 1998.

Marx, Karl. "Critique of Hegel's Philosophy of the State." In Karl Marx, *Writings of the Young Marx on Philosophy and Society*, translated and edited by Loyd D. Easton and Kurt H. Guddat, 151–202. Indianapolis: Hackett Publishing Company, 1997.

Matsunaga, Daigan, and Alicia Matsunaga. *Foundation of Japanese Buddhism*. 2 vols. Los Angeles: Buddhist Books International, 1974.

May, Burkhard. "Die Religionspolitik der ägyptischen Fatimiden, 969–1171." Doctoral diss., Hamburg University, 1975.

McCutcheon, Russell T. *Manufacturing Religion*. New York: Oxford University Press, 1997.

McDougall, William. *An Introduction to Social Psychology*. Boston: John W. Luce, 1908.

McGinn, Bernard. *The Foundations of Mysticism*. Vol. 1. New York: Crossroad Publishing Company, 1991.

———, ed. and trans. *Apocalyptic Spirituality*. New York: Paulist Press, 1979.

McLellan, David. *Marxism and Religion: A Description and Assessment of the Marxist Critique of Christianity*. New York: Harper & Row, 1987.

McMullin, Neil. "Historical and Historiographic Issues in the Study of Pre-modern Japanese Religions." *Japanese Journal of Religious Studies* 16, no.1 (1989): 3–40.

Meissner, William W. *Psychoanalysis and Religious Experience*. New Haven, CT: Yale University Press, 1984.

Merton, Robert K. *Social Theory and Social Structure*. 1938. Reprint, New York: Free Press, 1956.

———. *Science, Technology and Society in Seventeenth Century England*. New York: H. Fertig, 1970.

Meyer, Birgit. *Translating the Devil: Religion and Modernity among the Ewe in Ghana*. Trenton, NJ: Africa World Press, 1999.

Minamiki, George. *The Chinese Rites Controversy from Its Beginning to Modern Times*. Chicago: University of Chicago Press, 1985.

Miyake, Hitoshi. *Shugendo: Essays on the Structure of Japanese Folk Religion*. Ann Arbor: University of Michigan Press, 2001.

Modder, Ralph P. *Chinese Temple Festivals*. Hong Kong: South China Morning Post, 1983.

Mooney, James. *The Ghost-Dance Religion and the Sioux Outbreak of 1890*. Chicago: University of Chicago Press, 1965.

Müller, F. Max, ed. *Sacred Books of the Buddhists*. Vol. 2. London: H. Milford, Oxford University, 1899.

Mulsow, Martin, and Richard Henry Popkin, eds. *Secret Conversions to Judaism in Early Modern Europe*. Leiden: E. J. Brill, 2004.

Mungello, David E. *Curious Land: Jesuit Accommodation and the Origins of Sinology*. Honolulu: University of Hawai'i Press, 1989.

Musurillo, Herbert, ed. *The Acts of the Christian Martyrs.* Oxford: Clarendon Press, 1972.

Al-Nawawi. *Al-Maqasid: Al-Nawawi's Manual of Islam.* Translated by Nuh Ha Mim Keller. Cambridge: Islamic Text Society, 1996.

Nelson, John K. *Enduring Identities: The Guise of Shinto in Contemporary Japan.* Honolulu: University of Hawai'i Press, 2000.

———. *A Year in the Life of a Shinto Shrine.* Seattle: University of Washington Press, 1996.

Newberg, Andrew, Eugene D'Aquili, and Vince Rause. *Why God Won't Go Away: Brain Science and the Biology of Belief.* New York: Ballantine Books, 2001.

Newman, John. "Eschatology in the Wheel of Time Tantra." In *Buddhism in Practice,* edited by Donald S. Lopez, 284–89. Princeton, NJ: Princeton University Press, 1995.

———. "Islam in the Kalacakra Tantra." *Journal of the International Association of Buddhist Studies* 21, no. 2 (1998): 311–71.

Nichiren. *The Writings of Nichiren Daishonin.* Tokyo: Soka Gakkai, 1999.

Nilakanta Sastri, K. A. *A History of South India from Prehistoric Times to the Fall of Vijayanagar.* Madras: Oxford University Press, 1958.

Nizami, Khaliq Ahmad. *Akhbar and Religion.* Delhi: Idarah-i-Adabiyat-i-Delli, 1989.

Nock, Arthur D.: *Conversion: The Old and the New in Religion from Alexander the Great to Augustine of Hippo.* Baltimore: Johns Hopkins University Press, 1933.

Nohl, Johannes. *Der schwarze Tod: Eine Chronik der Pest 1348–1720, unter Benutzung zeitgenössischer Quellen.* Potsdam: Kiepenheuer, 1924.

Nyanaponika, ed. *Die Lehrreden des Buddha aus der Angereihten Sammlung: Anguttara-Nikaya.* Translated from the Pali by Nyanatiloka. Vol. 2. Brunswick: Aurum Verlag, 1984.

Nyanaponika, Bodhi, and Hellmuth Hecker. *Great Disciples of the Buddha: Their Lives, Their Works, Their Legacy.* Boston: Wisdom Publications, 1997.

Oldenberg, Hermann. *The Religion of the Veda.* Delhi: Motilal Banarsidass, 1988.

Oldenberg, Hermann, and Heinz Bechert, eds. *Die Reden des Buddha: Lehre, Verse, Erzählungen.* Freiburg: Herder, 2000.

Olin, John C., ed. *The Autobiography of St. Ignatius Loyola.* New York: Fordham University Press, 1992.

Otto, Rudolf. *The Idea of the Holy: An Inquiry into the Non-rational Factor in the Idea of the Divine and its Relation to the Rational.* New York: Oxford University Press, 1958.

———. *Kantisch-Fries'sche Religionsphilosophie und ihre Anwendung auf die Theologie.* Tübingen: Mohr, 1909.

———. *Mysticism East and West: A Comparative Analysis of the Nature of Mysticism.* Translated by Bertha L. Bracey and Richenda C. Payne. New york: Macmillan, 1970.

Ownby, David: "Chinese Millenarian Traditions: The Formative Age." *American Historical Review* 104, no. 5 (1999): 1513–30.

Padwick, Constance. *Muslim Devotions: A Study of Prayer-Manuals in Common Use.* London: SPCK, 1961.

Paper, Jordan D. *The Spirits Are Drunk: Comparative Approaches to Chinese Religion.* Albany, NY: State University of New York Press, 1995.

Parker, Robert. *Athenian Religion: A History.* New York: Oxford University Press, 1995.

Parsons, Talcott. "Christianity and Modern Industrial Society." In *Sociological Theory, Values and Sociocultural Change,* edited by Edward A. Tiryakian, 33–70. New York: Free Press, 1963.

Patai, Raphael. "Folk Islam." In Eliade, *Encyclopedia of Religion* (see above), 5:382–85.

———. "Folk Judaism." In Eliade, *Encyclopedia of Religion* (see above), 5:378–82.

———. *On Jewish Folklore.* Detroit: Wayne State University Press, 1983.

Pattanayak, Amiya Kumar. *Religious Policy of the Imperial Gangas.* Delhi: Discovery Publishing House, 1988.

Perera, G. Ariyapala. *Buddhist Paritta Chanting Ritual.* Dehiwala, Sri Laanka: Buddhist Cultural Centre, 2000.

Philippi, Donald L. *Norito: A Translation of the Ancient Japanese Ritual Prayers.* Princeton, NJ: Princeton University Press, 1990.

Picken, Stuart D. B. *Essentials of Shinto.* Westport, CT: Greenwood Press, 1994.

Piyadassi, Thera. *The Book of Protection: Paritta.* Kandy, Sri Lanka: Buddhist Publication Society, 1975.

Polanyi, Karl. *Primitive, Archaic, and Modern Economies, and Other Essays.* Boston: Beacon, 1948.

Pollack, Detlef. *Säkularisierung—ein moderner Mythos? Studien zum religiösen Wandel in Deutschland.* Tübingen: Mohr-Siebeck, 2003.

———. "Vom Tischerücken zur Psychodynamik: Formen außerkirchlicher Religiosität in Deutschland." *Schweizerische Zeitschrift für Soziologie* 1 (1990): 107–34.

Poo, Mu-chou. *In Search of Personal Welfare: A View of Ancient Chinese Religion.* Albany, NY: State University of New York Press, 1998.

Post, Paulus Gijsbertus Johannes. *Disaster Ritual: Explorations of an Emerging Ritual Repertoire.* Louvain: Peeters, 2003.

Prophetic Medical Sciences: The Saviour. Delhi: Dini Book Depot, 1977.

The Qur'an. Translated by M. A. S. Abdel Haleem. New York, Oxford: Oxford University Press, 2004.

Ramachandran, V. S., and Sandra Blakeslee. *Phantoms in the Brain: Probing the Mysteries of the Human Mind.* New York: William Morrow, 1998.

Rambo, Lewis R. *Understanding Religious Conversion.* New Haven, CT: Yale University Press, 1993.

Rawski, Evelyn S. *The Last Emperors: A Social History of Qing Imperial Institutions.* Berkeley: University of California Press, 1998.

Raymond of Capua. *The Life of St. Catherine of Siena.* Translated by George Lamb. New York: P. J. Kennedy, 1960.

Reader, Ian. *Religious Violence in Contemporary Japan: The Case of Aum Shinrikyō.* Honolulu: University of Hawai'i Press, 2000.

———. *The Simple Guide to Shinto.* Haarlem: Becht, 1998.

Reeves, Marjorie. *The Influence of Prophecy in the Later Middle Ages: A Study in Joachimism.* Notre Dame, IN: University of Notre Dame Press, 1993.

Reichert, Eckard. "Elvira, Synode von." In *Religion in Geschichte und Gegenwart,* vol. 2, edited by Hans Dieter Betz, 1242–43. Tübingen: Mohr-Siebeck, 1998.

Reischauer, Edwin O. *Ennin's Travels in T'ang China.* New York: Ronald Press, 1955.

Ricci, Matteo. *The True Meaning of the Lord of Heaven.* Translated by Douglas
   Lancashire Guozhen and Peter Hu. St. Louis: Institute of Jesuit Sources, 1985.
Ricci, Matteo, and Nicolas Trigault. *China in the 16th Century: The Journals of Matthew
   Ricci: 1583–1610.* Translated by Louis J. Gallagher. New York: Random House, 1953.
Riesebrodt, Martin. *Die Rückkehr der Religionen: Fundamentalismus und der "Kampf
   der Kulturen."* Munich: C. H. Beck, 2000.
———. *Pious Passion: The Emergence of Modern Fundamentalism in the United States
   and Iran.* Berkeley: University of California Press, 1993.
———. "Was ist 'religiöser Fundamentalismus'?" In *Religiöser Fundamentalismus: Vom
   Kolonialismus zur Globalisierung,* edited by Clemens Six, Martin Riesebrodt, and
   Siegfried Haas, 13–32. Innsbruck: Studien Verlag, 2004.
Ritter, Adolf M., ed. *Kirchen- und Theologiegeschichte in Quellen: Alte Kirche.* Neu-
   kirchen: Neukirchener Verlag, 1994.
Rizzuto, Ana-Maria. *The Birth of the Living God: A Psychoanalytic Study.* Chicago:
   University of Chicago Press, 1979.
Rotermund, Hartmut O. *Die Yamabushi: Aspekte ihres Glaubens, Lebens und ihrer sozi-
   alen Funktion im japanischen Mittelalter.* Hamburg: Cram, de Gruyter, 1968.
Russell, Norman. *The Lives of the Desert Fathers: The Historia Monachorum in Aegypto.*
   Translated by Norman Russell; introduction by Benedicta Ward. Cistercian Studies
   Series, vol. 34. Kalamazoo, MI: Cistercian Publications, 1981.
Sachedina, Abdulaziz Abdulhussein. *Islamic Messianism: The Idea of Mahdi in Twelver
   Shiism.* Albany, NY: State University of New York Press, 1981.
Sadr, Muhammad B qir al-. *The Awaited Saviour.* Translated by Mustajab A. Ansari.
   Karachi: Islamic Seminary Pakistan, 1979.
Sahlins, Marshall D. *How "Natives" Think: About Captain Cook, for Example.* Chicago:
   University of Chicago Press, 1995.
Sakade, Yoshinobu. "Divination as Daoist Practice." In *Daoism Handbook,* edited by
   Livia Kohn, 541–66. Leiden: J. E. Brill, 2004.
Sansom, George. *A History of Japan to 1334.* Stanford: Stanford University Press, 1958.
Saso, Michael R. *Blue Dragon, White Tiger: Taoist Rites of Passage.* Honolulu: University
   of Hawai'i Press, 1990.
———. *Taoism and the Rite of Cosmic Renewal.* Seattle: Washington State University
   Press, 1972.
Savonarola, Girolamo. *Selected Writings of Girolamo Savonarola: Religion and Politics,
   1490–1498.* Translated and edited by Anne Borelli and Maria Pastore Passaro. New
   Haven, CT: Yale University Press, 2006.
———. *A Guide to Righteous Living and Other Works.* Translated and introduced by
   Konrad Eisenbichler. Toronto: Centre for Reformation and Renaissance Studies,
   2003.
———. *O Florenz! O Rom! O Italien! Predigten, Schriften, Briefe.* Translated by Jacques
   Laager. Zürich: Manesse, 2002.
Schimmel, Annemarie. *The Empire of the Great Mughals: History, Art, Culture.* Trans-
   lated by Corinne Atwood. London: Reaktion Books, 2004.
———. *Mystical Dimensions of Islam.* Chapel Hill: University of North Carolina Press,
   1975.

———. *Sufismus: Eine Einführung in die islamische Mystik.* Munich: C. H. Beck, 2000.

Schipper, Kristofer. *The Taoist Body.* Translated by Karen D. Duval. Berkeley: University of California Press, 1993.

Schleiermacher, Friedrich. *On Religion: Speeches to Its Cultured Despisers.* Translated by Richard Crouter. New York: Cambridge University Press, 1996.

Schmidt-Glintzer, Helwig. *Das Hung-ming chi und die Aufnahme des Buddhismus in China.* Wiesbaden: F. Steiner, 1976.

Scholem, Gershom. *Sabbatai Sevi: The Mystical Messiah, 1626–1676.* Princeton, NJ: Princeton University Press, 1973.

Seidel, Anna. "Taoist Messianism." *Numen* 31, no. 2 (1984): 161–74.

———. "Yü-huang." In Eliade, *Encyclopedia of Religion* (see above), 15:541.

Selinger, Reinhard. *Die Religionspolitik des Kaisers Decius: Anatomie einer Christenverfolgung.* Frankfurt am Main: Peter Lang, 1994.

Sharma, Sri Ram. *The Religious Policy of the Mughal Emperors.* London: Asia Publishing House, 1940.

Sharot, Stephen. "Beyond Christianity: A Critique of the Rational Choice Theory of Religion from Weberian and Comparative Religions Perspective." *Sociology of Religion* 63, no. 4 (2002): 427–54.

———. *A Comparative Sociology of World Religions.* New York: New York University Press, 2001.

———. *Messianism, Mysticism, and Magic: A Sociological Analysis of Jewish Religious Movements.* Chapel Hill: University of North Carolina Press, 1982.

Shimazono, Susumu. "Conversion Stories and Their Popularization in Japan's New Religions." *Japanese Journal of Religious Studies* 13, nos. 2–3 (1986): 157–75.

———. "Traditional Japanese Religious Society." In *The Oxford Handbook of Global Religions,* edited by Mark Juergensmeyer, 133–39. Oxford: Oxford University Press, 2006.

Simmel, Georg. *Die Religion.* Frankfurt am Main: Rütten & Loening, 1906.

———. *Soziologie: Untersuchungen über die Formen der Vergesellschaftung.* Leipzig: Duncker & Humblot, 1908.

———. "Religion." In *Essays on Religion,* edited and translated by Horst Juergen Helle and Ludwig Nieder, 137–214. New Haven, CT: Yale University Press, 1997.

Singh, Sundar. *With and Without Christ.* London: Harper & Brothers, 1929.

Smilde, David A. *Reason to Believe: Cultural Agency in Latin American Evangelicalism.* Berkeley: University of California Press, 2007.

Smith, Jonathan Z. "Religion, Religions, Religious." In *Critical Terms for Religious Studies,* edited by Mark C. Taylor, 269–84. Chicago: University of Chicago Press, 1998.

Smith, Margaret. *Rabi'a the Mystic and Her Fellow-Saints in Islam.* Cambridge: Cambridge University Press, 1928.

Smith, Robert J. *Ancestor Worship in Contemporary Japan.* Stanford: Stanford University Press, 1974.

Smith, Wilfred Cantwell. *The Meaning and End of Religion: A New Approach to the Religious Traditions of Mankind.* New York: Macmillan, 1963.

Snow, David A., and Richard Machalek. "The Sociology of Conversion." *Annual Review of Sociology* 10 (1984): 167–90.

————. "The Convert as a Social Type." *Sociological Theory* 1 (1983): 259–89.

Snow, David A., and Cynthia Philipps. "The Lofland-Stark Conversion Model: A Critical Reassessment." *Social Problems* 27 (1980): 430–47.

Sperber, Dan. "Apparently Irrational Beliefs." In *Rationality and Relativism*, edited by Martin Hollis and Steven Lukes, 149–80. Cambridge, MA: Harvard University Press, 1982.

Spiro, Melford E. *Culture and Human Nature*. Chicago: University of Chicago Press, 1987.

————. "Religion: Problems of Definition and Explanation." In *Anthropological Approaches to the Study of Religion*, edited by Michael Banton, 85–126. London: Tavistock Publications, 1966.

Staal, Frits. "The Meaninglessness of Ritual." *Numen* 26, no. 1 (1975): 2–22.

Stark, Johann Friedrich. *Tägliches Hand-Buch, in guten und bösen Tagen*. Reutlingen: Brockhaus, 1855.

Stark, Rodney. *The Rise of Christianity*. Princeton, NJ: Princeton University Press, 1996.

Stark, Rodney, and William Sims Bainbridge. *A Theory of Religion*. New Brunswick, NJ: Rutgers University Press, 1996.

Stein, Leopold, ed. *Seder ha-avodah: Gebetbuch für israelitische Gemeinden; nach dem Ritus der Hauptsynagoge zu Frankfurt a. M.* Frankfurt am Main: J. Lehrberger, 1860.

Steinschneider, Moritz. *Polemische und apologetische Literatur in arabischer Sprache zwischen Muslimen, Christen und Juden, nebst Anhängen verwandten Inhalts.* Abhandlungen für die Kunde des Morgenlandes, vol. 6, no. 3. Leipzig: Brockhaus, 1877.

Stepanchuk, Carol, and Charles Wong. *Mooncakes and Hungry Ghosts: Festivals of China.* San Francisco: China Books & Periodicals, 1991.

Sugirtharajah, Sharada. *Imagining Hinduism: A Postcolonial Perspective.* London: Routledge, 2003.

Tabari, 'Ali. *The Book of Religion and Empire.* Translated by A. Mingana. Lahore: Law Publications, 1970.

Takei, Jir , and Marc P. Keane. *Sakuteiki, Visions of the Japanese Garden: A Modern Translation of Japan's Gardening Classic.* Boston: Tuttle Publications, 2001.

Tambiah, Stanley J. "The Buddhist Arahant: Classical Paradigm and Modern Thai Manifestations." In *Saints and Virtues*, edited by John Stratton Hawley, 111–26. Berkeley: University of California Press, 1987.

————. *The Buddhist Saints of the Forest and the Cult of Amulets.* Cambridge: Cambridge University Press, 1984.

Tanakh: The Holy Scriptures. Philadelphia and Jerusalem: Jewish Publication Society, 1985.

Taussig, Michael T. *The Devil and Commodity Fetishism in South America.* Chapel Hill: University of North Carolina Press, 1980.

Teiser, Stephen F. "Introduction: The Spirits of Chinese Religion." In *Religions of China in Practice*, edited by Donald S. Lopez Jr., 3–37. Princeton, NJ: Princeton University Press, 1996.

————. *The Ghost Festival in Medieval China.* Princeton, NJ: Princeton University Press, 1988.

Thomas, Keith. *Religion and the Decline of Magic.* New York: Scribner, 1971.

Thompson, Laurence G. "Chiao." In Eliade, *Encyclopedia of Religion* (see above), 3:239 40.

Trainor, Kevin. *Relics, Ritual, and Representation in Buddhism: Rematerializing the Sri Lankan Theravada Tradition.* Cambridge: Cambridge University Press, 1997.

Troeltsch, Ernst. "Der Deismus." In *Gesammelte Schriften,* edited by Hans Baron, 4:429–87. Tübingen: Mohr, 1925.

Turner, Stephen. *The Social Theory of Practices.* Chicago: University of Chicago Press, 1994.

Tylor, Edward B. *Religion in Primitive Culture.* New York: Harper 1958.

Uddin, Inam, and Abdur-Rahman Ibn Yusuf. *Reflections of Pearls: A Concise and Comprehensive Collection of Prophetic Invocations and Prayers.* Santa Barbara: White Thread Press, 2005.

Van der Leeuw, Gerardus. *Religion in Essence and Manifestation: A Study in Phenomenology VII.* Translated by J. E. Turner. 1938. Reprint, Gloucester, MA: Peter Smith 1967.

———. *Der Mensch und dieReligion.* Basel: Hans zum Falken, 1941.

———. *Phänomenologie der Religion.* Tübingen: J. C. P. Mohr, 1933.

Waardenburg, Jacques. "The Problem of Representing Religions and Religion." In *Religionswissenschaften und Kulturkritik,* edited by Hans G. Kippenberg and Brigitte Luchesi, 31–56. Marburg: Diagonal Verlag, 1991.

Waardenburg, Jacques, ed. *Muslim Perceptions of Other Religions.* New York: Oxford University Press, 1999.

Walshe, Maurice, ed. *The Long Discourses of the Buddha: A Translation of the Digha Nikaya.* Boston: Wisdom Publications, 1995.

Warner, Stephen. "Work in Progress toward a New Paradigm for the Sociological Study of Religion in the United States." *American Journal of Sociology* 98 (1993): 1044–93.

Weber, Max. *Economy and Society.* Edited by Guenther Roth and Claus Wittich. Berkeley: University of California Press, 1978.

———. *The Protestant Ethic and the "Spirit" of Capitalism and Other Writings.* Edited and Translated by Peter Baehr and Gordon C. Wells. New York: Penguin Books, 2002.

———. *The Religion of China: Confucianism and Taoism.* Translated and edited by Hans H. Gerth. Glencoe IL: Free Press, 1951.

———. "Science as a Vocation." In *From Max Weber,* translated and edited by H. H. Gerth and C. Wright Mills, 129–56. New York: Oxford University Press, 1946.

———. "The Social Psychology of the World Religions." In *From Max Weber,* translated and edited by H. H. Gerth and C. Wright Mills, 267–301. New York: Oxford University Press, 1946.

Weinstein, Donald. *Savonarola and Florence: Prophecy and Patriotism in the Renaissance.* Princeton, NJ: Princeton University Press, 1970.

Wiesberger, Franz. *Bausteine zu einer soziologischen Theorie der Konversion.* Berlin: Duncker & Humblot, 1990.

Wilson, Liz. *Charming Cadavers: Horrific Figurations of the Feminine in Indian Buddhist Hagiographic Literature.* Chicago: University of Chicago Press, 1996.

Winchester, Simon. *A Crack in the Edge of the World: America and the Great California Earthquake of 1906.* New York: HarperCollins, 2005.

Wohlrab-Sahr, Monika. *Konversion zum Islam in Deutschland und den USA*. Frankfurt am Main: Campus, 1999.

Wong, Eva, trans. *Seven Taoist Masters: A Folk Novel of China*. Boston: Shambhala, 2004.

Woodward, Kenneth L. *The Book of Miracles: The Meaning of the Miracle Stories in Christianity, Judaism, Buddhism, Hinduism, Islam*. New York: Simon & Schuster, 2000.

Wuthnow, Robert. "Spirituality and Spiritual Practice." In *The Blackwell Companion to Sociology of Religion*, edited by Richard Fenn, 306–20. Oxford: Blackwell Publishers, 2001.

Yampolsky, Philip B., ed. *Selected Writings of Nichiren*. New York: Columbia University Press, 1990.

Yoshio, Yasumaru. "Millenarianism in Omotokyo." In *Millenarianism in Asian History*, edited by Ishii Yoneo, 3–24. Tokyo: Institute for the Study of Languages and Cultures of Asia and Africa, 1993.

Young, Lawrence A, ed. *Rational Choice Theory and Religion*. New York: Oxford University Press, 1997.

Zeilinga de Boer, Jelle, and Donald Theodore Sanders. *Earthquakes in Human History: The Far-reaching Effects of Seismic Disruptions*. Princeton, NJ: Princeton University Press, 2005.

Zürcher, Erik. *The Buddhist Conquest of China: The Spread and Adaptation of Buddhism in Early Medieval China*. 2 vols. Leiden: E. J. Brill, 1972.

———. "'Prince Moonlight': Messianism and Eschatology in Early Medieval Chinese Buddhism." *T'oung Pao* 68, nos. 1–3 (1982): 1–75.

INDEX